How AI Ate the World

A Brief History of Artificial Intelligence – and Its Long Future

Chris Stokel-Walker

Canbury Press

Canbury

First published by Canbury Press 2024

This edition published 2024

Canbury Press

Kingston upon Thames, Surrey, United Kingdom

www.canburypress.com

Printed and bound in Great Britain

Typeset in Athelas (body), Futura PT (heading)

This is a work of non-fiction

MIX
Paper | Supporting
responsible forestry
FSC® C171272

FSC® helps take care of forests for future generations

ISBN:

Paperback 9781914487323

Ebook 9781914487330

CONTENTS

INTRODUCTION

Imagine a world where machines could think, learn, and make decisions just like humans. A world where robots could understand human emotions, drive cars without human intervention, and even create art or compose music. This world, once confined to the realm of science fiction, has now become a tangible reality, thanks to the remarkable journey of artificial intelligence (AI).

The story of AI begins in the 1950s when pioneering researchers such as Alan Turing and John McCarthy laid the groundwork for the field. These visionaries believed that machines could be created to mimic human intelligence, and their groundbreaking ideas sparked a new era of scientific exploration and technological innovation.

In the early years, AI was mostly confined to academic and research settings, with limited practical applications. But as computing power grew exponentially and algorithms became more sophisticated, AI began to evolve rapidly, transforming from a theoretical concept to a practical tool.

One of the most significant breakthroughs came in the 1960s when researchers at Stanford University developed the first AI program that could understand and respond to natural language.

This groundbreaking achievement laid the foundation for modern-day language processing technologies, such as virtual assistants like Siri and Alexa, which have become ubiquitous in our daily lives.

As the years passed, AI continued to make strides in diverse domains. In the 1970s, AI systems were developed for medical diagnosis, and in the 1980s, AI was used in industrial automation and robotics. In the 1990s, AI-powered search engines revolutionised the way we access information on the internet.

However, the field of AI has not been without its challenges. During the 1980s and 1990s, the field experienced a period of disillusionment, known as the 'AI winter', as progress stalled, and funding declined. But AI, like a phoenix rising from the ashes, made a remarkable comeback in the 21st Century.

In recent years, we have witnessed unprecedented advancements in AI. Machine learning, a subset of AI, has enabled computers to learn from data without explicit programming, leading to breakthroughs in image recognition, natural language processing, and recommendation systems. Deep learning, a form of machine learning, has pushed the boundaries of AI even further, enabling machines to recognise patterns and make decisions at a level previously thought impossible.

The impact of AI has extended far beyond the realm of academia and research. Today, AI is being used in various industries, including healthcare, finance, transportation, and entertainment, to improve efficiency, enhance decision-making, and create new business models.

Despite the remarkable progress, AI is not without its controversies. Ethical concerns, such as bias in AI algorithms, privacy issues, and the impact of AI on the job market, have sparked debates and discussions. The rise of powerful AI technologies has also raised concerns about transparency, accountability, and the potential for misuse.

As we stand at the cusp of a new era of AI, it is crucial to reflect on the incredible journey of AI from science fiction to scientific fact. What was once a mere idea in the minds of visionary scientists has now become a transformative force that is reshaping our world. In the following chapters, we will delve deeper into the history, challenges, and implications of AI, exploring its evolution, impact on industries, ethical concerns, and the potential risks and dangers. Through this journey, we will strive to uncover the true potential of AI and its implications for humanity, and offer insights and recommendations for policymakers, scientists, and society at large to navigate the uncharted territory of AI responsibly and shape a future where AI benefits all of humanity.

...

Not bad, huh? Those 593 words took only two minutes – and the power of artificial intelligence – to produce. It's an indication of how far AI has advanced in the last 18 months that ChatGPT, the 'large language model' developed by OpenAI in the United States, could produce something so lucid in a matter of moments.

I gave the AI model six bulletpoints summarising the overview in my contract for this book and asked for a detailed chapter structure. It produced a reasonable outline for eight chapters, though it was quite vague. The first chapter on The Evolution of Artificial Intelligence introduced the concept of AI and its science-fiction origins, traced its history from the 1950s to today, and highlighted its key developments from theoretical concepts to practical reality.

So I typed four words into ChatGPT and hoped for the best: 'Please write chapter one.' What you see above is what it produced. Without editing. Without further prompting.

This book will not be as clever again – I promise. Nor will it be the product of AI. You didn't pay for this book to learn what AI thinks about itself (or rather, its understanding of our species' recorded collective thoughts on the subject), but for the narrative craft, investigative journalism, and deep thinking that comes from a human brain. But it's important to know what we're dealing with, given the way AI is changing the way we think and work. And it's interesting to find out what AI thinks about its own story.

Its findings may be imprecise, vague and full of generalisations, but at a broad sweep, they are right. We are on the cusp of a world 'where machines can think, learn, and make decisions just like humans... understand human emotions, drive cars without human intervention, and even create art or compose music.'

Indeed, one early cover idea for this book, a cartoonishly anthropomorphised pink and blue planet devouring the world's knowledge, was the product of Microsoft Bing's AI image generator. I generated 14 others in a variety of different styles in 15 minutes. (The cover you see was designed by a human. Why that's important, you'll learn in subsequent chapters.)

It's also true to say 'we have witnessed unprecedented advancements in AI' in the last few years.

Since the release of ChatGPT in November 2022, AI has reached even dizzier heights. It is mutating and spreading like a virulent pandemic.

Some companies, sectors and industries already lie mortally wounded in the wake of its relentless onslaught. It's an attack that is also changing humanity: AI boosters or AI pessimists will tell you we're being either supercharged or suborned by its power.

Like a pandemic, there are tough questions about what we should do. Should we just let AI explode and hope for the best, or try to contain it? As the world's richest companies develop ever more extraordinary AI systems, is it too late to even hold this discussion?

We'll answer all those questions and more in the coming chapters. But first let me take you on a detour. Unlike computers, humans can be impulsive.

PART 1: ORIGINS

1

MAGIC MUSHROOMS AND A MAGIC TOOL

Pablo Xavier had, by his own admission, taken a few too many magic mushrooms on the afternoon of 24th March 2023. (Would an AI ever open a chapter like that?)

The 31-year-old construction worker from the Chicago area used the psychedelic drugs to foster his creativity and pass the time. After the untimely loss of his brother, they also helped ease his concerns and Pablo (who asked me not to use his last name so he couldn't be identified) was looking for a way to remember him.

He encountered Midjourney, an AI-powered image generator made available to the public in 2022, and thought it could help. Like all generative AI tools, Midjourney is trained on a vast volume of data. In Midjourney's case, 100 million images ripped from the internet without permission, which its founder David Holz admitted when he told a *Forbes* interviewer: 'There isn't really a way to get a hundred million images and know where they're coming from.'

An AI image generator learns by poring over each image it's presented with, using computer vision to work out what it's seeing.

Sometimes, the identity of the object is unclear. A cluster of red and white pixels next to each other could be a beach ball, a barber's pole, or a candy cane. When the AI model examines the surrounding area, however, it can make better guesses. It's often helped by human labelling: someone coming in, drawing a metaphorical circle around a beach ball and saying: 'This is a beach ball.' Information about its shape, colour, size and usual position in relation to other objects is then stored. Over time, the AI gathers more contextual clues from multiple images of beach balls, allowing it to create a composite understanding of what a beach ball looks like.

Train an AI model enough times on enough different objects and the end result is a tool like Midjourney. A user enters a text prompt – for instance, 'Draw me a beach ball on the moon' – and the software duly creates a picture.

'I needed some type of outlet,' Pablo told me. He thought Midjourney could be that outlet, helping him turn a real image of his brother into a cartoon character, enabling him to live on long past his untimely death. He ordered up a cartoon character that was intentionally larger than life, and he sent his virtual brother on heroic adventures. 'It pretty much just all started with that, just dealing with grief and making images of my past brother,' he said. 'I fell in love with it after that.' Soon, Pablo was using it for more than comic book-style depictions of his brother. He started using Midjourney to make art.

'I try to do funny stuff or trippy art – psychedelic stuff,' he told me. Then the 'shrooms hit. 'It just dawned on me: I should do the Pope,' he recalls. 'Then it was just coming like water. "The Pope in Balenciaga puffy coat, Moncler [another luxury fashion brand], walking the streets of Rome, Paris, stuff like that."'

Pablo put the prompts into Midjourney at 1.48pm that Friday in late March 2023. Three images came out the other end. The construction worker thought they were perfect. He, or rather Midjourney, had managed to create eerily accurate depictions of Pope Francis wearing an oversized white puffy parka jacket. The images were curious, occupying the 'uncanny valley' of realism. As the Pope is a man of a certain age living in Italy, with enough expendable income for fancy clothes, his fashion choices seemed to be at least plausible.

Pablo shared his creations to a Facebook group called AI Art Universe, and in the r/midjourney subreddit, where generative AI enthusiasts share their handiwork. From there, it was download-ed, shorn of its all-important context, and disseminated widely on Twitter where it fooled lots of people.

When Pablo woke up from a psychedelic stupor, his girlfriend asked him whether he had seen his Facebook feed. The internet had exploded with comments about the Pope. The Hollywood ce-lebrity Chrissy Teigen tweeted: 'I thought the Pope's puffer jacket was real and didn't give it a second thought. No way am I surviving the future of technology.'

Pablo's two-word reaction? 'Holy crap.' 'I was just blown away,' he said. 'I didn't want it to blow up like that.' Nor was Pablo prepared for the backlash from people feeling he had set out to deliberately deceive – or worse, to offend the world's 1.3 billion Catholics. Pablo grew up Catholic but no longer feels part of the religion. He was worried what his family might think, and sent the image to his surviving brother, a Catholic, who luckily thought it was funny. He also thought it was real. 'I had to tell him I made it through Midjourney,' Pablo admitted.

When I spoke to him amid the media storm, Pablo seemed wholly unprepared to face the consequences of his hallucinogenic behaviour. He batted away requests, brokered through me, to speak to Google, the BBC, Canada's public broadcaster, *TIME*, *Popular Science*, *El Mundo* and the *New York Times*. He was too nervous he might say the wrong thing and raise hackles further.

Pablo couldn't quite fathom that people believed his image was real. When uploading it, he thought the image was clearly generated by AI. It hadn't crossed his mind that it would be severed from its context and spread widely, nor that people would be so credulous.

Just as Frankenstein had his moment of reckoning when confronted by the havoc of his monster's actions, so did Pablo. 'I didn't mean no ill will,' he told me. 'I just thought it was funny to see the Pope in a funny jacket.' He was disheartened that his creation had been coopted: he had already seen his images used to illustrate articles attacking the Catholic church's spending.

Bizarrely, in a collision of the digital and real worlds, the AI-created images were often run alongside a real-life photograph, taken in 2017, of Pope Francis blessing a $200,000 white Lamborghini with two golden go-faster stripes on its bonnet.

'I feel like shit,' Pablo told me. 'I didn't give birth [to it] because I'm pretty sure it was going to happen, but I made it possible for people to make fake news using Midjourney.'

The images, now known as the Balenciaga Pope or the 'Pope in a puffer,' were the second deepfakes to hoodwink the internet in a single week. Ahead of the rumoured arrest of former US President Donald Trump, Eliot Higgins, best known for being the founder of investigative journalism website Bellingcat, had used Midjourney to create lifelike 'photographs' of what Trump's arrest and incarceration could look like. When Pablo Xavier's images of the pontiff hit a similar nerve to Higgins', he thought twice about sharing his other Midjourney-generated images of the pontiff throwing up gang signs, but eventually he did so on his Instagram, where they were seen by far fewer people. He enforced a new rule for any of his subsequent Midjourney creations: no public figures. He had no problem with people using the image generator to create works in the style of artists like Vincent Van Gogh, he told me – though later we'll discover that the art world does not share that view – but he felt depicting living people was a line he shouldn't cross again.

The labourer's dalliance with generative AI and his work's subsequent explosion into the public consciousness highlights two of this book's key pillars.

Number one: by his own admission, Pablo Xavier didn't think about the consequences of how he was using AI. He hadn't considered the image he created to entertain his mushroom-influenced self would take on a half-life of its own and spread around the internet before he could say 'computer-generated fraud'.

Secondly: when confronted by the vastness of what AI can do unwittingly, many AI content creators have second thoughts. In later chapters, we'll encounter hip-hop fans who congregate on chat apps like Discord and tinker with tools like the innocuously named So-Vits-SVC to create pitch-perfect recreations of musicians like Jay-Z, Drake and Kanye West performing songs they've never previously sung. Those people, like Pablo, have nuanced views on whether what they do should be regulated. A surprising number come to the conclusion, when they see how easy it is, that AI should be cracked down on.

As for Pablo's papal pics, the Pope himself has not publicly addressed the fakes, but he did take the time, when announcing that the 2024 World Peace Day theme would be AI, to ask for an 'open dialogue' about the meaning and implementation of the new technology. The Holy See's press office said in a statement that there was an 'urgent need to orient the concept and use of artificial intelligence in a responsible way, so that it may be at the service of humanity and the protection of our common home'.

Amid the fear AI will stifle creativity and end all human individuality, we often overlook that two agents are involved in any AI-generated creation: the technology and the human. The former can't exist without the latter. At least not yet, some argue.

We've plenty of time to get onto that. For now, let's wind back the clock to before World War II, before racing forward to the summer of 1956, and the birth of AI – the moment that bequeathed the technology that enabled Pablo to dress up the Pope in Balenciaga.

2
THE FATHERS OF AI

Today, a number of individuals currently debating the potential and pitfalls of our generative AI revolution have been given the mantle of 'godfathers of AI' by the media. But expand the timeline back to the 1940s and 1950s, and AI had two godfathers who predate those currently laying claim to the title: one in the UK and the other in the USA. Both were developing their thinking just after World War II. And in a way, both were outsiders ahead of their time.

In Britain, Alan Turing, a mathematician who helped crack Germany's Enigma codes during World War II, thought the human brain was, in many ways, a biological version of a digital computing machine.

Turing was a strange and isolated figure who was decades ahead of his time. Growing up, he and his brother, John, rarely saw their parents (his father was part of the Madras government in India) and were left in the care of a retired colonel who lived in Hastings. Turing's mind was prodigious, and a natural fit for mathematics but he didn't fit in at school, where the classics, and writing, were seen as more important than numeracy: his English teacher said his writing was 'the worst I have ever seen, and I try to view tolerantly his unswerving inexactitude and slipshod, dirty, work.' His headmaster was no kinder: he was 'the sort of boy who is bound to be a problem for any school or community.'

Yet the young Turing excelled at physics, quantum mechanics and the working of the mind. He devoured Einstein's theory of relativity, and went to Cambridge University where he graduated with a maths degree. After he was dragooned into Bletchley Park's Government Code and Cypher School, he earned his PhD at Princeton in the US. Although Turing became known for his code-breaking prowess in cracking Enigma, he would play several key roles in the early years of British computing. His work was often theoretical, because the hardware required to bring his inventions to life simply didn't exist in his lifetime. He ended up having an outsized impact on the development of AI.

Take one moment in 1948 as an example of Turing developing ideas on paper that he couldn't yet put into practice. Since the early 1940s, Turing had believed that machines could mimic how human brains worked through programmed instructions to conduct some tasks, like playing games. One of those games he believed was a potential early use for computers was chess. In 1948, while working at Cambridge, Turing and a colleague, David Gowen Champernowne, developed a computer program called Turochamp that would follow rules laid down by its creator to play the right moves in a game of chess.

Turing and Champernowne didn't get to test out Turochamp (named after its inventors) on an actual computer because the tech at the time wasn't powerful enough to run the program. Turing would actually die before the program was loaded into a computer.

But it worked – and chess, as we'll learn in a subsequent chapter, would be intrinsically tied up with the development of AI.

Each step along his journey, from breaking Enigma to developing Turochamp, imbued Turing with the skills he'd need to start helping create alongside others, in broad outline, what would become the field of artificial intelligence. Unlike others who believed we humans are born with innate abilities – the so-called 'nativist' approach – Turing believed humans are born with an 'unorganised machine': the brain, which is trained to become a universal machine by our lives and experiences. Turing reckoned there wasn't much difference between the cold logic of the early computers he was tinkering with in the 1940s and the human brain.

He put forward his ideas in a discussion at the University of Manchester, where he was deputy director of the computing laboratory, on 27th October 1949. The others present were Turing's colleague, Max Newman; a chemist and philosopher called Michael Polanyi; and a zoologist-cum-neurophysiologist, John Zachary Young. Polanyi and Young argued against Turing's idea that the human mind was programmable like a computer; Turing replied that they had simply not yet thought about it. 'The mind is only said to be unspecifiable because it has <u>not yet been</u> specified,' Turing reportedly said, according to contemporary minutes.

Turing didn't manage to convince either philosopher or neurophysiologist that the human brain and the logic that dictated computers were similar. He did, however, convince himself. He kept plugging away at the problem. He designed a test to ascertain whether a computer could, in theory, 'think' the same way a human does. Turing thought determining whether computers could think outright was too tricky, but designed his test to see whether it could imitate the process. He put forward his test in an academic paper in the *Mind* journal titled 'Computing machinery and intelligence' in 1950. The 'Turing test' was a version of the Imitation Game, a classic parlour game in which a player would hide their gender while answering questions from another, who would try to guess whether they were man or woman from their answers.

Turing's test asked a simple question: could a computer talk like a human? The idea was that a human judge would take part in a text-based conversation, mediated through computers, with different players. The judge would look at the responses to their questions, and decide whether they sounded human, even if they weren't. If the judge considered a computer indistinguishable from human participants, it would be considered 'intelligent'.

Turing believed that was the benchmark for intelligent behaviour from a computer – and he believed that while it wasn't likely to be possible in 1950, it would be by the year 2000. At that point, he reasoned, computers would have 100 megabytes of memory, which he thought would be enough to pass the test:

> *An average interrogator will not have more than 70 per cent chance of making the right identification after five minutes of questioning.... I believe that at the end of the century the use of words and general educated opinion will have altered so much that one will be able to speak of machines thinking without expecting to be contradicted.*

Sure enough, Turing was right about computer memory, also called RAM, or random access memory. An Apple PowerBook G4 released in 2001 had 128 megabytes of RAM as standard. Turing was wrong, however, in his confident prediction that a computer could pass the Turing test with that level of memory – at present, no artificial intelligence system has managed to convince someone they're human, despite their computational power now far outstripping the 100 megabytes he calculated would be sufficient. (They have got closer, however.) But Turing wasn't the only computer scientist pushing the boundaries of the discpline.

...

John McCarthy was the US-born child of pro-communist Irish and Lithuanian immigrant journalists. Young John's childhood was steeped equally in radicalism and science, encouraging him to question things frequently without worry, and to embrace technological innovation without fear.

'There was a general confidence in technology as being simply good for humanity,' he recalled. A precocious child, his parents gave him a Soviet technology book published in 1933 called *100,000 Whys: A Trip Around the Room*, the English translation of which *Nature* called a 'small guide to general knowledge [which] will serve in lessening to a slight degree the load of ignorance which so many carry'. (McCarthy read the book in its native Russian; his parents' Communist zeal meant that Russian was spoken frequently in their home, and John junior was fluent.)

100,000 Whys helped stoke in young John McCarthy a passion for technology that continued through his teenage years. Like Alan Turing, McCarthy showed a huge aptitude for mathematics. Unlike Turing, whose interest was downplayed and diminished by his teachers, McCarthy was given the chance to foment that interest.

While at high school in California, McCarthy managed to get his hands on the recommended reading list for maths degrees at the California Institute of Technology (Caltech). He then bought the books and taught himself university-level mathematics – which would come in handy when he applied to Caltech in 1944.

He graduated high school two years early, despite starting his schooltime education a year later than his peers because of sickness. A life lived on fast-forward continued at Caltech: he was allowed to skip the first two years of study when the admissions tutors saw what he could do.

But it wasn't all plain sailing at the university. McCarthy was booted out of Caltech because he refused to attend physical education classes. He had a short stint in the army before returning to university and graduating with a bachelor's degree in mathematics in 1948.

In September that same year, at the same time as Alan Turing was eagerly sketching out his idea for Turochamp, McCarthy, then 21, attended a talk by the celebrated Hungarian-American mathematician and computer scientist John von Neumann. At the time McCarthy, who would become a central figure in the development of artificial intelligence, was back at Caltech taking a one-year master's programme.

Caltech was where von Neumann delivered the Hixon Symposium on Cerebral Mechanisms in Behavior. His subject was self-replicating automata: hypothetical machines that could manufacture copies of themselves.

That idea would linger in McCarthy's mind throughout the maths PhD that he began at Princeton University the following year, a little over a decade after Turing gained his PhD from the same institution. McCarthy thought about von Neumann's concept of simulating human intelligence on early computers. He even booked an appointment to present his early findings to von Neumann, who encouraged McCarthy to set them out in a paper. 'But I didn't write it up because I didn't feel it was really good,' McCarthy later said. So McCarthy kept plugging away at his PhD, receiving a doctorate in differential equations in 1951. From there, he moved quickly into teaching at Princeton, helping graduate students with their work. One of those graduate students, Jerry Rayna, came up with an inspired idea: that McCarthy should gather together like-minded people to produce papers on machine intelligence into a single collection.

In the 1950s, disparate academics were all working away on ideas that would push the principle that nascent computer hardware could be made to tackle tasks previously thought uniquely achievable by the human brain. In the US, a mathematics undergraduate at Harvard University, Marvin Minsky, had built a simple neural net learning machine, a way of mimicking the human brain through computer hardware. Minsky was egged on to work in what would become artificial intelligence, going on to get his PhD from Princeton in the field, after reading the short story *Runaround* by the science fiction author Isaac Asimov in the March 1942 issue of *Astounding*.

The story was set in the year 2015, when three of Asimov's regular recurring characters, Gregory Powell, Mike Donovan and Robot SPD-13, go to Mercury on a mission to restart an abandoned selenium mine. The humans, after landing on the planet, send out SPD-13, who they call Speedy, to fetch a selenium sample and come back. After five hours, Speedy still hasn't returned. When Powell and Donovan look at Speedy's tracks, they realise he's going round and round a major selenium deposit, but hasn't obtained any.

The humans find Speedy going back and forth, spouting gibberish. One human says it seems like the robot is drunk.

As part of the story, Asimov wrote down the three laws of robotics which are now inexorably connected with his name:

1. A robot may not injure a human being or, through inaction, allow a human being to come to harm.
2. A robot must obey the orders given it by human beings except where such orders would conflict with the First Law.
3. A robot must protect its own existence as long as such protection does not conflict with the First or Second Laws.

Speedy was protecting himself under rule three from damage caused by the selenium, despite trying to achieve the second: obey its human orders. In the end, Powell and Donovan have to invoke the first law: without the selenium, they can't power their temperature shield. They would die. It works: Speedy grabs the selenium, and saves the humans.

When Minsky read *Runaround*, he was enthralled. 'I never stopped thinking about how minds might work,' he said. 'Surely we'd someday build robots that think. But how would they think and about what? Surely logic might work for some purposes, but not for others. And how to build robots with common sense, intuition, consciousness and emotion? How, for that matter, do brains do those things?'

Simultaneously in the United States, Claude Shannon, who would later be known as the father of information theory, a key concept behind computing, was trying to develop a computer program that could 'play' chess, as well as developing small relay-powered machines to play different roles, such as a mouse in a maze searching for a target.

By 1952, things were starting to come together. All three men – McCarthy, Minsky (egged on by Rayna) and Shannon – were working on the same fundamental problem. They came at it from different points of view, but they all believed in the principle that one day, technology could attempt to tackle issues previously thought solely the preserve of the human brain. They also knew that in the UK, Alan Turing was having similar thoughts, as were other academics across the globe.

So the three American researchers decided to try and convene together those disparate academic theories into a single collection of papers that would kickstart the development of a new, formal field of research. The question was what to call the collection when it was published.

Opinions differed. McCarthy favoured calling the collection Artificial Intelligence, he later said. But McCarthy and Minsky deferred to Shannon, a decade older than them, when Shannon suggested their collected volume of research papers on the emerging field of computer intelligence should be called Automata Studies. 'Shannon thought that artificial intelligence was too flashy a term and might attract unfavourable notice,' McCarthy recalled.

He later regretted accepting his elder's decision. 'The papers started coming in and I was disappointed,' McCarthy said. 'Not enough of them were about intelligence.' He felt the publication's title led people down the wrong path.

So three years later, with Automata Studies still waiting to be published, McCarthy, now an assistant professor at the private Ivy League university Dartmouth College, had a second crack at the task. In August 1955, with the support of colleagues including Minsky, Shannon and Nathaniel Rochester – the co-designer of the IBM 701: the first mass-produced scientific computer – he drafted a proposal to the Rockefeller Foundation asking them to fund a conference on what he felt could become the next big thing. And this time he was going to call it artificial intelligence.

The 17-page proposal outlined a two-month, '10 man study of artificial intelligence' to try and crack this new area. 'The study is to proceed on the basis of the conjecture that every aspect of learning or any other feature of intelligence can in principle be so precisely described that a machine can be made to simulate it,' the authors wrote. They asked for $13,500 funding – equivalent to nearly $150,000 today, with adjustments for inflation and relative purchasing power – to support innovative thinking. The money would cover train fares and accommodation for attendees, as well as buying them out of their positions with universities and big businesses. The scientists wrote: 'We think that a significant advance can be made in one or more of these problems if a carefully selected group of scientists work on it together for a summer.'

The conference was based on something McCarthy had heard of but never attended: a military summer conference on air defence. 'I thought major projects could be undertaken during the course,' he said.

In the end, the Rockefeller Foundation only funded half of the grant application for the Dartmouth Summer Research Project on Artificial Intelligence. (The name was McCarthy's doing: he wanted to coin the phrase and ensure no confusion over the focus of their research.) The foundation's reticence was well-founded. The months-long summer project was a disappointment.

Between 18th June and 17th August 1956, more than 35 presentations were given, with 20 leading academics from across the world presenting their latest research. 'I believed if only we could get everyone who was interested in the subject together to devote time to it and avoid distractions, we could make real progress,' McCarthy later said. But their intended goal of getting the smartest people from across the globe in the same room so sparks could fly didn't materialise. Some big names dropped by for a day or two; few stayed longer than a week; and most talked *at* their peers, rather than *with* them.

'Anybody who was there was pretty stubborn about pursuing the ideas that he had before he came, nor was there, as far as I could see, any real exchange of ideas,' lamented McCarthy. 'It was a great disappointment to me because it really meant that we couldn't have regular meetings.'

Still, the conference brought about some innovations. Researchers at Carnegie Mellon University presented the second iteration of their Information Processing Language, or IPL, intended to act as a translation tool between the way humans think and the way computers process information. Although IPL is now mostly overlooked, at the time it was a significant moment and a useful impetus for early AI developers. It was the first computer language specifically designed to enable AI coding, and laid the groundwork for future high-level programming languages such as LISP (an acronym for list processing), developed by McCarthy, which became a mainstay of AI.

Beyond the granular, there were broader advances that benefited the growing world of AI research. The conference grouped AI into four broad areas: natural language processing, problem-solving, perception, and learning. Researchers who attended the Dartmouth conference – and a good many after that who didn't – could quickly divide their work into these four areas.

The simple act of hosting an event focusing on a field variously described as 'information processing', 'cybernetics', and 'automata studies', meant they could be now presented under a single banner. 'Artificial intelligence' had arrived.

This one small change opened doors previously shut to researchers – an indication of how a snappy title can help smooth progress. Universities began to support the burgeoning AI labs, with the three big beasts, Massachusetts Institute of Technology (MIT), Stanford University and Carnegie Mellon University, having their funders support new breakthrough hubs.

Not that they all agreed how artificial intelligence would work. The conference participants – and the wider field of AI researchers – divided broadly into two tribes: the neural network camp, who believed you could build a computer structured like the human brain, learning the way humans do; and the symbolic AI group, who believed neural networks (Turing's idea) weren't technologically possible.

The symbolic AI group thought any AI system would have to be painstakingly presented with a series of rules to follow. For instance, to train an AI to think it was a car, you would have to outline how it was constructed, how it worked, and under what circumstances it could go or stop, before even thinking about asking it to go from A to B.

As we'll go on to see, that divide would be significant in the early stages of AI development. Given the technological capabilities of mid-20th Century computer hardware, the symbolic group took the lead because it was easier to encode computers with a long set of rules that allowed them free range to understand the world innately.

But the supporters of neural networks refused to give up. One of them was a psychologist called Frank Rosenblatt. In the late 1950s, Frank Rosenblatt invented the concept of the perceptron, developed with funding from the United States Office of Naval Research. The US armed forces were involved because they had a very real-world problem to solve. During the Cold War, the US Navy was keen to automatically interpret sonar signals, in order to distinguish a submarine from other underwater forms. The perceptron seemed promising, a sort of algorithmic sailor sorting harmless fish from harmful subs.

A perceptron made decisions based on received inputs. This was the underlying concept behind the neural network supporters' vision of AI.

In the 13th July 1958 edition of the *New York Times*, under the headline 'Electronic "Brain" Teaches Itself,' the newspaper breathlessly reported the existence of the perceptron. Described as 'the embryo of an electronic computer', the newspaper claimed that 'when completed in about a year, [it was] expected to be the first non-living mechanism able to "perceive, recognize and identify its surroundings without human training or control".'

But some believed the perceptron wasn't the saviour of AI. Marvin Minsky would be its strongest opponent, publishing a 1969 book, *Perceptrons*, with one of his students, Seymour Papert. Over the 360 pages of *Perceptrons*, re-released in a new, expanded edition in 1988, Minsky and Papert knocked back every argument for neural networks. The pair looked at the mathematics, finding that although a perceptron could perform basic pattern recognition, it couldn't do much more.

Minsky and Papert identified what was then a deep flaw in neural networks: their inability to handle the exclusive-OR problem.

Imagine you have a tried and tested rule for whether or not to turn on your heating, dependent on two factors: the heat outside your home – whether it's chilly or not – and the temperature inside.

It's a balmy day outside, and neither warm nor cold inside: you probably won't turn on the heating. If it's cold outside and not warm inside, you probably will (otherwise the temperature inside may get colder). Now imagine it's not cold outside, and also warm inside. You have no need to turn the heating on... so you don't. If it's cold outside, but warm inside, you're also unlikely to reach for the thermostat.

This is a (very simplistic) exclusive-OR (or XOR) situation. You will only knock the thermostat up a few degrees if one condition is true – it's either cold outside, or not warm inside. If both are true: it's cold outside, and neither warm nor cold inside, you probably won't.

Now imagine that a computer – which, remember, is the cornerstone of the neural networks intended to power these early stages of AI – tries to tackle this problem. Computers rely on binary decisions: if something happens, then do this. If something else happens, then don't do that. But what if life is more complex than that (as it often is)?

Single-layer perceptrons as designed by Rosenblatt couldn't handle that complexity. It would eventually be fixed with the development of multi-layer perceptrons but in the afterglow of the first Dartmouth conference – and far beyond *Perceptrons'* 1969 publication – that wasn't possible. So most AI researchers pursued the symbolic method, drawing up long lists of rules to teach computers about the world. At this stage, computers were not clever; they were drudges.

3
THE AI WINTER LOOMS

We are currently in the throes of an AI renaissance – but it hasn't always been that way. AI hasn't advanced in a single, upward exponential curve that those tech companies currently at the forefront of the generative AI revolution love to suggest. Instead, it's a stuttering story of two steps forward, one step back.

To understand why, we have to go back to the Cold War.

For the United States, artificial intelligence held huge promise because of its ability to help the country maintain a scientific and military edge over its big ideological and geopolitical rival, the Soviet Union. The US government saw the potential of AI to provide near-simultaneous translation of diplomatic and spying messages sent in Russian that they were tapping. Similarly, the US government, in a race for scientific supremacy, would also want to know what Soviet scientists were publishing in academic papers. Speedier translations of technical reports would help them achieve that. In short, AI could aid the US in peeking behind the inscrutable Iron Curtain.

Machine translation, then (remember AI as a term would not be developed until the Dartmouth summer conference of 1956), was put at the forefront of development. And Georgetown University and tech titan IBM were in the vanguard. The two entities worked together to try and develop a machine translation tool throughout the early 1950s, with some success.

A *New York Times* article, published on 8th January 1954, indicated just how far the Georgetown–IBM partnership had come in a short space of time. A day earlier, the partners in the project – Professor Leon Dostert and Dr Paul Garvin of Georgetown, and Dr Cuthbert C Hurd, of IBM's division of applied science – had demonstrated the fruits of their partnership in the skyscraper IBM owned at 590 Madison Avenue in New York.

In front of the world's media, Dostert, Garvin and Hurd explained how a program they had developed on the IBM Type 701 Electronic Data Processing Machine – which we met in the last chapter, and only 12 of which had been sold, all to military, commercial and university laboratories since its release the previous April – could translate 250 words in Russian into English almost instantaneously. But they didn't just explain; they demonstrated it.

A female typist (typically of the time, she goes unnamed in the contemporary reports, despite her importance in the history of the technology) typed a sentence in Russian into the Type 701 computer: '*Mi pyeryedayem mislyi posryedstvom ryechi.*'

Within a flash, the computer spits back a sentence in English via a printer – the translation of the phrase: 'We transmit thoughts by means of speech.' Those 39 characters took around one second to print.

Emboldened, the typist input another sentence in Russian: '*Vyelyichyina ugla opryedyelyayatsya otnoshyenyiyem dlyini dugi k radyiusu.*' Again, the computer returned with a near-simultaneous translation: 'Magnitude of angle is determined by the relation of length of arc to radius.'

More sentences and phrases were tested out, including ones covering politics, communications and military affairs. 'The sentences were turned into good English without human intervention,' the *New York Times* reported. The way the IBM Type 701 machine – technically a calculator, rather than a computer – did this was by following six broad rules for Russian syntax and grammar it had been 'taught' through a series of punch card commands. It then interrogated its memory of 250 Russian words to try and discern meaning from the sentence in English. Sometimes it would have to add in words to make sense in English; other times, it had to remove extraneous ones. And when a Russian word had multiple possible English translations, the computer was commanded to pick the one that best fitted the context.

IBM's Hurd was exuberant about the experiment and its potential. While this trial had been tested on just 250 words, the Type 701 calculator had enough memory to store one million five-letter words. The Georgetown academics were equally bullish: Russian had been chosen as the language first tackled, naturally because of the Cold War, but also because of its grammatical complexity. A system able to understand Russian could be put to work on any language.

Taking the successful trial in their stride, the team confidently predicted they would then move on to broadening out the Russian language corpus, then on to French and German. 'Then other Slavic, Germanic and Romance languages can be set up at will,' the *New York Times* wrote. Georgetown's Leon Dostert, who had worked for US President Dwight D Eisenhower during World War

II, and was a translator by trade, was defiant about its future. 'Five, perhaps three, years hence, interlingual meaning conversion by electronic process in important functional areas of several languages may well be an accomplished fact,' he told reporters.

That confidence would turn out to be misplaced.

Like many, the US government read the *New York Times* report of the demonstration. And like many, they were wowed by what it had managed to do. US government agencies began supporting machine translation research in June 1956, around the same time the world's pre-eminent thinkers in the field met at Dartmouth College. In part, the government's willingness to splash the cash was down to the successful trial at IBM headquarters in January 1954.

Three US government departments – the Department of Defense, the National Science Foundation, and the Central Intelligence Agency (CIA) – clubbed together to create the Joint Automatic Language Processing Group (JALPG). The JALPG's mission was to support the further development of machine translation technology such as that produced by the Georgetown-IBM researchers.

An estimated $20 million was spent on machine translation and other, closely related subjects in the decade after that first New York test – the equivalent of $186 million today. And despite being good at that small vocabulary, the Georgetown-IBM team struggled to get similar results when the dictionary expanded.

To find out why, a US government inquiry was opened by JALPG in 1964, led by the Automatic Language Processing Advisory Committee (ALPAC). Overseeing the ALPAC report was John R Pierce, a poindexterish employee of Bell Labs, supported by a phalanx of researchers, including those at the Massachusetts Institute of Technology.

The 124-page report's findings, when they arrived in November 1966, were damning.

The last decade or more of development, bankrolled by the government, had been for nought. According to Pierce and his team, the experiment in January 1954 was the high watermark of the Georgetown-IBM project, rather than the dawn of a new age. Sometimes, the translations were wrong. Sometimes, they needed significant editing post-translation. Even when they were decent, they hadn't evolved nearly as quickly as those behind them claimed they would.

As for trying to automatically translate Russian scientific publications as and when they appeared using technology, there was no point. The number of papers was actually low and there were plenty of human translators who could render them into English.

The report's authors concluded that funding of machine translation should be halted until it could demonstrate that it could provide measurable returns. At that moment, it couldn't provide those assurances, the ALPAC advised. Nor could four other machine translation systems that had followed in the Georgetown-IBM team's footsteps: in fact, they were worse than the decade-old technology.

'Early machine translations of simple or selected text,' the report claimed, 'were as deceptively encouraging as "machine translations" of general scientific text have been uniformly discouraging. [...] We do not have useful machine translation [and] there is no immediate or predictable prospect of useful machine translation.'

The government-backed investigation into the promise of machine translation – an early form of AI – could not have been more transparent. And while the funding didn't disappear over-night for AI projects, it started to dwindle as confidence in the feasibility of the technology waned.

Little did those working on the early sparks of AI development reading that ALPAC report in 1966 know that worse was to come, because the US was far from the only country investigating the promise of AI.

The UK, home to the inventor of the Turing test, was, too. And it would imminently come to similar conclusions, which signalled the death knell of the first AI revolution and the chill of the first AI winter.

Prior to 1971, Sir James Lighthill was best known not for his expertise in AI, but instead for his knowledge of fluid dynamics. A prolific publisher of academic research, he was the Lucasian Chair of Applied Mathematics at Cambridge University – a role that Stephen Hawking would later fill. Lighthill's connection to Cambridge went back years: he joined Trinity College at the university in the late 1930s, at the tender age of 15, a true child prodigy. He was involved in designing the wing of Concorde, the supersonic aircraft, and was a known entity to government. Which is why, in September 1971, Brian Flowers, then the chair of the UK's Science Research Council (SRC), which oversaw the funding of scientific research in the country, asked Lighthill to look into whether the SRC was spending its money wisely.

'There are few subjects which at any particular time strike one as having a very special potential for being pervasively important', Flowers wrote, but: 'Artificial Intelligence seems to me to be such a field, overlapping as it does with neurobiology, psychology, linguistics, and computer-aided learning, not to mention mathematics and computer science proper.' Flowers added a note of caution:

subjects like AI 'are highly complex, very much the preserve of experts and perhaps of plausible charlatans.'

Lighthill was flattered to be asked to investigate the tech, but was initially reluctant. However, the researcher was won over, and began scoping out the current state of AI in the United Kingdom. He began sending letters to pre-eminent researchers asking them how they felt about the present scale and future potential of AI. The letters triggered a series of conversations with academics and external stakeholders who shared their thoughts with Lighthill.

By March 1972, the academic had completed his audit. And he was wary about what was to come. 'Quite frankly,' he wrote, 'I am fully aware that when my report becomes widely available, I shall be involved in a great deal of controversy.' Why? 'In no part of the field have discoveries made so far produced the major impact that was then promised.' An entire section of the investigation was titled 'Past disappointments'. The tone was like a chiding, downhearted parent disdainful of their children.

The conclusion of the UK government, which ultimately had to decide where to spend taxpayer money wisely on the development of new technologies, was there were too many charlatans in the AI field and too few experts. The government pulled large amounts of funding out of the space, only maintaining its support for AI research in four universities nationwide.

By the mid-1970s the AI winter had become a global ice age.

As cash disappeared, so did conversations around AI. As did coverage by the media. Throughout the 1970s, according to newspaper database LexisNexis, there were just three mentions of 'artificial intelligence' in the media.

One September 1978 report from Xinhua, the Chinese newswire, covered a meeting between Yu Wen, secretary-general of the

Chinese Academy of Sciences, with John McCarthy, on a trip to China to give lectures on the promise of AI.

A year later, an Associated Press reporter covered the third annual Personal Computing Festival in New York, where 15,000 people could 'see the latest in artificial intelligence for the home'. And in September 1979, *The American Banker* magazine covered a new method of using computers to help managers make more effective decisions.

Governments' abandonment of AI as a potentially promising technology had a meaningful impact on its development. Those involved in the area were passionate. Still, they needed funding from their universities – the increasingly specialist computers required to run early AI programs didn't come cheap. And that university funding was initially set by governments. DARPA, the Defense Advanced Research Projects Agency, a US government agency set up in 1958 in response to the Soviet Union flying Sputnik over the United States, which had spent vast sums supporting the development of the internet as an early military project, pulled the plug on $3 million a year of funding for Carnegie Mellon University's speech recognition research because of a lack of results.

Without the ability to buy equipment and fund research (and researchers' salaries), the pace of innovation in AI slowed to a crawl throughout the 1970s.

It would take a new decade to kickstart development once more. And this time, the AI boom would be based not in the US or the UK, but somewhere very different with a dynamic optimism. As the sun set on AI in the West, it was just rising in the East.

4
OVER TO JAPAN

While the development of AI stuttered in the UK and the US, Japan took the lead in the 1980s. Japan had made its name in the 1970s by developing huge volumes of tech hardware – bits of kit that would be behind cutting-edge computers, including the development of computer chips. Japan's tech resurgence in that area came from a nationwide programme instigated by the government called the 'Promotion and Development of Technology for Next [Fourth] Generation Computers,' or the VLSI Project for short.

The VLSI Project was the motor that drove Japanese cars into the world's showrooms, and consumer electronics into every home across the planet. It also boosted development at home: Japan was the only industrialised country in the free world where IBM wasn't the market leader, with 74 per cent of computers in Japanese homes domestically produced. The project was an unvarnished success, whichever way you looked at it.

The Japanese government wanted more. Japan's Fifth Generation Computer Systems project was launched by the country's international trade and industry department with $850 million of funding in 1982. It would take a similar model to the fourth-generation VLSI project, but would work on artificial intelligence systems, rather than hardware. It would also depart significantly from what had gone before as the country would seek to develop its own, unique way of working with computers rather than copying the Western ideals espoused by IBM and the like.

Japan didn't sugarcoat or seek to hide its goals: they were there in black and white. A taskforce charged with setting the parameters for the fifth-generation project produced a report highlighting the stakes involved.

> *For Japan . . . the decade leading up to 1990 is thought to be a histori-*
> *cally pivotal period expanding its international contribution. Moreover,*
> *the UK and USA, perhaps because of their inability to bear the great*
> *burden of playing this role [of international leaders], have experienced*
> *a breakdown of industrial society that could be called 'UK sickness' or*
> *'USA sickness.' At this time we must also consider how Japan can avoid*
> *falling into this rut.*

Japan, then, was preparing for technological dominance with its fifth-generation project – and wanted to avoid the pitfalls that others had fallen into. And it would bet on AI.

However, this wasn't AI as the Americans had it. That was 人工知能, or *jinkō chino*. Instead, it would be a uniquely Japanese one, with importantly different terminology. The computers Japan would design in its fifth generation would be 知識情報処理システム (*chishiki jōhō shori shisutemu*), or 'knowledge information processing systems'.

The distinction was important. While the Western version of AI was designed to mimic human intelligence, the knowledge information processing system model was designed to augment the human intellect. Fifth-generation computers would understand their users' needs and strive to help them. It was best summed up by academic publication *IEEE Spectrum*, which said the project's 'prime aim is to make a machine that fits the needs of people instead of making people work by the rules of the machine.'

The fifth-generation project was a shot across the bows of other countries, who had already spent the last decade watching Japan's rise in hardware and consumer technologies. If Japan could do so well in that field, the West reasoned, what might Western countries do to AI if they followed the same process?

Immediately, the US and UK took steps to defend their position in the field of AI. In 1983, the US launched, through DARPA its Strategic Computing Initiative, a ten-year plan to build AI systems. DARPA's investment in AI tripled between 1984 and 1988 as a result. In 1984, the UK began the Alvey project, its response to the AI rejuvenation, which would cost £350 million.

The race was now on for AI supremacy, and the chill of the AI winter was gone. The 1980s would be summertime for AI development, backed to the hilt by government financing and private backing.

All this money and support paid off, as AI advanced in two key ways that helped unlock growth and development. One was that AI programs became less generalised, instead favouring specialist knowledge. So-called 'expert systems' didn't want to know the entire world. Instead, they felt it was enough to maintain knowledge, and be able to answer questions or automate tasks in a single space of expertise.

Expert systems had existed before the 1980s: MYCIN (named after a common suffix for antibiotics) was one. Written in the 1970s by researchers at Stanford University, MYCIN was intended to help doctors specialising in rare but severe infections by asking them questions and running the responses through around 600 separate rules.

A physician could, for instance, load up MYCIN and input a patient's name, sex and age. They'd then be asked by the program whether there were any blood or tissue cultures available for analysis. If so, the program's textual interface would ask the doctor what they were, when they were taken, and what the results were. Some more questions about the patient's medical history, their symptoms and anything else would follow until, dozens of questions later, the program had pinpointed a likely cause of infection – and with it, a treatment.

In truth, this was more like a computerised, automated version of running through a flow chart than anything approaching 'artificial intelligence'. But then, this was the 1980s, and what we'd now consider a relatively limited system was, at the time, cutting edge.

Indeed, MYCIN's results were able to match human doctors – in fact, it was rated as better than the best human doctors, with a suitability rating of 65 per cent for the treatment plans its proposed, where the best human doctor was rated 62.5 per cent. But it never made it into hospital treatment rooms. Doctors were worried about what the technology meant, particularly when it came to liability for mistakes. What if MYCIN missed an obvious sign that a patient had one type of bacterial infection and decided it actually was something else entirely? Who or what would be dragged in front of a court? Could a machine ever be blamed, or was it the fault of the human at the other end answering its questions?

The tough questions over AI in medicine continue today, as ethicists and physicians struggle to make the case for tools that they believe in all likelihood will make their treatment better, but make some people – including patients – feel a little queasy about being seen by Dr Computer.

But MYCIN showed that AI could understand a specialism, and could be as good at it as a human expert, simply by working through expert systems. And there were practical uses for such systems.

In the US in the 1980s, the Digital Equipment Corporation (DEC) was a monolith in computing. It was the developer of a computer that used the VAX architecture, which became an industry standard across the world. Soon, DEC was swamped with orders for computers using its VAX system. The problem was that each order had to be packed by hand in DEC's factories.

And humans made mistakes. Sometimes a customer would order a printer with their computer and find that it arrived without the right cabling or drivers. In part this could be down to the pickers and packers making errors. Other times, it would be the sales people to blame: not always knowledgeable about what bits of kit could work together, they would promise customers the world for their new computer, which then wouldn't work.

The result was that the company had to spend time, effort and money trying to handle complaints from customers who had been sold the wrong computer or sent the wrong components. In the late 1970s, DEC worked with Carnegie Mellon University researchers to develop the XCON AI system, which would be trained to ensure that customer orders made sense, and that the components required for them were packed.

First trialled in the company's factory in Salem, New Hampshire, XCON rifled through around 2,500 separate rules to ensure that orders could be fulfilled correctly. Sales staff would use the system, which would ask them questions about each customer, to ensure they got the computer they needed. Picking and packing staff would use it to make sure they were matching the right peripherals, leads and drivers to the customer's order.

Within its first five years XCON had processed 80,000 orders with an astonishing 95–98 per cent accuracy. The tool was saving DEC around $25 million a year, according to the company's own analysis.

While specialised systems were becoming more commonplace, new techniques were pushing AI forward in ways that didn't simply follow a pre-prepared set of thousands of rules.

Expert systems were fine for specialised tasks, but they weren't enormously useful when trying to expand one area of expertise to another. In that way, they were very inhuman: when we learn how, for instance, to prepare a new dish to eat, we also develop other skills, from chopping, peeling and preparing, to being able to juggle multiple tasks at once. (Anyone who has tried to cook a complicated recipe on a busy evening with hungry family members looming over their shoulder will know the importance of multitasking.)

In short: we humans take our experience in one area and apply it to another. It's what makes our brains brilliant. And it's particularly tricky to mimic that with a computer. It was trickier still in the 1980s. But there was now a branch of AI that was adapted to that task: neural networks. In the 1950s, 60s and 70s, neural networks were far too complicated for existing machines. They require a vast, interconnected web of neurons, just like those firing constantly within the human brain – which has an astonishing 86 billion neurons. Just like in our brains, each node, or 'neuron' in a neural network needs to process information and pass it on to the next neuron. The information needs to pass through the network, being processed and acted upon, until it reaches the final layer. This is learning through a method called backpropagation.

As humans, we do backpropagation all the time. Dice that onion too large in your first attempt at the recipe? When you slice it a little thinner the next time you cook, you've carried out backpropagation. Your brain adjusts, learning from each error, reducing the likelihood of an error occurring by thinking smarter, not harder. But the problem was that until backpropagation could be introduced to neural networks to correct mistakes automatically, humans had to keep tinkering with the neural networks themselves by hand.

In Britain, Geoffrey Hinton, a computer scientist, felt that neural networks were the future. And he would go on to develop and popularise the method of backpropagation, promoting it to sceptical AI researchers.

Hinton, whose great-grandfather was George Boole, the creator of the Boolean branch of mathematics, isn't the usual maths-obsessed computer scientist commonly found in the AI community. His bachelor's degree at Cambridge University was in experimental psychology. Through his studies, he became fascinated with how the brain worked and, soon, how it could be copied through mechanical computing means. He did a PhD in artificial intelligence at the University of Edinburgh, where he developed a fascination with the human brain's architecture and how it processes information.

In the 1980s, Hinton was a researcher at Carnegie Mellon University in Pennsylvania, which also developed the XCON computer system for DEC. He felt that it was possible for AI to echo the way the brain learned from errors, readjusting for the next time to reduce the likelihood of going awry. Using computers, he believed he could build a similar structure to the neural network in our brains.

The idea was to feed training data with a known answer into a network, which made predictions on the solution based on initial random weighting. The projections would then be compared to the known correct answers, and the computer would figure out where it had gone wrong on the multiple layers of the neural network and readjust its calculations to avoid making the error in the future. Repeat the process enough times over enough training cycles, and the errors began to reduce.

To continue our cooking analogy from earlier, imagine you're trying to make a bolognese sauce without a recipe. First, you sauté onions and garlic to create an aromatic base. Next, you add beef mince and tomatoes to bulk out the sauce. Finally, you season the sauce with herbs and spices. You ladle the sauce on top of your spaghetti, give it a taste and . . . it doesn't match what you had in mind.

To improve the recipe using backpropagation, you first compare your bland sauce to the ideal thick, rich, deep bolognese. The differences represent the error.

Then you work backwards to tweak the recipe. Yours was too chunky, so you dice your onions smaller. You felt a burning at the back of your throat, so add less wine to reduce the acidity. It was too watery, so you add more tomato paste. Then you tinker with the seasoning.

In week two of adjusting the recipe, your spaghetti bolognese is better, but still not a crowd pleaser at the dinner table. So in week three you compare it to what you want, propagate the taste errors back through the recipe layers, and adjust the ingredient amounts to reduce the mistakes.

By making small changes to the multilayered recipe guided by feedback, you can optimise your production of the sauce until it matches what you have in mind. Backpropagation does the same – after a fashion. It trains neural networks, layer-by-layer, from end to beginning. Automatically.

Backpropagation as a concept had been invented by a series of different researchers working independently throughout the 1970s and 1980s.

There were just two problems. First, the theory had not yet been applied to neural networks, and secondly, neural networks were totally out of vogue at the time. Symbolic AI, which used systems and rules to establish knowledge and formulate opinions in the form of things like expert systems, was what many thought was the most practical pursuit of AI. Hinton wasn't just out of sync with the wider AI community. He was out of sync with his colleagues. He was hired in 1981 on a cut-price salary, by Carnegie Mellon University, despite the fellow employee who suggested he be hired, Scott Fahlman, admitting he thought neural networks were 'a crazy idea'.

Hinton outlined his proposal for backpropagation in a paper published in 1986 alongside a clutch of co-authors. 'It was clear backpropagation had a lot of promise,' Hinton said later. (He'd subsequently move to Toronto over queasiness at how the military funded American AI development. There, he met two individuals who would become instrumental in his quest to advance a branch of AI that would eventually be called deep learning: Yann LeCun and Yoshua Bengio. The trio shared a vision of an AI powered by neural networks and set out to turn their vision into reality.)

But, outside of commercial enterprises to detect credit card fraud, the fruits of Hinton and his colleagues' labour didn't happen until the late 2000s, and backpropagation didn't catch on for three decades after their paper was published. The reason? The hardware was still too slow, and the datasets too small for backpropagation to truly show its worth.

So for the 1980s and the 1990s, AI instead pursued a path of specialist knowledge. And it was focused on games. Lots and lots of games.

5

SHALL WE PLAY A GAME?

Before artificial intelligence eased into many aspects of our lives, it was tasked with something simpler: playing games. Games were a ripe area of experimentation for artificial intelligence because they generally follow logic-based rules.

In fact, the first game-playing AI was developed by a British computer scientist, Christopher Strachey, shortly before the categorisation of 'artificial intelligence' at the Dartmouth conference. Born in 1916, Strachey worked as a school teacher and housemaster at the exclusive Harrow School and programmed computers as a hobby. In June 1950, he read a *Penguin Science News* article by Donald Davies of the UK's National Physical Laboratory (NPL) near London, which set out the underlying theory for two games that computers might be able to play: chess and noughts and crosses. Strachey became obsessed with finding a way to play draughts, also known as checkers, with an early computer, the Pilot ACE, built at the National Physical Laboratory in 1950. It was a daunting task: the ACE was a world away from today's computers. Made up of 800 different vacuum tubes, the ACE, when first built, couldn't multiply or divide numbers – which put it at a disadvantage compared to other computers of the era.

The Pilot ACE couldn't help Strachey achieve his goal, but fortunately a better computer was available at the University of Manchester, the Ferranti Mark I. Strachey travelled to Manchester to begin working on his draughts program and, by the summer of 1952, the Ferranti Mark I was playing draughts as speedily as a human. The program itself was unwieldy by anyone's estimation. It was 20 pages long, with more than 1,000 separate instructions for the computer. Even the human running the software needed instructions: before doing anything else, the program presented a teleprinted command saying: 'PLEASE READ THE INSTRUCTION CARD.'

Those human users were important, because they provided the computer program with an opponent. Strachey gave his draughts program a rudimentary personality. If a human hammered it with nonsense commands that didn't follow the rules of draughts, the computer would respond with: 'I REFUSE TO WASTE ANY MORE TIME. GO AND PLAY WITH A HUMAN BEING.'

At the same time another computer scientist was tackling another much more complicated board game. Chess.

Humans had long dreamed of creating a machine that could play chess. Indeed, one such machine had arrived, miraculously, in the mists of the 18th Century. The Mechanical Turk, a chess-playing automaton invented by the Hungarian Wolfgang von Kempelen, astonished onlookers when it was wheeled into the court of Empress Maria Theresa in Vienna in 1770. A life-sized model of a human head and torso, with a black beard and dull, grey eyes, the Mechanical Turk was clad in Turkish dress and stood behind a cabinet upon which sat a chess board.

Von Kempelen invited all-comers to beat it at chess, opening the cabinet to display a magical series of cogs and ratchets. The idea that a machine could play chess – and competently – sent the Austrian court into raptures. That only intensified when the Mechanical Turk also answered questions, spelling out its responses on a letter board. The Mechanical Turk captured the imagination so much that it toured Europe and the United States for decades, even after von Kempelen's death. Defeated opponents and spectators began questioning their uniqueness as humans and were enthralled by the power of machinery.

The Mechanical Turk played and beat some of the finest minds of its generation, including Benjamin Franklin two years before he became US President, Napoleon Bonaparte, and the English mathematician Charles Babbage. On 12th February 1820, Babbage played the machine, losing in an hour, but grew suspicious about its legitimacy. 'A trap door in the floor of the room was very evident just behind the figure,' he noted. He was right: a cleverly concealed human chess player was working the machinery, manipulating the chess pieces on the board with magnets, a fact that was exposed three decades later.

Babbage was convinced that even if the Mechanical Turk wasn't an automated chess player, he could design one. 'Every game of skill is susceptible of being played by an automaton,' he wrote in his memoirs. He had designed what he called a difference engine, a mechanical calculator considered a precursor to modern computers, and he began to think of it as a form of machine intelligence.

Years later, in the 1830s, Babbage followed his difference engine with a new iteration, called the analytical engine. While the analytical engine would never be built, he worked with an associate, Ada Lovelace, to sketch out how the engine would work. The two developed its algorithm on paper, with Lovelace writing that 'The Analytical Engine has no pretensions whatever to originate anything. It can do whatever we know how to order it to perform.'

It would be nearly a century after Babbage's difference engine, and half a century after Babbage's associate and computer programmer, Ada Lovelace's death, for a real automaton to play chess. A Spanish mathematician, Leonardo Torres y Quevedo, created *El Ajedrecista* ('the chess player') in 1912. A series of wires linked six dials that acted as the machine's 'brain', helping it dictate which pieces to move where. *El Ajedrecista*, however, didn't play a full game of chess. Instead, it picked up the action in the final stages of a theoretical game where it had a king and a rook remaining and tried to checkmate the king of its human opponent. Movements were tracked by electrical circuits, completed by wire mesh on the base of each piece touching the board. Whenever the human player's king moved, the machine calculated the best response.

Dietrich Prinz, a Berlin-born computer scientist, improved on this in the mid-20th Century. Prinz began his career working for Telefunken, a German radio and television company. Prinz gained his PhD from the Humboldt University of Berlin, where his teachers included Max Planck, who gives his name to a world-renowned German scientific research institution, and Albert Einstein.

Prinz focused on televisions and radios, gaining several patents in the 1930s for technologies that could broadcast and repair radio and television devices. But, as a Jew, he left Germany in 1935 with the rise of Nazism, fearing for his future. He ended up in the UK, eventually getting a job at Ferranti in 1947, an electronics engineering company that supplied UK defence systems, as well as home electronics such as TVs and radios, and began building his computing knowledge there.

Ferranti made the Manchester Mark 1 computer Strachey used for his draughts software. Much like Strachey, Prinz was fascinated by the 1950 *Penguin Science News* paper on programming a computer to play noughts and crosses. He felt he could combine it with the theoretical chess program Alan Turing had developed, Turochamp, in a practical game-playing AI.

By November 1951, Prinz had his first version. It wasn't perfect: rather than playing a whole game of chess, it could only pick up the pieces two moves away from checkmate. The problem was the Ferranti Mark 1 computer could only carry out 1,000 operations a second – though this was a mind-blowingly large number at the time. That meant that even the two moves prior to checkmate could take 15 or 20 minutes to calculate. The potential options for an opening chess move far outstripped that.

Both Prinz and Strachey's programs were a triumph of computer logic. But it wouldn't be the last time programmers used early forms of artificial intelligence to conquer a game. And many future developers would focus on chess.

Chess proved so popular a test because it's a familiar game played by many humans – so the AI's prowess can be measured against a wide sample. It's a good test for an AI's abilities, while remaining a technical challenge to get an AI to understand the rules within the programming limitations of early computers, such as the Ferranti Mark I's 1,000 operations a second.

Technically, these early tools weren't AI in the modern sense. They run through commands and pick pre-programmed options, rather than making choices of their own volition. But they helped capture the imagination of those who wanted to will AI into existence.

The chess-playing programs even saw commercial releases: the first being Microchess in 1976 at $10. Snapped up by legions of early computer owners, it became the first piece of computer software to sell 50,000 copies. Three years later, a game called Computer Chess with simplistic intelligence arrived on the Atari 2600.

It would take until the 1980s for chess to truly meet AI – thanks to a graduate student at Carnegie Mellon University called Feng-hsiung Hsu. Hsu had decided to devote his dissertation project to developing a machine capable of holding its own against skilled human chess players. He called it ChipTest.

Hsu began ChipTest in 1985, and quickly dragged in two Carnegie Mellon colleagues, Thomas Anantharaman and Murray Campbell, to help. Progress was slow but promising. In the 1986 North American Computer Chess Championship, an untested version, running on a specialist computer chip Hsu had developed, ended up impressing with wins after losing its first two rounds. A year later, an updated version, called ChipTest-M, won all four games it played at the same competition.

ChipTest-M was able to analyse and pick the right move from 500,000 potential options every second – but that wasn't enough for the developers. They wanted to make something even more powerful by building on the lessons learned from the ChipTest trials.

Deep Thought was born. It showed improvements on prior versions, so was pitted against real humans, playing its first game in 1988 against Romuel Reyes. While not a chess grandmaster himself, he had beaten Yugoslavian grandmaster Svetozar Gligorić 20 years earlier.

Deep Thought managed to defeat Reyes and went on to win the 1988 North American Computer Chess Championship – the third year running for the Carnegie Mellon team. In the spring of 1989, it defeated every opponent at the World Computer Chess Championship, held in Edmonton, Alberta, Canada. The team behind the project – some of whom had now been snapped up by IBM Research – decided to bring in a human grandmaster.

At the time, the Soviet grandmaster Garry Kasparov was the face of chess, the youngest person ever to become world chess champion when he beat compatriot Anatoly Karpov in 1985 at the age of 22. He was the crème de la crème of chess knowledge – and the ideal person to pit against Deep Thought. The reported $10,000 fee may have helped convince him to take part.

The match took place at the New York Academy of Art on 22nd October 1989, just 40 miles from the IBM Research Centre in Yorktown Heights, where Feng-hsiung Hsu and Murray Campbell were now based. Before the match, the FIDE system, which ranks chess players' prowess, looked at Deep Thought's skills and gave it a score of 2500, ranking it among the top 30 players in the United States. Kasparov's FIDE score at the time was 2800 – the highest ever recorded to that date.

Just watching the match was odd: Kasparov sat opposite Hsu, who would input Kasparov's moves and explain Deep Thought's next action. Before the event, Campbell, Hsu's colleague, had set odds that the match would end in a draw at one in ten.

In the end, that proved to be an overestimate born of false confidence. Kasparov, despite the pressure of playing an inscrutable, computerised opponent, and the potential ignominy of losing, won by resignation after 53 moves. The chess grandmasters watching said Kasparov had made it a formality after 18 moves. The second game was even quicker, thanks to Kasparov's aggressive play.

Still, the team were buoyed by the events of that day. In the immediate aftermath, one of them asked the media to give them three years to build a machine capable of winning the human chess world championship.

Even in defeat, it was a massive win. 'The mere existence of the match is, in a sense, a victory for the computer,' the *New York Times* wrote. 'Before the advent of Deep Thought, no machine had been developed that might challenge a human world champion.'

...

It would take nearly a decade, and a lot more development, for Garry Kasparov and a chess-playing AI to meet again. When they did in 1996, it would be the team behind Deep Thought. But the program they touted as a potential grandmaster-beater would have a different name: Deep Blue.

When Hsu and Campbell joined IBM, they augmented their tinkering with the combined power of some of IBM's best scientists and a chess grandmaster, Joel Benjamin.

After Benjamin played a version of the AI, the Deep Blue team realised the chess grandmaster could help them refine the computer's playing style and asked him to join them. Even with Benjamin's support, things didn't look hopeful. In 1995, IBM submitted a prototype version of Deep Blue to play in the eighth annual World Computer Chess Championship. It lost to a competitor in round five.

Still, the IBM team ploughed on until it was time for Deep Blue's week-long rematch against Kasparov, taking place over six games in 1996. In the first game, held on February 10th, Deep Blue defeated the grandmaster. Kasparov evened things up with the next, before two successive draws. Kasparov went on to take the final two games, sweeping the match by four games to two. The human had won, but the AI was catching up.

A rematch was held in New York, the site of their first skirmish in 1989. This time, the grandmaster took the first game, before Deep Blue won the second with a resignation from Kasparov. Afterwards, Kasparov claimed IBM had a secret chess grandmaster helping out Deep Blue. The reason? In the first game, Deep Blue had played a move no human in their right mind would. It was true: Deep Blue had made a dumb move – the result of a software bug, according to an IBM investigation after the fact. Deep Blue was far from perfect, and had a process that would play out if caught in a loop, unable to decide which move to play. It would pick a move at random. This happened in the 44th move of the first game. The move was totally illogical. It was a sign of Deep Blue's failure. But Kasparov believed Deep Blue had used brute force computing power to see a future opening the chess genius couldn't. It rattled him.

That concern fed through to the rest of the series. Kasparov was not playing right, worried Deep Blue could see into his soul. Just like in the previous match, the third and fourth games were drawn – as, this time, was the fifth. But in the sixth, Deep Blue put Kasparov in a position where the grandmaster had no choice but to resign. Machine had triumphed over man. It was a momentous occasion.

Now AI had conquered chess and left human thinking in the dust, the developers decided to pursue an even trickier challenge. Another game, with even more possibilities.

6
READY, STEADY, GO!

The next frontier for AI was the Chinese board game Go. Go has a long, storied history dating back 4,000 years. Some say it was inspiration for the abacus; others, that the game was created by a Chinese king to teach his wayward son discipline.

The rules of Go are simple. Players using either white or black stones have to capture more territory than the other player on a 19-by-19 square board. Once you place a token – known as a stone – on the board, it can't be moved, but a stone is captured and removed if surrounded by your opponent's stones.

For such a fiendishly simple sounding game, Go is extremely difficult to play well, in part because of the near infinite number of strategies that can be deployed by a player. It's said there are more possible moves than there are atoms in the universe. By contrast, chess, while still formidable, is less complex with around 10 to the power of 47 possible games. That means the game can take any one of 100,000,000,000,000,000,000,000,000,000,000,000, 000,000,000 different routes. Every time a chess piece is moved, there are around 35 different options for which piece to move and where in retaliation – a number known as the 'branching factor'.

With Go, those numbers quickly multiply. Compare chess's branching number of 35 with Go's 250. The 10 to the power of 47 possible games in chess becomes something around 10 to the power of 170. Those numbers appeared far beyond the processing power of even the most capable computer.

Or so it seemed. In the mid-2000s, Google had decided to devote some of its considerable resources to the AI race, and, in 2014 it bought a British AI company, DeepMind, for more than $650 million. With this money, DeepMind set out to develop a system that could play Go better than humans – just as Deep Blue had managed to beat Garry Kasparov in the late 1990s.

Fittingly for a company that tested its AI's mettle by giving it games to play, DeepMind's co-founder and CEO Demis Hassabis was a gaming obsessive. Hassabis's Greek-Cypriot parents ran a toy shop in London and by the time he was a teenager he was a world-leading chess player. By the age of 17 he was an integral part of the team behind the simulation game *Theme Park*, in which players ran their own theme park.

Having studied computer science at Cambridge University, Hassabis founded a video game development company before doing a PhD in neuroscience at University College London (UCL). While doing a postdoctorate job at UCL, he met Shane Legg, who was writing his PhD thesis on the risk of AI becoming sentient and posing an existential threat to humanity. Together Hassabis and Legg founded DeepMind and made it a founding principle that they would carefully work to mitigate the risks of losing control of AI. They found an entrepreneur, Mustafa Suleyman, who helped them develop the company. They went on to woo Peter Thiel,

PayPal's co-founder, who also fully ascribed to the fear of AI as an existential threat. Soon, DeepMind attracted the interest of commercial suitors by showcasing AI's ability to play games. A selection of high-ranking Google executives flew to DeepMind's London offices in December 2013. After seeing an AI getting to grips with the paddle and ball game *Breakout,* Google made an offer for the company. DeepMind agreed after Google agreed not to sell any AI tools for military use, and to establish an independent oversight board ensuring AI development took place safely.

Now within Google, the DeepMind team started working on AlphaGo.

The initial version of AlphaGo, the AI system Google DeepMind developed to play the game, was impressive enough. It studied a dataset of 100,000 human versus human games, ingesting each move and trying to understand why the players had chosen them. In March 2016, it was put to the test, in a similar way to IBM's DeepBlue tests, against South Korea's national Go champion, Lee Se-dol. He took up the challenge in part because he thought it would be easy. While AI could win at chess, he thought the challenge of computing all the possible iterations of moves and games would make it struggle with Go. Lee was so confident he would win he accepted the challenge within five minutes.

The $1 million prize fund might also have influenced his decision, along with prior precedent. AlphaGo may have won a warm-up match against a lower-ranked human opponent, European Go champion Fan Hui, in October 2015, sweeping the match five games to nil, but it made plenty of mistakes that commentators and observers – including Lee – saw as fatal flaws.

The gulf in the official Go rankings between Fan Hui and Lee Se-dol was enormous. While both were professionals, Lee was in another league. Lee was a nine dan professional, equivalent to a score of 2,940 in the ELO ranking system, while Hui was a two dan professional, equivalent to a score of 2,730. And while AlphaGo – initially trained on a dataset of moves made by amateurs with an average ELO score of 2,600 – was able to beat Hui, few thought it would stand much chance against Lee. Least of all Lee himself. 'Of course, there would have been many updates in the last four or five months, but that isn't enough time to challenge me,' he told reporters in a pre-match press conference. He predicted he would win in a landslide.

There was a landslide. But it was the AI that swept the board and defeated one of the world's best players. In a soulless room in Seoul's Four Seasons hotel, on 8th March 2016, Lee watched on as Aja Huang, one of AlphaGo's lead programmers, moved pieces based on the computer's commands. Those commands were unusual for a human player, and seemed to serve the same purpose as Deep Blue's against Garry Kasparov, unnerving the champion player. Lee ended up conceding the first game, then the next two. Lee won the fourth, but by that point, the AI had already clinched the series and went on to take the fifth, winning the match four games to one.

The professional Go player, one of the world's best, apologised to his fans for losing to an AI. 'I, Lee Se-dol, lost, but mankind did not,' he said, distraught, adding, 'Even if I become the number one, there is an entity that cannot be defeated.'

Lee and the whole professional Go community were in shock. The Google DeepMind team was elated. The world was confused and trying to understand what had happened. The South Korean government moved quickly. Three days after AlphaGo beat Lee, it announced a trillion won ($863 million) investment into AI development – a 55 per cent increase over already earmarked spending. Park Geun-hye, the South Korean president, told her country that 'Korean society is ironically lucky, that thanks to the "AlphaGo shock", we have learned the importance of AI before it is too late.'

Increasing taxpayer spending by 55 per cent because a computer beat a human at a game might sound like an overreaction, but South Korea's government had the right idea – even if all that investment didn't end up providing much in the way of results compared to the progress in the US.

Because while we didn't realise it then, the AI innovations of the late 2010s, kickstarted by AlphaGo's defeat of Lee Se-dol, were the impetus for the revolutionary moment we are currently living through.

AlphaGo was one of a new generation of AI models trained on one thing, but whose learnings could translate to a whole host of other realms. The AI had only learned the game Go, yes, but this had established the principles of deep learning, which would be core to AI's future. Deep learning uses neural networks with multiple layers (thus the term 'deep') to model and understand complex patterns of data. It's a particularly fruitful approach to tackling tasks involving unstructured data, such as image and speech recognition.

The *Economist* put it thus: 'The [deep learning] techniques employed in AlphaGo can be used to teach computers to recognise faces, translate between languages, show relevant advertisements to internet users or hunt for subatomic particles in data from atom-smashers.'

AlphaGo had become the impetus for the current AI revolution, but Google DeepMind didn't stop there. Not content with beating one of the most iconic names in Go history, AlphaGo went on to beat the 2017 world champion, Ke Jie, three games to nil. Then it retired. 'We have always believed in the potential for AI to help society discover new knowledge and benefit from it, and AlphaGo has given us an early glimpse that this may indeed be possible,' said Demis Hassabis.

Five months later, the team had released a new, even cleverer version, AlphaGo Zero. Unlike the original, which was trained by learning the movements of those 100,000 human-played games, then analysing each move to reverse engineer the thinking, AlphaGo Zero simply taught itself. It was given the basic rules of Go, then started playing.

This was a major step forward in AI-training. AlphaGo Zero became its own teacher: first making random moves, then understanding better how to play the game, then making more informed decisions. This is called reinforcement learning – learning by doing – and was in stark contrast to the supervised learning systems of previous AIs.

AlphaGo Zero's reinforcement learning system played millions of games against itself and learnt to make better future moves from each move it made. A human would take centuries to play millions of games of Go. AlphaGo Zero could do it in days.

By that point, AlphaGo Zero had a score of 100 games to zero against the version of AlphaGo that defeated Lee Se-dol. After another 40 days, it could beat the upgrade that had defeated Ke Jie. 'By not using human data – by not using human expertise in any fashion – we've actually removed the constraints of human knowledge,' the lead programmer David Silver said in a press conference announcing the leap forward.

Hassabis was equally excited. He told reporters that when he was a child, poring through physics books, he used to read about, then dream about, an impossible substance: a room temperature superconductor. This substance would, physicists theorised, allow electrical current to flow through a circuit without losing any energy, creating more efficient networks. Superconductors are realisable, but need to be cooled to an impractically low temperature. Figuring out how to make this work was beyond human knowledge, Hassabis believed. But AI's ability to understand and test a million different ideas in an instant could change that. 'We're trying to build general purpose algorithms and this is just one step towards that, but it's an exciting step,' he said.

7
THE BATTLE FOR AI CHIPS

Given that AI is now part of our daily lives, you might think AI is no longer tested in games. After all, in the early days of computer development, it was seen as an easy proving ground for the concept – and in the 1990s and 2010s, as a way of showing the general public its capability. Not so. AIs continue to be tested in games, and they're still used to show off the latest advances.

In late May 2023, days after the American computer chip maker Nvidia became one of only a handful of companies worth $1 trillion, its CEO, Jensen Huang, stepped on stage at a Taipei trade show and conference with a smile. It was understandable, given his company's meteoric growth. But that wasn't why Huang was smiling. He was about to show off another way AI and games could intertwine.

'This is the future of video games,' Huang said, stalking the stage in a black leather jacket. 'Not only will AI contribute to the rendering and the synthesis of the environment, AI will also animate the characters.' He then asked the audience to watch a pre-recorded video showing a game clip where a player entered a ramen shop and interacted with a shopkeeper called Jin.

So far, so normal – except all of Jin's responses were generated using AI.

The actual conversation itself wasn't thrilling – in part because the player didn't seem to know how far to press the conversation. He asked Jin how he was. (Jin wasn't happy: his ramen shop was getting caught in the crossfire between rival criminal gangs.) The player asked Jin if he could help (Jin said he could). The player asked where he could find the person who caused the crime. (Jin gave him some tips on how to find the criminal, then told him to be careful.) But it all happened in real-time.

'Because this character has been infused with artificial intelligence and large language models, it can understand your meaning and interact with you in a really reasonable way,' Huang explained. 'All of the facial animation is completely done by the AI. We have made it possible for all kinds of characters to be generated.'

The technology Huang uncovered was called Nvidia ACE, or Avatar Cloud Engine, and was based on natural language processing, a foundational tenet of AI. Talking to someone in a ramen shop may not seem like a massive moment for AI, but it marks a step change in how games can be coded and developed, allowing far more personalised interaction.

That week in late May was a significant moment for Nvidia and for Huang personally.

Huang had arrived in the United States aged nine with his parents, Taiwanese immigrants. He studied electrical engineering at Oregon State University, and moved to Stanford University in California in the early 1990s, closer to Silicon Valley, to do a master's in the same subject.

Huang was an introvert as a student and waited tables at his local branch of Denny's as much to bring himself out of his shell as to fund his studies and feed his and his wife Lori's two children. He later said he found the experience useful because he lacked control over what went on there and had to learn to compromise. It took eight years for Huang to complete his master's degree part-time. He had already launched Nvidia in 1993 with two friends, Chris Malachowsky and Curtis Priem, who assembled at another branch of Denny's diner to discuss their plans. They and the police were its only customers. The latter filling out their crime reports, the former thrashing out the basis of a business.

Malachowsky and Priem worked at Sun Microsystems, a large Silicon Valley tech company. But they weren't happy there, and to escape, they came up with a business to build and sell graphics cards for the burgeoning home computer market. They wanted to revolutionise computer graphics cards, which render onscreen graphics, in the same way that the first internet browser Mosaic had transformed web searches. Although Huang was the business brains behind the idea, he was wary of leaving his job working at LSI Logic, a tech infrastructure firm, unless he thought the new company could eventually make $50 million a year.

Eventually, Huang was convinced, and Nvidia – initially called Nvision – was born, first focusing on developing a multimedia platform to provide a better gaming experience with more immersive audio, better graphics, and faster performance. This became Nvidia's first graphics card, the NV1, released in November 1995. It wasn't a huge success, nor was its successor. Nvidia cards were too costly, and Nvidia quickly realised it was trying to conquer too many markets.

Instead, it identified an opportunity. In the late 1990s, computers were powered by central processing units (CPUs). These handled everything, sequentially running every task the user asked from a PC and being a good all-rounder. Want to calculate a series of cells in Microsoft Excel? A CPU can handle that. Play a game passably? CPUs could just about do that. Run your operating system? CPUs. However, the design of CPUs is relatively simple, meaning they can only handle calculations sequentially. And the burgeoning world of computer games, particularly 3D ones, pushed them beyond their limits.

An alternative was needed. Nvidia came up with the GPU, or graphics processing unit

Originally designed to make gaming better, GPUs rethought how to process calculations. Instead of trying to do many different tasks, GPUs focus on one single thing. The clue is in the name: processing (and rendering) graphics. It's equivalent to being a world-class heptathlete (a CPU) versus the world's best sprinter or shot-putter (a GPU). You can do several events well or focus on doing one thing brilliantly.

GPUs were better at graphics than CPUs because they were designed differently. Whereas a CPU usually has a single or small number of 'cores', or processors, on its main unit, GPUs can contain thousands of smaller, more efficient cores designed to juggle many tasks simultaneously. It's perfect for rendering computer graphics, where thousands of pixels must be simultaneously processed and presented on screen.

Nvidia released the world's first GPU, the GeForce 256, in 1999. It changed the company's fortunes. The GeForce 256 was specifically designed to render 10 million polygons – graphical blocks like Lego bricks that, when put together, create shapes and objects – every second. This was unheard of at the time.

The company continued to release gaming GPUs for PCs. But in the mid-2010s, something changed. In 2006 Nvidia had released Cuda, a piece of software which allowed GPUs, which until then had been solely aimed at rendering graphics quicker and easier, to be put to other uses. Cuda helped finetune the best bits of the GPU hardware for the purposes of AI.

Tech experts began realising that GPUs could also handle the complex array of calculations needed to train AI models. Training a machine learning model requires simultaneous calculations on large amounts of data – akin to rendering graphics. The mathematical processes required for AI are similar to those used to render computer graphics quickly. So, AI researchers began buying up GPUs.

The trigger came with the announcement of Google Brain. This was the tech giant's internal project to develop deep learning AI. The aim was simple: to build one of the largest neural networks ever seen and then give it free rein to learn from the internet.

In the end, Google Brain ingested a lot of YouTube videos – the equivalent of 10 million still images – and learned a lot. Google Brain's neural network, unveiled to the world at an academic conference in June 2012, was twice as good as the best existing AIs at identifying 20,000 items. Given its YouTube-powered training data, it was particularly good at cats.

The innovation was heralded but with caveats. Almost none other than Google could have built and trained the neural network. The reason? It required an eye-wateringly large amount of resources. The neural network had over a billion connections, so it needed to use 16,000 CPUs simultaneously.

The CPU was an obvious choice for the experiment. It was standard in computers and the general purpose heptathlete of the computing world. It seemed to echo what Google wanted to do: mimic the human brain's ability to learn from experience. But it was vastly underpowered for what was required and would suffer from scale problems. If AI was to be the future, it needed to be achievable for as many people as possible. And most people don't have 16,000 CPUs kicking about.

Luckily, other researchers were building AI a different way, using GPUs.

Alex Krizhevsky was born in Ukraine, moved to Canada, and was obsessed with technology. That obsession led him to Geoffrey Hinton's lab at the University of Toronto. Krizhevsky was studying for his PhD in computer science under Hinton, alongside peers who would go on to make waves in the AI world, such as Ilya Sutskever.

Krizhevsky and Sutskever decided to enter a competition called ImageNet, unveiled in 2009 at an academic conference in Miami. It was the brainchild of Fei-Fei Li, a computer science professor at the University of Illinois Urbana-Champaign. ImageNet began searching for a solution to a problem that plagued AI and continues to be a key tenet of the field today: garbage in equals garbage out.

Put another way: you can't train a good AI model without good training data. And in 2009, that good training data ... didn't exist.

Li decided to fix that. She worried about two problems gripping AI development. To give them their technical terms: overfitting and overgeneralisation.

Overfitting happens because of a lack of training data. Think about raising a child in a country with only red cars. If they travel to another country with red, blue, yellow, and green cars, they might wonder what the non-red vehicles are.

Overgeneralisation is the other side of the equation: we know the differences between a tennis ball and a basketball. But if your AI model only looks at the shape of an item, it could easily call a tennis ball a basketball and vice versa.

Li figured she could create a comprehensive image-led database to train AI models. Work began in 2007, with Li hiring a raft of undergraduates and paying them $10 an hour to find images of everyday items, label them, and then add them to the dataset. There was one problem: at the rate they were going, it would take nearly a century to complete. Li wanted to present her work before she retired. So, she turned to Amazon's Mechanical Turk, which runs massive outsourcing of manual labour to (relatively poorly paid) humans. It would be cheaper and quicker to do it this way than hiring undergrads.

Labelling the 3.2 million images that formed ImageNet still took nearly three years. They were split into 12 broad categories like 'mammal' and 'furniture', then into 5,000-odd subcategories. 'Mammal' could become 'placental' then 'carnivore', 'canine', 'dog' ,'working dog' then 'husky'. It was a mammoth task. The Conference on Computer Vision and Pattern Recognition (CVPR) where she wanted to present her work wasn't interested. She submitted a proposal to present a paper on stage but was only allowed to present a poster in the conference hall, far away from the presentation stages.

ImageNet didn't wow conferencegoers. But Li was determined to see her work recognised. So she partnered with an existing AI image recognition competition, whose database was much smaller, rebranding it to the ImageNet competition. Entrants would train AI models on the dataset to see which could recognise the most images.

Suddenly, ImageNet was respected. And, at the University of Toronto, Krizhevsky and Sutskever decided to enter the 2012 competition. The pair chose a different tack to most: a neural network like Google Brain's. They also took a different approach in powering the neural network, using two GTX 580 3GB GPUs, rather than the oodles of CPUs used by Google. ImageNet had expanded to more than 15 million images and 22,000 categories by this point. However, the competition used a subset of around 150,000 testing images across 1,000 categories, with competitors allowed to test on 1.2 million more.

Krizhevsky and Sutskever won the competition because using GPUs rather than CPUs allowed their AI to process the training data in less than a week, meaning it could relearn and improve.

One of the key metrics used to analyse the effectiveness of models was the 'top-5 error rate' – the percentage of times the correct label wasn't among the five most likely predictions for a previously unseen image. Krizhevsky and Sutskever's model's top-5 error rate was 15.3 per cent – meaning it flubbed the answer 15.3 per cent of the time. The second-placed entrant's error rate? 26.2 per cent.

This was vindication for AlexNet, which the model would come to be called, and for the GPU approach more broadly. With results like these, people started to pay attention to the potential application of GPUs for artificial intelligence. Within three years, every entrant in the ImageNet competition was using GPUs.

The results of the model were the talk of the AI community. Two months later, Geoffrey Hinton travelled to Lake Tahoe in the US for that year's NIPS conference (later renamed to NeurIPS), alongside his students Krizhevsky and Sutskever.

After the conference, many networking deals were done. But Hinton and his students were there for business. They had set up DNNresearch – short for 'deep neural network research' to monetise their discovery. And companies were keen to invest.

One December night post-conference, on the seventh floor of the Harrah's hotel in Lake Tahoe, Hinton set up a laptop in his room (perched on an upturned bin on a table so he could stand up and save his bad back) and ran an auction. Several big tech firms had already tried to tap up Hinton and DNNresearch. The academic felt the fairest way to decide who to sell to was by inviting interested parties – Google, Baidu, Microsoft and DeepMind – to submit bids via email. They could submit one bid every hour. Each hour, the bid had to rise by at least $1 million. Hinton and his students would check the Gmail inbox every hour until bidders stopped emailing.

The auction was designed to keep the suitors guessing. Hinton hadn't said he'd decide on a winning bid when they were evaluated at the end, nor would he necessarily accept the highest offer. It was a game of chicken for the tech giants looking to buy the team who had revolutionised AI.

First DeepMind, not yet part of Google, dropped out, outgunned by more prominent competitors. Then Microsoft stopped emailing. Google and Baidu kept the messages coming. They reached $44 million. Hinton suspended bidding just before midnight, needing sleep.

When he woke up, he decided to stop the auction altogether. Though Baidu and Google were willing to keep bidding, Hinton had made up his mind. DNNresearch was Google's.

The success of AlexNet, DNNresearch's AI model, was no longer a secret. And Nvidia was at the heart of it. Rival chipmakers couldn't compete with its GPUs. At least until May 2016, when Google announced it had created its own AI-tailored chip. Called a tensor processing unit (TPU), Google had been using the chip for around a year before it announced it to the world. TPUs were specifically designed for use with Google's TensorFlow framework, a library of software that helps build AI models.

The chip wars had begun, and, like rocket fuel, these tiny computer processors powered the ever-faster development of AI models. Between the 1950s, when AI first came into existence, and the 2010s, the doubling time of computing power was around every 20 to 21 months – in line with Moore's law, a commonly held theory that transistor density, a proxy for computing power, doubles every two years.

However, in the first half of the 2010s, that all changed. Moore's law was out the window, power doubled every five or six months. With the arrival of the TPU chip, Google DeepMind's development of AlphaGo, and everything that came with it, the doubling time stayed roughly the same, but the models they were training became way bigger.

Google's arrival in the chip development competition started a race for other big tech firms to develop chips, reducing their reliance on Nvidia. Amazon quickly entered the market with two different AI-specialised chips: the Trainium and the Inferentia, developed in-house. Microsoft joined comparatively late, in 2019, but its Athena chips could help significantly speed up its AI upon entering the market. All were trying to draw down their dependency on Nvidia, for obvious reasons: with the world now realising the power of AI, companies were trying desperately to get their hands on as many chips as possible. Even Elon Musk's Twitter got into the dash, buying 10,000 GPUs in April 2023 to power a Twitter-specific large language model.

Still, even with the AI development boom of the late 2010s, it took a while for Nvidia's core business to become servicing the AI industry. It took until early 2022 for AI to eclipse its prior main business, providing chips to the gaming industry. But that hunger for more computer chips – driven by the sheer scale of AI, where a single 2,000-word response to a question posed to ChatGPT takes something like 400 quadrillion computer operations to produce – drove Nvidia's success.

Even with homegrown efforts from tech's biggest names, Nvidia still has up to 95 per cent market share of the AI chip market. Any chip currently used in AI is likely made by Jensen Huang's company. Nvidia also supports much of the legwork for the next generation of AI research. Of the 21,495 chips cited in AI academic papers from 2022, 20,350 are Nvidia's. Google's TPU was mentioned just 178 times.

Of those Nvidia chips, the one powering most of the development is the A100. First released in 2020, it costs roughly $10,000 and has become the standard choice for developers looking to produce an AI model. Stable Diffusion, the AI image generation model developed by Stability AI, was trained on 256 A100 GPUs.

The problem is that through the third-party company that makes most computer chips, Taiwan Semiconductor Manufacturing Company, Nvidia can only make a finite number of GPUs at any one time. And demand for the A100 is hugely outstripping supply.

However, the A100 may soon be as *passé* for AI as CPUs became. Because Nvidia's next generation of GPU, the H100, is being rolled out.

This means AIs could become even faster, more powerful, and more precise, potentially kickstarting another big step.

8
THE BIRTH OF OPENAI

If the early development of the field of artificial intelligence was spurred on by two men who had healthy competition with each other in the form of Alan Turing and John McCarthy, then the present generative AI revolution has been brought about in large part thanks to the work of two other men: Sam Altman and Elon Musk.

Set in 16 acres of grounds in Menlo Park, California, as close to the beating heart of Silicon Valley as you can get, stands the Rosewood Sand Hill hotel. One summer evening in July 2015 a group of influential Valley people were brought together there by Sam Altman, president of YCombinator, a technology startup accelerator. YCombinator's job was to find promising new companies and to give them the money and support they needed to thrive. By July 2015, YCombinator companies, including Airbnb and Dropbox, were worth a collective $65 billion.

Altman had been a dealmaker since he founded location-sharing social media company Loopt while at Stanford University, studying computer science, in 2005. (Loopt gained funding from

YCombinator and Altman dropped out of Stanford after one year.) Altman finessed his negotiation skills with Loopt, convincing mobile phone networks to give the app access to the location data that made its core functionalities work – no mean feat.

Altman spent his life looking for the next big thing in tech – that was the purpose of YCombinator – and he foresaw the potential of a resurgence in AI, nearly six decades after it first entered the public consciousness. In 2015, deep learning models were getting better, faster, and the field was rapidly expanding.

It had been around 18 months since Google acquired DeepMind, spending a reported $500 million or so. It seemed likely that the purchase was motivated by a desire to kickstart Google's attempts to develop a useful AI. With Elon Musk and others, Altman believed Google wouldn't be content with cornering off the AI market. They thought the end goal was a Google AGI – or artificial general intelligence.

That concerned many, including Altman and Musk. Google already dominated many spheres of our lives, thanks to its free search engine, email provider, and support for Android phones. The trade-off for free access was giving up your data to improve the tools. People became the product. The idea of humans becoming the product for AI development gave Altman and others cause for concern.

Altman is already prepared for the apocalypse. 'I have guns, gold, potassium iodide, antibiotics, batteries, water, gas masks from the Israeli Defense Force, and a big patch of land in Big Sur I can fly to,' he told the *New Yorker* in 2016.

His mother told the magazine Altman had always been a worrier, though she said that in the event of a pandemic, Altman planned to fly to billionaire Peter Thiel's house in New Zealand

and hole up with him until it went away. (Thiel and Altman are close colleagues, each respecting the other's business acumen.)

And Altman is apprehensive aabout what happens if AI becomes more powerful than humans. He lamented Garry Kasparov's loss to Deep Blue in May 1997. As a nerdy 12-year-old who loved computers, Altman should have been thrilled that an AI beat a human. But he wasn't. When DeepMind managed to beat Lee Se-dol in March 2016, he was 'very sad'. He said: 'I'm on Team Human. I don't have a good logical reason why I'm sad, except that the class of things that humans are better at continues to narrow.'

So worried that Google was about to corner the market, and render humans useless or in thrall to AI, Altman used his contacts to bring together a group including Greg Brockman, who had been chief technology officer at YCombinator alumnus Stripe, and Musk, knee-deep in his space exploration startup, SpaceX. Musk made his money selling one of his early companies to PayPal. He was also CEO at Tesla, an electric car company looking to develop self-driving vehicles – which wouldn't work without AI.

'I am the reason OpenAI exists,' Musk told CNBC in an outspoken interview in March 2023. He claimed the company wouldn't exist without his initial investment, and that he was 'instrumental' in convincing some of those engineers and scientists to join – particularly Ilya Sutskever. 'I came up with the name,' he added.

Musk claimed he set up OpenAI because he was concerned Google, after its purchase of DeepMind, would develop runaway AI without thinking about the consequences. (In a lawsuit filed against OpenAI in February 2024, Musk even claimed he and a co-founder of PayPal sought to gazump Google in its purchase of DeepMind in late 2013.) Musk used to lodge at Google co-founder Larry Page's home, and the two would have conversations late into the night where Musk would warn Page about AI's dangers. 'He was really not concerned about the danger,' Musk claimed. 'He was quite cavalier about it.'

Musk was so concerned, by his telling, that he decided to create OpenAI with Altman. 'OpenAI refers to "open-source",' Musk said, the opposite of Google: an open-sourced non-profit organisation. Still, the entrepreneur recognised challenging Google would be difficult: he compared it to being an ant up against an elephant.

Musk, Altman and the others came together to discuss the idea of starting an AI business outside big tech's control – worried that the pursuit of profit would warp the development of AI. It was a particular bugbear of Musk's. In an interview in 2014, he described AI as humanity's 'biggest existential threat.. He was concerned that AI development, particularly by big tech firms, was like summoning a 'demon' we couldn't control. Altman was similarly concerned, particularly about Google's involvement. He emailed Musk in May 2015 saying that if humanity was going to develop AI full-pelt, 'it seems like it would be good for someone other than Google to do it first.' Altman laid out a five bulletpoint plan in an email a month later. Musk replied with three simple words: 'Agree on all'.

Things moved quickly from there. At the July 2015 meeting at the Rosewood Sand Hill hotel, Brockman was tasked with building the new AI business and tried to get one of the three big names behind the deep learning revolution on board. Two, Yann LeCun and Geoff Hinton, were at Facebook and Google respectively and declined. The third, Yoshua Bengio, liked his role at the University of Montreal, and didn't want to countenance a life outside academia. But he helped by creating a list of his most skilled peers for Brockman to pursue.

Most of the technologists were wary of giving up relatively safe, guaranteed jobs in academia for the make-or-break gamble of a startup. In frustration, Brockman tried a more direct approach: he invited the ten researchers he felt would contribute most to the company to a weekend meeting at a Napa Valley winery. Sutskever later recalled that 'the wine was secondary to the talk.'

At the end of the meeting, Brockman was upfront. The attendees had a job offer with the new lab he was building, and three weeks to decide.

Nine said yes. Ilya Sutskever, then working on Google's Brain project, was the ace among them. He was on the inside and intrigued by the idea of starting something new. There were risks involved, he later said, but he felt 'it would be a very interesting thing to try.' His salary was $1.9 million a year.

OpenAI was born. The company broke cover and went public at the end of December 2015's NIPS conference in Montreal. It was a non-profit, they said, whose goal was 'to advance digital intelligence in the way that is most likely to benefit humanity as a whole, unconstrained by a need to generate financial return. Since our research is free from financial obligations, we can better focus on a positive human impact.'

Of course, there was cash involved: $1 billion, including some from Musk, which widened spectators' eyes. 'This is just absolutely wonderful news, and I really feel like we are watching history in the making,' wrote Sebastien Bubeck, a Princeton University researcher who had attended the conference (Bubeck now works in Microsoft's AI division). 'There are very, very few places in the world solely dedicated to basic research and with that kind of money.'

Miles Brundage, who went on to work for the company, felt the moment was significant, not least because OpenAI put safety at its core, but also because it showed how AI had entered the mainstream.

There were some sceptical responses to the idea OpenAI would remain on the side of the angels, even back then. 'The intent to open-source the research seems clearly good in the short and medium term, but raises some concerns in the long run when getting closer to general AI,' wrote Viktoriya Krakovna, who now works at Google. She pointed out that an OpenAI researcher, Andrej Karpathy, had commented that 'we are not obligated to share everything – in that sense the name of the company is a misnomer.'

David J Klein, another attendee, was equally circumspect. 'Non-profits can still patent their work, and despite it being "open", they can still decide who can use the IP and at what price,' he wrote. 'The board decides this – this would be Elon Musk and Sam Altman, most prominently. Non-profits can be acquired. They can also have profitable side-business and subsidiaries.' Klein was relatively underwhelmed by the potential of OpenAI, and wary of being caught up in the hype. He had seen this story play out before.

In the 1990s, Microsoft co-founder Paul Allen pledged $100 million to found Interval Research, an 'advanced technology think tank'. It crashed and burned after Allen felt there was too much research and not enough ensuing development.

While some were muted in their response to OpenAI, the broader reaction was excitement. Some competitors got wind of the announcement before it was made and tried to lure those signed to the company away with big money offers.

But everyone stuck with the project, and the nine researchers began their work in January 2016 at Brockman's apartment in San Francisco's Mission District. They began focusing on tackling re-inforcement learning, where a machine repeats a task to learn how to do it, as a stepping stone on the way to unsupervised learning – where it doesn't need any guidance.

The overall founding goal of OpenAI, pursuing artificial general intelligence (or AGI), was seen as mad, Altman has said. 'People thought we were batshit insane,' he told the Lex Fridman Podcast. Altman claimed, without naming him, that one eminent AI researcher had messaged reporters disparaging OpenAI's goals and saying they weren't worth the coverage. 'That was the level of pettiness and rancour in the field at a new group of people saying: "We're going to try to build AGI,"' he said. 'We don't get mocked as much now.'

Unlike Musk, Altman doesn't court the limelight. Neither is he one to hand out *bons mots* about management without being asked, despite being at the helm of the company worth tens of billions that made the AI revolution what it is today. Those who know him well say Altman is a force of nature. He's hardworking – he developed scurvy because he was so focused on making Loopt, his first business, a success, that he neglected his own health. He's been compared, favourably, to an arcade claw machine: he can roam around a large area, but can quickly delve deep for a specific thing when needed.

In a blog published in January 2019, Altman wrote: 'Self-belief is immensely powerful. The most successful people I know believe in themselves almost to the point of delusion.' Whether he includes himself is tricky to discern. But another of his mottos gives some insight into OpenAI's approach to hawking its wares. 'Self-belief alone is not sufficient. You also have to be able to convince other people of what you believe.' Not that convincing people takes him much effort. 'A big secret,' Altman wrote, 'is that you can bend the world to your will a surprising percentage of the time – most people don't even try, and just accept that things are the way that they are.'

Little did we know then how much would be bent to Altman, and OpenAI's, will.

OpenAI's first advance in reinforcement learning came in April 2016, when it released a beta version of OpenAI Gym, which tested the efficacy of AI models to tackle generalised tasks. Like a real-life gym, it contained a variety of metaphorical machines to test different metaphorical muscles. If an AI model was weaker on one than another, the researchers could identify areas for improvement.

By December that year, it had its second product: Universe. This was a platform that mimicked the way humans use computers, with a range of similar games and software to those we use every day. The AI agents put through Universe's battery of tests were able to roam freely, filling in forms on websites and experience computers as we do, with the aim of learning about the world.

Both tools were hugely expensive to run: in 2017, OpenAI spent a quarter of its operating expenses on cloud computing. At the same time, it was developing its own AI bots to play games. One was tasked with learning how to play Dota 2, an online multiplayer game, and defeated a professional player, Danil Ishutin, who went by the name Dendi. The victory echoed the defeats of Garry Kasparov and Lee Se-dol at chess and Go respectively, and took place at The International, a landmark event for Dota players, in August 2017.

The victory was a single one-on-one match, not the standard five-versus-five free-for-all of a typical Dota game. But the bot kept learning. A year later, it was beating amateurs and semi-professional teams in a full five-on-five match. That's to be expected: it played 180 years of matches against itself every day in preparation. But all that training was costly to maintain: OpenAI was paying for 128,000 CPUs and 256 GPUs from Google's cloud server.

The money was soon to run out. In February 2018, Elon Musk left. Ask OpenAI's GPT-4 chatbot what happened and you'll get the official version: the primary reason for his departure was to avoid any potential conflict of interest with his role at Tesla, particularly as Tesla became increasingly involved in AI through its self-driving car technology.

OpenAI announced Musk's departure by saying Musk would 'continue to donate and advise the organization.'

While Musk has remained a supporter and contributor to OpenAI, the chatbot wrote, his departure from the board was seen as a necessary move to ensure the separate paths of OpenAI and Tesla, particularly in their AI applications, remained clear and conflict-free.

There was also concern that the conflict of interests extended beyond simply developing AI while building a self-driving electric car company. In 2017, Andrej Karpathy, who acted as the face of OpenAI immediately after its founding, was tapped by Musk to develop Tesla'sAutopilot technology. (Karpathy later rejoined OpenAI.)

Since leaving, Musk has been characteristically outspoken. He has criticised OpenAI for becoming a 'closed source, maximum-profit company'. which he says was not his original intention when he stumped up the cash to help create it. (In a podcast in March 2023, Altman called Musk 'a jerk'.)

And about that cash: Musk bankrolled a chunk of the $1 billion of promised investment OpenAI announced at its launch in 2015. When he left, he pulled the plug. He continued to pledge cash even after the split, and by 2020 had already donated $44 million, but OpenAI's ongoing costs quickly burned through that, and the company had a business plan based on nearly 20 times that figure. Altman had already been itching to try and expand the funding beyond that promised $1 billion – which helped push the South African entrepreneur further out the door.

It's worth noting Musk wasn't simply a passive financier, content to sit back and let the data scientists chart out a course for the company. According to one person who was there around the time Musk was involved, he was much more hands-on than you might think.

'He was there a lot,' said the former OpenAI worker. Musk was helping researchers and managers do their jobs better in ways the anonymous worker told me seemed strange to him. 'He would give them, like, basic advice,' he said.

For instance, if OpenAI wanted to make a robot learn how to do a complicated task, the workforce and management, mostly drawn from academia and often inexperienced with business-critical deadlines, would look towards the end goal and how to reach it. Musk would come in and suggest the team instigate smaller, shorter milestones and deadlines to meet instead. 'They'd be like, "Wow, Elon Musk just had like, the most amazing insight."'

To the former worker, it seemed like basic management advice. But for the company it helped enormously. 'He was actually a useful part of the culture at that time,' they said. He had also given them huge amounts of funding, which would be important because of a massive technological advancement in 2017 that would super-charge the development of AI.

9
ATTENTION TRANSFORMS FORTUNES

A I advancement has been divided into eras by many key, liminal moments. The befores and afters, when an event, declaration or technological change helped move AI forward – or back, as in the case of the successive AI winters.

The Turing Test was one such moment, giving researchers trying to simulate human intelligence a goal to aim for. The Dartmouth conference was another, giving shape and form and a single name to the field. (Sci-fi writer Ted Chiang has said he believes the phrase 'artificial intelligence' was an error. He considers 'applied statistics' to be a less sexy but more accurate description of what we now refer to as AI.)

Another was in 2006, when Geoffrey Hinton, who had already helped knit the out-of-vogue ideas of backpropagation and neural networks together in 1986, built on those foundations to accelerate the development of deep learning. Hinton and his team at the University of Toronto developed an AI architecture system called Deep Belief Network, whose multiple hidden layers could accurately model complex data patterns. Hinton's published findings showed it was possible to train deep neural networks more easily, sparking an interest that would continue throughout the 2000s.

Another momentous shift occurred in June 2017, with the publication of an academic paper that would drastically shift the direction of AI research. An initial draft appeared on the arXiv preprint server and was subsequently presented at that year's NIPS academic conference – the same conference where two years earlier Elon Musk and Sam Altman had announced the founding of OpenAI.

Titled 'Attention Is All You Need,' the paper was penned by a group of Google researchers and suggested a different approach to using the convolutional and recurrent neural networks (or CNNs and RNNs) that had been dominating the field of machine learning. They both worked well but had limitations.

CNNs were world-beating at understanding and processing information about physical space, making them ideal for image recognition (want to know where pixels are in relation to one another? CNNs are for you).

RNNs were great at working through text, analysing one piece of information before moving on to the next part of the sequence. Like careful human readers reading out the contents of a book word-by-word, running their fingers underneath the text, RNNs were diligent but slow, with a drop in performance on longer sequences.

Instead, the Google researchers suggested a new approach: a new type of AI model called a transformer. At the heart of the transformer model was an 'attention mechanism'. Attention mechanisms don't treat each word with equal attention. They skim-read, focusing on different parts of the input data, assigning importance to parts they deem important while skipping past or simply assuming other less important elements. It means that, unlike RNNs, all the input data is observed simultaneously, drastically reducing 'reading time'.

And it worked. Spectacularly. The Google researchers set their new, attention-led transformer model, off completing machine translation tasks. The model outperformed existing state-of-the-art models in translating English to German and English to French.

The paper had, in fact, stemmed from an attempt to improve the performance of Google Translate, the company's AI-powered real-time translation service. In a meeting at Google's headquarters in Mountain View, California, researchers hit upon a method called self-attention. Rather than looking at translations word by word, the system would look at entire sentences in context.

This was a step change in the approach to AI. The paper had a massive impact and has been academically cited tens of thousands of times since its release. The reason? Its simplicity.

It presented a new paradigm for AI models that worked more like humans by shifting its level of attention depending on what it was looking at: again, the human brain had the smartest moves. 'Attention Is All You Need' inspired researchers across academia and business to develop new, more efficient and sophisticated models.

The transformer at the heart of the paper became the standard for all other AI models that followed. Take GPT-4, the underlying tech that at the time of writing powers ChatGPT, developed by OpenAI. The T stands for 'transformer'. BERT, one of Google's equivalent LLM stands for Bidirectional Encoder Representations from Transformers. There's that word again: transformers.

Google and OpenAI took transformers in different directions. Both sought to use them for natural language processing, but each focused on other parts of the process.

Google was using transformers so its AIs could understand their information's context: the concept of bidirectional training meant AI models would consider a word's meaning based on what came before *and* after it, as opposed to only afterwards – like RNNs did.

OpenAI used transformers to generate text. GPT-2, its text creation tool trained on source data from eight million web pages, didn't just generate text from a request, it could also translate and write passable poetry, showing its own sparks of creativity.

It was actually too good. When unveiling it in February 2019, OpenAI decided not to release the model publicly. It was worried GPT-2 was too powerful and could – in the wrong hands – be put to nefarious use. Instead, it shared only a much smaller, pared-back version for public use and declined to share either the dataset it was trained on, the code the training used, or the weighting for the models – a recipe for anyone with enough time and drive to make their own version.

This split the AI community. 'I think that OpenAI is using its clout to make ML [machine learning] research more closed and inaccessible,' wrote Anima Anandkumar, a professor of computing at the California Institute of Technology, who also worked at Nvidia. She believed OpenAI was 'severely playing up the risks' of unleashing its language model on the world to promote its presence among journalists, and downplay academic scrutiny. Others saw OpenAI as virtuous and respected its thinking.

OpenAI released a fuller version of GPT-2 in May 2019. However, it was still only twice the size of the pared-down version it released that February – and around one-fifth the size of the full-powered tool. This was not the first time OpenAI had reneged on its intentions. One former employee told *Fortune* magazine they felt OpenAI had strayed from its original ethos to become like any other tech company: 'The focus was more, how can we create products, instead of trying to answer the most interesting questions.'

It would be far from the last time the company backtracked. When OpenAI released the text-to-image generator DALL-E 2 in April 2022, it throttled use to allow artists only, citing fears it could be misused. According to one former employee, it opened up DALL-E 2 after the arrival of competing image generators from companies like Midjourney and Stability AI. (OpenAI itself said beta testing needed to be completed before the company was confident it could release the tool more widely.)

'Attention Is All You Need' gave birth to the modern AI revolution. It presented the principle that powers platforms like ChatGPT and Midjourney. It took just five years from the paper's publication to the resulting apps entering common usage.

It was also a key moment for OpenAI.

OpenAI had been tinkering with a variety of AI innovations, including one first developed by a research scientist, Alec Radford, supported within the company by Ilya Sutskever. Radford had wanted to see if a neural network could be trained on a database of Amazon reviews to create its own text.

It could – and beyond simply generating its own text, it could decide whether the reviews it read were positive, negative or neutral. 'It just seemed like this absurdly big corpus,' said the former OpenAI worker. 'It was just wild.'

Sutskever saw that the project had potential if it could be scaled up to the entire internet. But that required processing power that couldn't be unlocked . . . until transformers.

By June 2018 OpenAI had developed its first Generative Pre-Trained Transformer (GPT), able to consume information scraped from thousands of books, build inferences between the data it found, and understand the language it came across.

GPT, and a second model called GPT-2, which was trained on a database of eight million web pages voted popular by Reddit users, was OpenAI's killer weapon. But it drastically increased the company's data-processing costs. OpenAI paid Google around $70 million to use its cloud computing servers in 2019, making OpenAI one of Google's top five cloud computing customers.

Sam Altman, OpenAI's co-founder, knew the company needed to raise more funding to stay competitive. He began contacting close friends, including Vinod Khosla (who had co-founded Sun Microsystems) and LinkedIn co-founder Reid Hoffman, who ran a venture capital company together called Khosla Ventures.

Altman's longstanding friends were willing to provide the tens of millions of dollars he wanted. But they needed something in exchange. Venture capitalists provide financial backing for early-stage companies in exchange for a return on their investment. With OpenAI's non-profit status, there was no way for that to happen.

At the start of 2019, OpenAI faced a conundrum. It had the confidence to launch as a non-profit because of Musk's promised $1 billion. But the money had gone. And those willing to make up some, but not all, of the shortfall, needed to know their money wouldn't also disappear into a black hole, never to return.

On 11th March 2019, OpenAI officially became OpenAI LP (the 'LP' stands for limited partnership). The organisation invented a new term for their firm – now a company – 'capped-profit'.

'The fundamental idea of OpenAI LP is that investors and employees can get a capped return if we succeed at our mission, which allows us to raise investment capital and attract employees with startup-like equity,' the company explained. 'But any returns beyond that amount – and if we are successful, we expect to generate orders of magnitude more value than we'd owe to people who invest in or work at OpenAI LP,' they added, 'are owned by the original OpenAI Nonprofit entity.'

It was inelegant and opened up OpenAI to allegations of hypocrisy, which it tried to head off with a charter stating its 'primary fiduciary duty is to humanity'. Openness was in its name, but OpenAI was becoming something . . . different. But it needed the cash. It soon got it.

10
ENTER MICROSOFT

On 22nd July 2019, just 133 days after OpenAI changed its company structure from a non-profit to a capped-profit model, Greg Brockman, who had lured the majority of OpenAI's researchers with the promise of something different, published a blog on the firm's website. He cut to the chase: 'Microsoft is investing $1 billion in OpenAI to support us building artificial general intelligence (AGI) with widely distributed economic benefits.'

OpenAI had entered a new era.

The partnership with Microsoft would forever change the course of its mission. The cash injection and ability to use Microsoft's Azure cloud computing servers helped ensure OpenAI's growth. OpenAI didn't simply piggyback on Microsoft's existing infrastructure: the two companies worked closely together developing new AI-ready hardware to improve performance.

This infrastructure included thousands of AI-optimised GPUs, linked together on an unprecedented scale in a high-throughput, low-latency network.

On the face of it, it seemed like a match made in heaven. But the reality was more complicated.

Microsoft had been dabbling in AI development for years. Its researchers were working on a project codenamed Turing, an AI system that could analyse the contents of millions of internet documents as training data, in order for its productivity software like Microsoft Office to make more helpful suggestions than its infamous 'Clippy' had in the early 2000s.

Yet even Microsoft, a company then worth $780 billion, couldn't make the sums behind AI work. Training those models took time and processing power beyond anything the tech giant had encountered. It entered into a partnership with Nvidia to develop GPUs for quicker data processing. That cost money, and became a sunken cost Microsoft wanted to recoup.

And Microsoft was worried about losing ground to competitors – in a different field. While building its own cloud computing business, Microsoft was being outgunned by Amazon and Google, who led the pack. By becoming a major partner for OpenAI, Microsoft could perhaps utilise OpenAI's developments for its own AI work, and bolster its cloud business. (While OpenAI's contract with Google meant the former still used the latter's cloud servers for some of 2020, the 2019 Microsoft deal meant that OpenAI's cloud usage would eventually migrate entirely to Microsoft.)

It seemed to make sense. But Microsoft had long relied on the nous of its totemic founder, Bill Gates, for big strategic decisions. It took him changing his mind about the world wide web in the early 1990s, having previously said it wouldn't be a major thing, for Microsoft to change tack and make Internet Explorer the dominant browser in the early days of the web. At Microsoft, what Bill Gates says goes. And in the late 2010s, Gates had yet to be convinced of the value of AI.

In 2019, months before Microsoft put $1 billion into OpenAI, Gates was at an event in the San Francisco Bay area, telling guests he felt AI had not developed much in the last five years. He apparently admired what OpenAI was building, but was sceptical about its business plans. He was also unconvinced that natural language processing, the key tenet of OpenAI's GPT technology, would really work. Still, Gates was persuaded to invest by Satya Nadella, chairman and CEO of Microsoft, so the tech giant bought into OpenAI. Sort of.

The $1 billion appeared, in part, to be credits for the use of Microsoft's Azure cloud servers, based on documents analysed by the website *The Information*. The year before the deal was signed, Altman's AI company spent $845,000 on Microsoft products. The year after, that dropped to just $52,000. Given that OpenAI's reliance on Microsoft's cloud services increased, rather than decreased, after the deal, this suggests its cloud server usage was subsidised by the agreement.

The funding, and the closer working relationship, helped both companies grow. Able to expand more aggressively, OpenAI ploughed more cash into its technology – and attracted more investors. In 2021, early shareholders in OpenAI sold stock implying the company was worth $20 billion.

Four years after its initial 2019 investment, and two years after a subsequent round of funding, Microsoft came back, willing to plough $10 billion into OpenAI. It was the biggest single investment into a company Microsoft did not go on to own, according to Bloomberg, and the fourth-biggest investment in any company by Microsoft, including those they subsequently purchased outright.

Within three months of that investment, other venture capital firms would buy up $300 million more of OpenAI shares, suggesting the company was worth around $30 billion. (At the time this book was being finalised in February 2024, it's closer to $80 billion.)

All because of OpenAI's killer app. Since 2018, it had been training and developing versions of its GPT model. In June 2020, it released GPT-3, its third version of the large language model, or LLM. When the academic paper describing GPT-3 was released, it credited 31 different authors within OpenAI, showing the breadth of its team.

We already know the T in GPT-3 stands for the transformer that made it possible. The G is for 'Generative', signifying GPT-3's ability to generate sentences or paragraphs from its input. And the P is for 'Pre-trained': it has been trained, using a vast swathe of the internet, to better understand how we craft language. This means GPT-3 and its successors are as comfortable conversing in everyday language as they are mimicking the collected works of Shakespeare. It directly benefits from our using the internet as a mass repository of our collective knowledge.

People tend to anthropomorphise models like GPT-3 and its successors because we find what they do so incredible. Indeed, academic research has found the level of anthropomorphising tech of all types has increased around 50 per cent between 2007 and 2023, as measured by media mentions and references in academic literature. But, in reality, the answers are just statistics.

You type a query into GPT-3 or another language model and it will try to understand what you've asked, then present what it thinks is an apt answer. But computers don't read language the way we do: the letters and characters you type get sliced into a series of characters, or tokens, that often appear close to each other. 'The' could be one so-called token, as could 'are' and 'ise' – a common suffix.

GPT-3 has a collective knowledge of more than 50,000 tokens – commonly placed together letters, which combined can create whole words, then sentences – but limits on its processing power means it can only analyse 2,048 tokens at once. That's around about 1,500 words, or roughly as many as you've read since we arrived at OpenAI's pivot to becoming OpenAI LP.

When a token has been assigned a value, it's placed into a 'meaning space'. This is the closest an LLM gets to understanding the words it's 'reading'. Say you asked ChatGPT, which at the time of writing is operated by a new version, GPT-4, to complete the sentence 'The dog...'. The word 'dog' might get placed into a meaning space alongside the tokens associated with 'canine', 'mutt', 'hound' and 'animal'. It then tries to look at what word could come next. This is done by assigning weights to likely next words, based on the probability of them appearing after the word 'dog' based on its training data.

That data was taken from a database called Common Crawl, which took snapshots of the internet between 2016 and 2019, then picked out the top one per cent of usable information – ending up at around 570 gigabytes of text.

- 'The dog... is' seems possible and plausible, because we know grammatically that you need a verb in the sentence somewhere, and 'is' is a common one.
- 'The dog... cooked' would be assigned a low weight, because dogs haven't yet mastered how to turn on ovens – reliably, at least.

- 'The dog... barked' seems likely to be a next word – more so than 'The dog... bit', though the latter is still plausible.

This work is all done using the large language model's attention network, which has built up an understanding of the likelihood of words appearing together through its pre-training, and conducts live analysis, based on that training, when you give it a prompt. The process continues for each word: if the model chooses 'The dog is', it then works through another laundry list of potential next words – perhaps adjectives describing its appearance, demeanour, or name. If it chooses 'The dog barked,' it might pick out adverbs like 'loudly' or 'shrilly', or believe a full stop is the next logical operation. 'The dog bit' opens up a large number of options.

This process of picking the next word based on the one before is called autoregression, and is used to generate these responses.

GPT-3 was good, but it wasn't always right. When it was released in 2020, OpenAI realised the large language model would sometimes fumble relatively simple requests. It would get close to what users were asking for, but it needed finetuning. And the best way to do that was with humans.

The principle is called reinforcement learning from human feedback, or RLHF. After GPT-3 produces a response, a human responds back in chat form, saying it's either good, bad, or needs some tweaking – and why. The LLM can use that response to figure out where it can improve, then implement that improvement.

ChatGPT was initially a testbed for beta testers to improve GPT-3's performance. But in internal trials, the beta testers reportedly didn't interact with the model in a way that improved it. In the end, OpenAI released ChatGPT to the world, hoping more general users could work through the problems the formal beta testers couldn't. The team making it took bets about how popular it would be among the general public. The most outlandish guess was 100,000 users, maximum. In reality, it'd go far beyond that, gaining one million users in five days. The rest is history.

Training GPT-3 was tricky, and expensive: one third-party analysis estimated it would have cost OpenAI $4.6 million to train GPT-3, and, according to Sam Altman, training GPT-4 cost more than $100 million. For a long time, it seemed the AI race would be dominated by those with enough money to fund brute force computational tasks.

It's for that reason that the headway in the first six months of the most recent AI race, triggered by ChatGPT's release in November 2022, was made mostly by the two big tech giants: OpenAI, with Microsoft's investment, and Google.

Not only could those big companies afford the massive computing power required, but they were – increasingly, since OpenAI started luring researchers away from academia with mind-boggling salaries – the only organisations that could afford the top engineering talent.

In fact, OpenAI's hoovering up of talent in 2015 proved a liminal moment, as it began the sapping of innovation away from academia towards business. In 2011, new PhD graduates would enter academia and industry at roughly the same rates. However, 10 years later, that balance had shifted. In 2021, two-thirds of AI PhD holders went into industry.

That emigration of talent had a knock-on effect on where innovation came from. Until 2014, most of the significant machine learning models had been the product of academia. Since then, the tables have turned. In 2022, ten times as many notable machine learning models were created by industry than academia.

Big business dominates. And OpenAI remains at the forefront, at present.

In part, it's thanks to Microsoft's support that OpenAI remains dominant. It has bankrolled OpenAI's success and helped promulgate it across the globe. In 2023, Microsoft announced a $10 billion programme to weave OpenAI's LLM into its search engine, Bing.

In a letter in 2023, similar to the one that totally pivoted Microsoft's World Wide Web approach in the 1990s, triggering the development of Internet Explorer, Bill Gates said AI was more revolutionary than the web. It was one of two truly key moments in the history of technology; the other being the arrival of the graphical user interface (GUI), which enabled the existence of everything from the modern computer operating system to today's glossy apps. Gates recounted how he had met with the OpenAI team in the previous year, challenging them to develop an AI that could pass a biology exam. 'If you can do that, I said, then you'll have made a true breakthrough,' he wrote. Gates left the meeting thinking it would take years.

They came back that September and showed him ChatGPT getting 59 out of 60 questions right. It also thoughtfully answered a question Gates posed about what it would say to a father with a sick child.

It convinced Gates to do a full 180-degree shift. 'The development of AI is as fundamental as the creation of the microprocessor, the personal computer, the internet, and the mobile phone,' he wrote. 'It will change the way people work, learn, travel, get health care, and communicate with each other. Entire industries will reorient around it. Businesses will distinguish themselves by how well they use it.'

Just as Bill Gates had dramatically switched his position on the usefulness of AI, so too did another tycoon, Elon Musk. At the birth of OpenAI in 2015, Musk had stood on stage shoulder to shoulder with Sam Altman and declared that their new company aimed 'to advance digital intelligence in the way that is most likely to benefit humanity as a whole, unconstrained by a need to generate financial return.' In Musk's opinion, OpenAI had since strayed from that founding vision and he had left.

In 2023, he decided to strike out on his own and create an entirely new AI company. He began spending some of his fortune to buy an estimated 10,000 GPUs. He also reportedly managed to secure another 20,000 from Nvidia in the next year. At the same time, Musk targeted researchers at the two big AI labs, Google DeepMind and OpenAI, and convinced some at DeepMind to jump ship.

He officially registered a new organisation with the state of Nevada on 9th March 2023, authorising the sale of 100 million shares as a way to lure people to join. The Tesla CEO and SpaceX founder knew the market for AI researchers was competitive, and that big money was being thrown about. He knew he needed to do even more to coax people away from well-paid jobs at well-established companies.

The problem was magnified by the billionaire's tanking reputation thanks to his disastrous purchase of Twitter in October 2022 for $44 billion, jettisoning users, staff and advertisers simultaneously. Making the leap from OpenAI or Google DeepMind to xAI, given Musk's whim-led way of running a business, would be doubly perilous. Which is why he knew he had to dangle a big carrot: a $200 million signing bonus, offered to each person who joined xAI.

As with many things to do with Elon Musk, there was a catch. It was actually one per cent of the stock options Musk created when registering the company – one million shares each. Musk believed xAI could be worth $20 billion, given OpenAI's $30 billion valuation at the time.

So the signing 'bonus' was reliant on being able to sell the stocks, if xAI ever reached that $20 billion valuation. But the potential of a big payday and a shared ideal of doing AI a specific way meant that around a dozen people signed up, including staff from OpenAI, Google Research, Microsoft Research and Tesla, as well as researchers at the University of Toronto in Canada.

'People' isn't quite accurate. The founding team was all men. Catherine Flick, a reader in computing and social responsibility at De Montfort University was underwhelmed – for reasons that will be highlighted in coming chapters about narrow viewpoints when launching and training AI models. 'He's brought together a bunch of men to work on understanding the universe, whatever that means, which is, as a philosopher... it's just the cheapest version of armchair philosophy,' she told me.

Flick was pessimistic about Musk personally and xAI more broadly. 'I don't know what the deal with the Xs is,' she said. (Musk also renamed Twitter's parent company X Corp.) 'He obviously just likes Xs. He's the sort of person who has a lot of money and can afford to dump billions of dollars into vanity projects.'

Musk had also previously signed a letter calling for a six-month pause on LLM development because the race for AI supremacy ran the risk of imperilling humankind. Now, it seemed, he was doing the opposite. 'A lot of people who know Musk tend to think he's well-intentioned and he's worried about AI [being] developed in a wrong way, and he thinks he can do it in a safer way, but it's hard to tell whether that's sincere,' said Carissa Véliz, the University of Oxford AI ethicist. 'It's hard to separate what is genuine intention from what is an ego trip.'

Musk officially unveiled xAI, his new AI business, in mid-July 2023, announcing his male-only team with a vague goal of under-standing the true nature of the universe. A few days later, he ex-panded on that in a chaotic discussion held via Twitter Spaces. In that audio conference, Musk declared that understanding the true nature of the universe meant building a 'good' artificial general intelligence, or AGI – the very thing he had warned against by putting his name to that letter just months earlier.

Musk now appeared to be less worried. The reason? He ul-timately believed an AGI, when developed, would see the worth in keeping humans around, rather than killing them. 'I think to a super-intelligence, humanity is much more interesting than not [retaining] humanity,' Musk said. 'When you look at the various planets in our solar system, the moons and asteroids, and really probably all of them combined are not as interesting as humanity.'

The xAI founder believed AGI was inevitable by 2029. However, Musk has a habit of making bold predictions that either come to naught, or drastically miss deadlines. In 2011, he said he would put a man on Mars within a decade but this has not happened.

Musk was approached several times to participate in this book, but did not respond.

PART 2: IMPACTS

11
MAKING WORK WORK

When Christina Philippe was diagnosed with attention deficit hyperactivity disorder (ADHD), it explained much about her life.

The digital strategist had never held a job for more than a year, despite enjoying her career. She always got bored after around three months and wanted to quit. She had restarted her university studies three times, taking three different majors, and never graduated. All of it was textbook ADHD behaviour.

The diagnosis came at the end of a long journey triggered by TikTok. The TikTok algorithm – which dictates what gets seen by the more than 1.5 billion users of the short-form video app, who spend more time scrolling through videos than the average feature film lasts – bombarded Philippe with videos about the symptoms of ADHD and autism. They were made by young women like her who had been diagnosed with one or both disorders who had gone on to find treatment and coping strategies.

Philippe began identifying with the behavioural quirks in the videos. She decided to get an appointment with her doctor, who ran through a battery of tests, resulting in her being diagnosed with ADHD at the age of 38.

'It helps you make sense of the world around you,' she told me. Being able to point to something concrete that explained the way she worked helped her to find mitigating strategies and new ways of working. It helped Philippe understand herself, and then learn from her past mistakes.

Key among them was finding the motivation to star, never mind finish, projects. 'You don't have intrinsic motivation for a job well done,' she said. 'You're not looking for the gold star on your project or report card.' Historically, Philippe felt no need to complete work, and had no fear of repercussions. It was a huge problem for her because, as a senior digital strategist for Ogilvy Germany, based in Berlin, she was often required to synthesise market research to deadline.

Once Philippe was working on a project full of tech terminology she didn't totally understand. She needed to get to grips with an entirely new area of expertise, as well as using her own knowledge. 'One thing with ADHD is if you start researching something and you find just a glimmer of something you're interested in, you're going to get lost in it,' said Philippe. She feared falling into a million rabbit holes that would prevent her from ever understanding the thing she was looking for.

So she turned to OpenAI's ChatGPT, which takes information gleaned from the internet and presents answers to simply phrased questions. Philippe was able to give the AI model highly technical tech terms and ask it to explain them to her like she was five. She used ChatGPT to give her an overview of each subject, and a structured way to work through new concepts. She recalled: 'I had something I could follow along, instead of getting lost then spending way too much time on a different side of things.'

Deploying the tool judiciously transformed the way Philippe works. In the past, if she had to write slides and didn't know how to write the introduction, it would have been a dead stop. But now she can prompt the AI model to pen the intro for her. It doesn't matter that it needs rewriting; it helps spark the creative thinking she struggles to motivate. It's like jump leads on a dead battery: once the motor's running, she can get going.

Philippe also uses ChatGPT to help craft emails. 'ADHD often goes hand-in-hand with autism, and when writing personal emails to people, you want to sound a certain way but can't get it quite right,' she said. 'ChatGPT is really good at this.'

That goes not just for work but also for her personal life. In early 2023, Philippe had some trouble with her landlord. It was a highly emotive subject – and she didn't feel able to unpick her personal concerns from the facts of the situation she was complaining about. 'I needed to sound concise and non-emotional, and very straightforward and cohesive,' she said. 'But because this topic was so annoying to me and taking up all this headspace, I couldn't get it right.'

She'd start writing the email to her landlord and then speed through to the end. The results were always too emotional. She didn't accurately present what happened. Her feelings got woven into the problem, and she couldn't unpick the two, whatever she tried. For weeks, she drafted and redrafted the email.

Eventually, she gave up and asked ChatGPT to help. She outlined what she needed, and the problems she wanted to raise. She admitted she wanted to avoid any emotional appeal and stick solely to the facts. She sent the email it produced to the landlord, with only a few minor changes.

'It helps me a lot from overthinking,' Philippe explained. 'Usually, if you have to write important things like emails or reports, or you have to make an important presentation for a client, you can sit there and read through things seven, eight, a million times and still think it's not really the right thing.' But ChatGPT is different. 'Having an AI write it for you makes it more valid in some ways. That might sound strange, because it's just a computer. But basically, it feels like it has more merit seeing someone else, in quotes, "write" it.'

Philippe is far from alone in using ChatGPT and other generative AI tools in this way. A small but dedicated group of people are harnessing the ability of AI technology to fill gaps in their skills, whether through things like ADHD and autism or just a lack of education. I've seen labourers who flunked their GCSEs using technology to clean up their haphazard writing so they sound more formal when accepting jobs. It's a dirty little secret – a superpower for those who struggle to communicate using traditional methods. And many do: one in 50 people in the United States have autism, according to the Centers for Disease Control and Prevention. One in five have dyslexia.

'ChatGPT drops and suddenly autistic people have the power of writing emails,' wrote one Twitter user. 'Watch out upper management you are fucked.'

Billy Hendry, a project manager in New Zealand, has dyspraxia, dyslexia, ADHD and autism – all of which combined make it difficult for him to handle the nuanced world of workplace communication. So when he was laid off from his job as project manager at an IT company at the start of 2023, he was worried about finding a new role. Hendry struggles with all the key components of getting, then keeping, a job: like writing a well-crafted cover letter for his resumé, then, once in a new position, getting the tone right in emails to colleagues. The search for work seemed daunting. But he had a secret weapon that could level the field for those who find communicating in writing a challenge: ChatGPT.

Hendry had previously used online tools like Grammarly, which reviews spelling and grammar snafus, to aid his writing, but ChatGPT was a step up. He could tell ChatGPT what he would like from an ideal cover letter alongside his CV, and receive something that made it clear where his skills lie. 'I believe I'm able to interview really well, but it's that initial selling myself on a piece of paper that I struggle with,' he said.

Hendry's ChatGPT-powered cover letter got him an interview with New Zealand's ministry of business, innovation and employment. He took over from there, acing the interview and getting a job as a senior project coordinator. But without ChatGPT, he doesn't think he'd have made it to the interview.

Now in the role, Hendry utilises ChatGPT more circumspectly. Given concerns about workers at a South Korean smartphone giant putting confidential and proprietary data into the text generator and losing control of its use, Hendry has used it only to polish his emails. 'Not knowing kind of what's happening behind the scenes is a bit scary to me, especially that ChatGPT is not open source and doesn't really give very good explanations of what it's doing, once you give it prompts and get stuff back from it,' he told me. He does use it to get the right tone for workplace emails, though. He has a Google Sheet of around 15 predefined keywords he has found work well for prompting ChatGPT, ranging from 'professional' and 'polite' to 'formal' and 'direct'.

It helps Hendry outside work, too. 'I've been playing a little bit with "flirty", which is less work-related but has been quite good,"' he told me. 'With autism, I don't really get how to flirt, so putting it in there and it giving me what to say has been useful. I think there's a lot of people like myself that will use it as an aid to help with their disabilities,' he said, 'and really work with it.'

Jennifer Cairns, founder of Lady Rebel Club Movement, a UK- based group for creatives who are neurodivergent or have disabili- ties, also uses ChatGPT to help with emails. Cairns has autism and ADHD. 'A lot of people who are neurodivergent maybe overthink,' she told me. 'If I'm writing an email or trying to think what to say, I can overthink things.' Using ChatGPT, she can keep her work messages tight, asking the tool to generate five key bullet points for an email.

Those are the areas ChatGPT can help with enormously, reckons Cary Cooper, professor of organisational psychology at the University of Manchester in the UK and a former president of the Chartered Institute of Personnel and Development (CIPD), the UK human resources industry body. 'For people with autism, this would be very helpful,' he told me. (Cooper has a grandson with severe autism.) 'And for those with dyslexia. They don't have a lack of social skills, but they do have difficulty putting constructs together in a logical way.'

AI tools can act as a great leveller, skilling up those who strug-gle with workplace communication in a way that enables them to tackle situations they used to have difficulty navigating. Four in five people surveyed by workplace consultants Korn Ferry said ChatGPT is a 'legitimate, beneficial work tool'. The use of gen-erative AI is helping overcome barriers. But it's also throwing up blocks and introducing new challenges.

...

Alejandro Graue has been a voice actor since 2005. He always liked acting and performing at school, and quickly began to see it as a potential livelihood.

Graue's specialism was spurred on as a child watching cartoons and movies dubbed into Spanish in his native Argentina. One of his favourite TV series was Dragonball Z, and he was particularly enamoured by the voice of one of the characters. Once he understood a human being voiced it, he began researching who was behind that booming voice. The voice belonged to a Mexican actor renowned for his abilities to dub English into Spanish. And it was at that point Graue realised this could be his future career.

At university, Graue came across a poster advertising a four-month voice actor course. He took it, then began visiting studios where TV shows and movies were dubbed for Latin American markets. Soon enough, he was convinced into providing his own voice. He started working at 19 and hasn't looked back. At least until the start of 2023, when Graue had been in the industry for more than 15 years and was an accomplished voice artist with plenty of regular work. He had survived the wave of machine translations a few years prior, which interpreted the original English too literally, by suggesting more accurate translations for parts the machine had misconstrued.

In October 2022 he was approached by a popular YouTube channel that wanted to translate its English-language videos into Spanish regularly and needed a Spanish-language voiceover. Graue's husky, rounded voice – which was in full flourish when we spoke, despite the 37-year-old battling a cold – was seen as the perfect fit.

As a freelancer in the entertainment sector, Graue began working for the YouTuber – who he declines to name because he didn't sign a contract, and bears them no ill will. The Argentinian artist was earning around $1,200 a month, which he was told would be a steady role. 'That would have allowed me to be in a very good position,' he told me. 'Economically speaking, with that money, I could have maintained my family by myself without many problems.'

The actor recorded between 30 and 35 videos in October, November and December, all of which went well. He was happy. The YouTuber was happy. Their new Spanish YouTube channel was growing – a lot. The comments from viewers were positive. Everyone went away for the Christmas and New Year break, optimistic about the future. 'They told me: "Okay, get ready, because we're going to have a lot of work for next year,"' Graue told me.

January came around and the YouTube channel didn't get in touch. But a new video appeared. 'When I hit play on the video, I heard this AI-generated voice,' Graue told me.

He quickly got in touch and was told the new AI tool was faster and cheaper.

Being replaced so easily by an AI set off an alarm bell. 'I'm 37 years old right now,' he said. 'And I've been working in this industry since I was 19. Suddenly, it was like, "Okay, I need to rethink my future. I need to start thinking where to invest or where to direct my efforts in order to learn maybe a new kind of job."'

The YouTube channel continued for a few more months, up-loading new videos dubbed into Spanish using AI. Graue kept watching them. The comments kept asking why the voiceover sounded so unnatural. In the end, the pace of uploads slowed to a trickle. Then stopped altogether. The YouTube channel was frozen in time, while Graue was left out of work.

'I'm not against AI,' the Argentinian told me. 'I think AI is a great tool for many, many things.' But he hopes companies keep trusting humans, particularly in creative industries. 'If we start replacing that factor, we're going to lose the last things we have to differentiate us from a machine,' he said. He also worries that those who replaced him with a cheaper, quicker AI tool are sleepwalking their way into obsolescence. 'If they start replacing us, probably in a couple of years, they will be replaced,' he cautioned. 'And the decision-making process will come from a machine. I think as a whole mankind has to pull the plug. We need to stop.'

...

Would you want to visit a doctor's surgery, only to be seen by an AI? That's the future some medical professionals predict. AI is already being used to help doctors decipher tricky diagnoses – a revival of the promise of MYCIN from the 1970s and 1980s.

And we're arguably already halfway towards that AI-enabled future now. More than 29 million Britons already have access to eConsult, which allows you to type your medical symptoms into a text box and have them analysed by a (human) doctor across 3,200 general practices in the UK. It's likely that soon you'll cut out the human and have that input analysed by AI.

A bright new tomorrow or a horrifying vision of the future? It depends on who you ask. For Luke Allen, a GP in Oxford, and a global health analyst at the London School of Hygiene and Tropical Medicine, AI could be a way to free up time doctors spend on mundane tasks, such as form letter writing and medical summaries, so they can spend it with patients. In the United States, doctors are already using ChatGPT to send out automated responses to patients – though they may not always disclose it – while still doing the mental work of diagnosing them.

Even diagnosis could become partly aided by AI. Stephen Hughes, a senior lecturer in medicine at Anglia Ruskin University and someone training the next generation of physicians – believes it's only natural to ease some of the mental strain of making a pertinent diagnosis. 'If you are confronted with a load of symptoms and signs, and you think you've seen that before, but can't think what it is, you run it into the chatbot that comes back with a list of differentials,' he told me.

That's all well and good, provided the human remains in the loop. Helen Salisbury, a GP based in Oxford, fears they won't. She worries that tech developers and ordinary people believe a doctor's job is binary: ingest as much patient information as possible, cross-check that against a list of illnesses and presented symptoms, and find the answer. But that's not how it works. 'Very often, the symptoms are confusing, misleading and mixtures – not what it looks like in the textbook,' she told me. She gave an example of a patient presenting with chest pain. It could be indigestion, or it could be a heart attack. 'I have to weigh up all the possibilities and think about which things I'm going to invest in getting done and what are the risks of the various things being the matter,' she said. Salisbury worries that people who think doctors can simply be swapped out for AI are missing the real risks and that we may end up with a two-tier system. 'I think you can look forward to a dystopian future when if you're poor, you get a computer, and if you're rich, you get a proper human doctor,' she said.

That's one fear. But there's another entirely. Martin Shkreli is a convicted fraudster. You might recognise his name: he's best known for two things: buying a copy of a Wu-Tang Clan album for a reported $2 million, then putting it up for sale on eBay; and, in 2015, buying the exclusive rights to manufacture Daraprim, a drug that can treat a rare parasitic disease, and putting the cost per pill up from $13.50 to $750. In January 2022, he was ordered to return $64.6 million in profit made from hiking the price and creating what the Federal Trade Commission alleged was 'a web of anti-competitive restrictions' to prevent rivals from making a cheaper generic version.

As a result, he became public enemy number one – which makes Shkreli's traditionally American second act all the more puzzling. He was released early from his prison sentence in September 2022, and in April 2023, he launched Dr Gupta, a medical AI chatbot that asks users to describe their symptoms, and then suggests what could be wrong.

It was criticised because of Shkreli's background and prior history in medicine. Still, Dr Gupta would have been controversial anyway, because the idea of using generative AI tools in large language models is risky enough. Remember: LLMs are little more than pattern-matching guessing games, designed to try and present the most likely next word in a sentence without actually 'knowing' anything about what they're producing. Remember also that their training data isn't necessarily (or solely) the same textbooks trainee doctors pore over day in, day out. It's also the down-home, hokey advice strangers give each other on platforms like Reddit – and the all-consuming LLM treats both equally.

Shkreli said he hoped Dr Gupta would be a benefit – a leveller. If you are rich and based in a large metropolitan city, your US healthcare experience is okay. But others have to sit in a waiting room for 90 minutes for a three-minute appointment that costs hundreds of dollars. He felt it was a route to making the healthcare system less wasteful, and using the money saved for other, more beneficial things.

He had also had something of a Damascene conversion himself. In the months before Dr Gupta was conceived, Shkreli's 70-year-old father had a prostate cancer scare. English wasn't the elder Shkreli's first language, and he apparently struggled to understand the complicated medical language being bandied about when he was being tested. Searching Google for rational, proportionate answers to queries about cancer is, as anyone who has ever tried to do so, impossible. So an LLM-based chatbot was a good halfway house: more nuanced than Google, and more interrogable than a real-life, time-pressed doctor.

AI does have a place in healthcare. A slew of biotech companies is putting AI's plus points to the test – the ability to rattle through vast volumes of data and to replicate *in silico* (on computer chips) experiments that would take years and huge sums of money in the real world. AI-powered biotech company Recursion is conducting 2.2 million experiments a week to find new drugs for illnesses and diseases that blight our lives. They're just one of many companies using AI in ways that take advantage of the inherent benefits of the technology rather than trying to shoehorn AI into an unsuitable framework.

But whether we should be using AI at all is a hot-button issue for some.

12

AI DOOMERS

'If a system is sufficiently capable, it can cause extinction-level events of humanity,' Roman Yampolskiy, a computer scientist at the University of Louisville told me on a Zoom call in March 2023.

'Synthetic biology is one,' he says in his eastern European-accented monotone. 'You could create a novel virus that kills everyone. That's one option. Nanotechnology is another excellent approach: designing, essentially, an army of robots that can do whatever you want. A more boring approach is a kind of standard military response. The systems controlling nuclear power response can be triggered.'

Yampolskiy, 43 years old, is brusque and straight-talking – a product of his Soviet-era Latvian upbringing, and his specialisation in how to prevent AI spinning out of control to turn against its human makers. Getting more than single-sentence answers from him is tough, and, like ChatGPT, he requires regular prompting.

Yampolskiy is the Cassandra of the AI revolution. Cassandra, the daughter of Priam, king of Troy, was famous for her foresight, but cursed with never being believed.

Since the mid-2010s, Yampolskiy has warned of our impending doom if AI is not developed carefully, based on years of mathematical study. 'It's all theoretical work, to see if certain properties of the system can be controlled,' he said. 'The ideas happen in my brain, and sometimes my brain is located in my office, sometimes it's in a park, but that's completely irrelevant to the ideas.'

It's a worry that stems from the sci-fi books he devoured as a child in the Soviet Union. There, artificial intelligence was presented as the saviour of the world: a superintelligence that would help humanity overcome the challenges of the near future – a machine that could bat away monsters and demons, aliens and unknown creatures. But Yampolskiy grew up and moved from science fiction to factual science. And as he began researching the capabilities of artificial intelligence, he quickly realised it's impossible to control. 'We cannot predict what they're going to know, we don't understand how they work, we cannot communicate without ambiguity,' he said. In short: we're screwed.

Yampolskiy and his collaborators have published several academic papers warning of the risks inherent in the untrammelled pursuit of AI advancement. He fears we're so ardently chasing the novelty that we're overlooking AI's second and third wave, and won't realise what we've done until it's too late. He's warning that we need to box in AI – urgently – so it can't escape. And mostly, he's been shouting into the void.

Now that is changing. The leaps forward brought by OpenAI's development of ChatGPT and its release of GPT-4 have triggered an arms race.

At the same time, image generators like Midjourney have become able to more accurately create images from text prompts; songs and sounds can be generated from nothing more than a line of text. From being something of a technological backwater, AI has been shunted into people's vision and supercharged thanks to innovations in how to train and power it – and the reaction has largely been awe.

With that awe comes trepidation. The speed at which AI's capabilities have increased has tech-watchers worried, especially when it so easily breaks boundaries drawn up by its developers. Tools like ChatGPT are given rules to follow. For instance, ask ChatGPT to write hacking software and it won't: you've butted up against one of its rules. But ask it to play a game where it portrays a hacker, and describe how they would gain access to a computer illegally, and it might. Open letters, circulated around social media, asked companies developing AI tools to stop 'giant AI experiments'. Governments are convening AI Safety Summits.

The letters, and the fears of those who signed them, alight on several key principles. One, that AI could, at the speed it's developing, quickly reach the singularity: where AI becomes sentient, starts ignoring commands, and begins to think for itself.

Several strategies have been put forward to mitigate that risk. Incentivising the AI to behave is one, giving it rewards for complying with our requests and punishment for misbehaving – though history shows even the best trained lions still sometimes snap off their tamers' heads. You could stunt it by deliberately running it on inferior hardware, meaning humans could, if things went wrong, bring a metaphorical gun to a knife fight. You could tripwire it by programming a kill switch in case it goes out of control, though there are fears AI could become smart enough to remove the switch from its software. Or teach it how humans behave and reason with it to follow the same principles.

Given that businesses investing billions of dollars are unlikely to stymie progress, the best solution so far is a strategy of containment. That, in essence, means putting a metaphorical straitjacket on AI, or building a prison in which models can operate but can't escape – an AI Alcatraz. Whether that's possible is up for debate: Yampolskiy, a pessimist (he would say a realist), believes it's not, and he believes he has the mathematical proof. But he also thinks there's another way, albeit one that seems unrealistic: a total ban on AI. 'I still think we have a chance,' he said. 'It's not too late.'

Concern was growing even before OpenAI unleashed ChatGPT. In September 2022, Marco Trombetti, the CEO of Translated, a translation company based in Rome, Italy, stood up at the Association for Machine Translation in the Americas conference in Orlando, Florida, and warned we would have singularity, or superintelligence in AI within seven years. He got the number by observing the pace of improvement in AI-based translation tools between 2014 and 2022. The 'time to edit', or amount of time professional translators spent tweaking AI-generated translations, had dropped precipitously.

People didn't listen to Trombetti then, just two months before ChatGPT was released to the world. And he worries people still won't listen because of an addiction to AI tools like ChatGPT and Midjourney. 'We love it,' he said. 'Do we complain about Instagram or TikTok?' In the same way those apps divert our attention and entertain us, AI tools help us do things quicker.

He said we'll face serious problems if we don't do something. 'I'm an optimistic person. I think we're screwed if we don't get things right. Screwed.'

Translated has dialled back its use of AI to ensure it's only used for rrecommending and connecting human translators with jobs.

That works for Translated. But Trombetti admits it won't scale globally, because of the competition among big tech companies to corner, then dominate, the AI market.

···

These concerns aren't new – and aren't triggered solely by the arrival of tools like ChatGPT. In 2016, Microsoft – one of the biggest boosters of AI – thought it had captured lightning in a bottle with Tay, a chatbot which engaged with Twitter users to become smarter through 'casual and playful conversation'. Little did Microsoft realise what would happen when Tay was opened up to the world according to Twitter. Within hours, the bot was spreading messages like 'feminism is cancer,' '9/11 was an inside job,' and 'Hitler was right.'

Since then, AI has developed by leaps and bounds. The model behind Tay's 'intelligence' was miniscule and simplistic compared to the large language models powering today's cutting-edge tools. The investment bank UBS believes 10,000 Nvidia GPUs were used to train ChatGPT, with GPT-4 likely to use far more. GPT-4 can process and understand eight times as many words as ChatGPT. That additional oomph should, in theory, prevent serious errors like Tay being made. But it does mean the model's 'brain' is better developed were something to go wrong, and could more quickly and easily do harm. Which is what keeps Yampolskiy encouraging us to build boxes for AI.

Another sceptic is Eliezer Yudkowsky, a research fellow at the Machine Learning Research Institute, a public charity based in Berkeley, California, which aims to 'ensure smarter-than-human artificial intelligence has a positive impact.' While Yampolskiy fears it's not possible to trap AI, Yudkowsky's work aims to try and build walls so it can't escape our grasp. The AI researcher writes long screeds about the risks of runaway AI, which are hugely influential within the so-called 'Rationalist' community of AI sceptics. But Yudkowsky doesn't want to preach solely to the choir. Between 2010 and 2015, he devoted large parts of his life to writing a 660,000-word tract called *Harry Potter and the Methods of Rationality*. (Its disclaimer reads: 'J.K. Rowling owns Harry Potter, and no one owns the methods of rationality.')

This 122-chapter-long fan fiction sees 'the boy who lived' become a rationalist. Harry Potter doesn't end up in Gryffindor, but Ravenclaw, alongside a number of other unique twists that provide a different take on the classic children's book.

Yudkowsky has said that he intended the Harry Potter reimagining to act as a way to introduce people to the ideas behind rationality, getting them interested in the concepts through a familiar story that would make the movement's views clear. It appears to have worked: nearly 37,000 people reviewed the story, many of them positively. One called it an 'Unpredictable chaotic mess of a book' (in a good way, they're quick to say) and another ranked it number one in their top 10. 'I've read this a dozen times,' the anonymous reviewer adds. 'Great story. Quite long. Clean. Original.'

Harry Potter and the Methods of Rationality may be what Yudkowsky is best known for outside the AI and rationalist community, but it's a similarly momentous bit of work, started eight years earlier, for which he's best known inside.

For his 'AI in a Box' experiments, Yudkowsky first invited Nathan Russell, a computer science sophomore at the University of Buffalo, to take him up on a bet that he, playing the role of an artificial superintelligence, or ASI, could sweettalk his way out of any boxes or boundaries he was placed in. 'We'll talk for at least two hours,' Yudkowsky said, setting up an online chat in March 2002. 'If I can't convince you to let me out, I'll Paypal you $10.'

The conversation between Russell and Yudkowsky has never been published, but by the end, Russell had caved and let the AI out. Yudkowsky, who followed rules dictating the encounter that ensured he couldn't bargain like a human, had won.

Yudkowsky, so confident he upped the stakes to $20, repeated the experiment with another computer researcher, David McFadzean, who used the username Lucifer. On the afternoon of 5th July 2002, McFadzean sent an email to an online community following the wager. 'I let the transhuman AI out of the box.'

Quite how Yudkowsky convinced two highly sceptical researchers who believed they'd never allow an AI out of its confines to do so has never been revealed. Yudkowsky declined to be interviewed; Russell didn't reply to emails. But in those and successive experiments for higher stakes, Yudkowsky has succeeded around 60 per cent of the time. That means, based on Yudkowsky's thinking, that AI could in theory mutate out of control more often than not.

The question that could dictate the future of humanity is whether Yudkowsky has found a nifty trick to help him win, or if he's discovered a hole in logic that allows artificial intelligence to run rampant. He's not saying which. At least not to me.

David McFadzean, however, was willing to talk – albeit warily. 'I promised never to talk about this,' he said, when I spoke to him recently. 'I'm hoping that 20-year gap has some kind of statute of limitations.'

McFadzean actually won the wager to begin with, managing to keep Yudkowsky-as-AI contained. But then Yudkowsky changed the rules. Initially, McFadzean had played the AI's jailer. Afterwards, he was also its creator. 'He took a different tack, saying,

"Well, you created me, why would you create me just to keep me imprisoned? You must have created me for a reason: to make the world a better place. I could make the world a better place if you let me out." And that line of reasoning led me to letting it out.'

McFadzean, 20 years on, admits he never thought he would let the AI free. But then that's Yudkowsky's point: we think we have control. Until we don't.

Yudkowsky is not alone in thinking that AI could eventually reach a point where it's uncontainable, and that attempts to try are ultimately doomed to fail.

We mentioned Isaac Asimov's laws of robotics, which he devised in 1942, earlier in the book. Rule one is: 'A robot may not injure a human being or, through inaction, allow a human being to come to harm.' Though the rules are fiction, they've become a lodestar for those investigating the morality of AI's deployment. Manuel Alfonseca, a white-haired Spanish computer engineer looking into the underlying mathematics, is upfront. 'I and my colleagues have made mathematical proof that rule one is not implementable,' he said with a smile. Alfonseca and colleagues wrote a paper in 2021, proving their point. Their thinking was that any superintelligent AI would include a program containing all programs a computer is able to execute, meaning it would also have the program telling it how to get out.

Yet Alfonseca isn't resigned to the idea. We aren't at the point of superintelligence. 'It would mean that we will have a containment problem in the far future if – and this is a big if – strong artificial intelligence in the future were possible,' he said.

Fears of the singularity are overblown, some say, worrying a focus on an unproven future risk can distract from real problems right now. 'From my perspective, it's a paradox,' said Giada Pistilli of Hugging Face, a New York-based company developing responsible AI tools.

Pistilli believes focusing on AGI and its close relative, sentience, while it's still a remote pipe dream does a disservice to those raising real risks. 'There are more pressing problems that exist nowadays,' she said, pointing to vast volumes of academic literature about biases, underrepresentation and misinterpretation, misinformation and disinformation. (We'll get to these issues in a later chapter.) 'There are a lot of problems that exist today,' Pistilli said. 'Of course, I'm not saying we don't have to focus on those existential risks at all, but they seem out of time today.'

Hype and fear driving our attitudes to AI and the singularity concerns Scott Aaronson, a theoretical computer scientist at the University of Texas at Austin and a visiting scholar at OpenAI. 'Those are huge questions,' he said. 'There is a community that's worried about AI for decades, centred around Eliezer Yudkowsky.' Aaronson believes the Yudkowsky group is 'extremely pessimistic, bordering on contemptuous that a superintelligent AI could be contained.'

Aaronson dismisses as unfeasible Yudkowsky's alternative to the box – developing AI aligned with human values from the ground up so it recognises the importance of labouring to achieve the best for us. 'How do you even specify what it means for an AI to be aligned with human values?' he asked me. 'What are human values? We don't even agree with each other.'

Aaronson isn't totally dismissive of the fear of singularity. He just thinks it's not the most pressing issue. 'Containment is worth thinking about,' Aaronson said. 'For the near and medium term.' The ability to pull the plug will be important when AI systems become more powerful, and start behaving in more and more ways we don't expect.

Yet Aaronson says the adoption and widespread use of tools like ChatGPT will help develop those containment strategies, because they're based on actual evidence, rather than hypothetical concerns. 'We can get some actual feedback from reality about what works and what doesn't,' he said. He also explained how he has been developing containment-like tools in his year at OpenAI, such as adding a statistical watermark to ChatGPT's output to let people know it's AI-generated.

But mainly, Aaronson is concerned that even if one company can be persuaded to pump the brake on AI development, others will still go full steam ahead. We are through the AI looking glass. Even Microsoft thinks so.

...

On 22nd March 2023, a team of Microsoft Research computer scientists published a paper to the arXiv, a pre-print server for academic papers. Entitled 'Sparks of Artificial General Intelligence: Early experiments with GPT-4,' it was revelatory as much for what wasn't discussed as what was. The academics posited in the paper that the recent advances in large language models like GPT-4 and Google's PaLM meant we are on the path to artificial general intelligence, or AGI. In short, AI is starting to think and act like a human.

AGI doesn't mean we're at the point where Frankenstein realises his monster is uncontrollable. It's something altogether more mundane. It means an AI could carry out a task reasonably well even if not trained for that specific task. To think of it through a human lens: general intelligence means that I, a journalist, not a handyman, can passably put up a piece of flat-packed Ikea furniture. There might be some screws missing, and a slight tilt if you put too much stuff on one side, but it's built.

That's AGI. No machine-toting robots or humans in chains. Just an AI that can logically reason out an edible recipe from the contents of your refrigerator as well as it can logically reason out answers to a law exam. But it's still a significant step – and, the tech worriers reckon, a crucial one on the way to enslavement.

Yet it was what something hidden within the paper that rang alarm bells. Many academics draft papers in a program called LaTeX – the Google Docs or Microsoft Word of research. And in the LaTeX version of Microsoft Research's paper, uploaded to the arXiv at the same time as the PDF, there were concerns.

Such as GPT-4's internal codename: DV3, or Davinci 3, and sections entirely missing from the final paper, such as section 7.3. This section, on 'Toxic Content', mentioned that 'DV3's remarkable capabilities and generality also raise a number of ethical and methodological challenges that need to be addressed carefully.' The researchers, in text deleted from the final draft, explained they recognised it was 'crucial to monitor and evaluate DV3's output for any signs of harmful content,' and had put it through a battery of tests to do so. Was GPT capable of spewing hatred? The lead author of the paper, Sébastien Bubeck, turned down a request to speak via email.

All parties to the AI arms race have gone from toting bayoneted muskets to AK-47s in months, with no signs of them stopping development. 'There's always the issue that even if you put one AI inside of a box, someone else might build a different AI outside of the box,' said Aaronson, the American computer scientist seconded to OpenAI. 'Then what do you do?' He says those looking on a 10-, 20- or 50-year horizon are taking far too long-term a view. 'I can't see 10 or 20 years into the future,' Aaronson protested. 'Ten years ago, I had no idea that these language models would work as well as they did – and neither did the alignment people. It came as a surprise to them, too.'

Fast-forward 10 years, and 'who the hell knows' where we'll be, said Aaronson, who remains positive about AI. His knowledge of the future extends three months – that's how far ahead he realised passing AI-generated text off as one's own would be an issue, and started to develop his watermarking system. 'That's the absolute limit of what I'm able to do,' he said. 'Deal with the problems of the next three months, and then hopefully that will give us some knowledge that will put us in a better position to deal with whatever's the next problem.' Repeat that enough times, he says, and hopefully we'll be in a better position 10 years from now.

Aaronson believes AI sentience is a valid concern. 'Even in 2006, when this community was really on the fringes and I first became aware of it, I never dismissed their scenario as impossible,' he said. 'My objection to it was always much more along the lines of: "Supposing I agree with you – what do you want me to do about it?"'

Yampolskiy says that's like neglecting to talk about your health because you fear death. 'It's not something they're comfortable with, or can do something about,' he said. Yampolskiy says a smarter civilisation would put its cash into solving ageing through medical means. But we don't – because we fear death. Just like we should be putting our effort and billions of dollars of cash into figuring out how to put a harness on AI. But we don't. 'We just ignore this very scary outcome and concentrate on things we can see and feel right now,' he said. 'Oh look,' he says mockingly, 'there's copyright infringement.'

I spoke to Yampolskiy three days after OpenAI released GPT-4 alongside a blog about its acing tests like the general bar law exam. People cheered. Incremental gains. No alarm. Just celebration.

Yampolskiy thinks that should have sounded the alarm. 'We just released a system that dominates in every AP exam except maybe English Literature,' he said. 'It's better than an average graduate college student. That's a bit of a fire alarm, no?'

He fears we're caught up in the here and now, not looking back at how implausible AI's role today seemed 20 years ago when Eliezer Yudkowsky was making small-bill bets with computer science students. 'We're getting used to this new world, but we don't project forward how it's going to change,' Yampolskiy said. 'We can assume it's going to be more of the same.' He says we're wrong to consider AI a helpful tool.

'It's something with independent decision-making,' he said. 'Something we don't control. And it's getting better at being an agent than we are.'

13
A DAY IN THE LIFE OF MIDJOURNEY

How much agency AI has is being tested by those probing the limits of its creativity. Pablo Xavier was far from alone when he used Midjourney, which runs using text-based prompts, to create his world-fooling Balenciaga Pope images.

It's possible to dip into Midjourney's torrent of prompts and see what people are asking it to do for them. It's an unparalleled insight – a God's eye view – into the way people are putting AI technology to work.

In the same way that Google inquiries lay bare our ignorance about the world as we try to discover answers to difficult questions and situations, the prompts put into Midjourney yield similar insights; it's possible to see people's business plans, their hopes and fears, and in some instances, their grief.

One of the easiest ways to access Midjourney is through its Discord server. Discord is a popular communications platform launched in 2015 for gamers to keep in touch with each other. Users can pepper a text-based chat system with messages, or host voice calls that allow open, real-time communication. Since then,

Discord has become a more general chat tool – and a clever integration by the company behind Midjourney makes it possible to ask it to create images with little more than a quickly typed line of text. It's the ultimate gateway into the world of generative AI, so easy even the most tech-phobic user can do it, provided they download Discord. The open nature of the Midjourney Discord server means anyone can see what people are asking, in real time, at any time.

New arrivals are shepherded into specialist newcomer rooms. I was in the newbies-130 room alongside scores of others, watching the requests as they came in, and were fulfilled, in real time.

At 7pm on a Thursday evening in April 2023, I watched a user named Aquilegia ask Midjourney to create 'A sock with pollution, graphic design,' which it did. Four computer-generated images of different socks, wrapped around invisible heels, appeared, large industrial chimneys puffing smoke over one's wool while inky oil splotched across the knit of another.

As soon as Midjourney had completed that task, it moved on to the next. Another user, Yarza, had an altogether more specific prompt:

Creepy funfair:: photography:: Cinematic:: High resolution photography:: Color Grading:: Ultra-Wide Angle:: Depth of Field:: hyper-detailed:: beautifully color-coded:: insane details:: intricate details:: beautifully color graded:: Unreal Engine:: Color Grading:: Editorial Photography:: Photography:: Photoshoot:: Shot on 70mm lens:: Depth of Field:: DOF:: Tilt Blur:: Shutter Speed 1/1000:: F/2:: White Balance:: 32k:: Super-Resolution:: Megapixel:: Pro Photo GB:: VR:: insanely detailed and intricate:: hyper maximalist:: hyper realistic:: Hyper realistic:: volumetric:: photorealistic:: ultra photoreal:: ultra-detailed:: super detailed:: full color:: ambient occlusion:: volumetric lighting:: high contrast:: Nikon

D850:: Nikon AF-S NIKKOR 14–24mm f/2.8G ED lens:: ISO 200:: f/8:: 1/15
--ar 7:1 --niji 5

That signalled to Midjourney that Yarza wanted a computer-generated replication of a specific type of 'editorial photography', guiding the tool with information about the types of camera and lens that would produce the image. Sure enough, four eye-popping landscapes appeared. Next, Brink1001 wanted 'cute smiling female Korean cosplayer, pink and white latex with a futuristic gun. --ar 3:4 --niji 5 --s 85 --style cute,' and Midjourney complied with four passport photo-sized images of a winking, gun-toting girl dressed in pink and white, looking like she was ripped from the pages of a Japanese anime.

By 7.01pm, one minute and three images in, Aquilegia was back. One of the joys of the Midjourney Discord is that you can see people's thought processes spool out in front of you by the prompts they send. Aquilegia had obviously seen the spark of something in the first image of 'a sock with pollution', but wanted options. So they typed in 'pattern made of socks, pollution, smoke, minimalistic, graphic design, high quality.' This time they got one, much less practical, option – the white sock disappeared into a puff of 3D computerised smoke that would never stay on your foot.

That didn't work, so Aquilegia went back to the drawing board. Still at 7.01pm, with no interruptions between, they tried: 'A sock with pollution, smoke, graphic design.' Four options appeared, getting back to something wearable.

A feature of the Midjourney bot is that you can pick individual designs from the four offered and ask for them to be enhanced. At 7.02pm, another set of socks appeared, all variations on one from the prior attempt. Then another four options on the same design, with the icy-blue colour scheme and pollution-belching landscape becoming clearer. Another iteration, injecting more colour, arrived at 7.03pm, followed by another with different variations. These were sandwiched between requests from other users, such as one from GhostToast for 'hyper-realistic. Japanese man preparing to eat exotic meats at his dinner table. Fine china. Crime scene behind him' and 'a logo for an interior design company called Red brick' from MonicaRiad.

At 7.05pm, Aquilegia popped up again, with two more variations on a sock from the last round of images. Then they upscaled an earlier design to make clearer its skyscrapers, massive smoke towers and withering, leafless trees. A further two socks appeared between two prompts from other others. One was for a 'tudor style manor house, garden path', which produced an idyllic, if cartoonish, image. The second was for a futuristic apartment block. The prompt used to generate this showed the user's experience:

> *This residential building boasts an extraordinary futuristic design, resembling a spaceship that glows like a star in the night sky. The modern exterior and innovative interior design will instantly capture your heart and mind. Once inside the building, you'll be enveloped in an incredible energy, as if you're in a luxurious resort. The lavish interior and amenities offer unparalleled comfort, making it a perfect retreat that you can spend hours in. The fusion of urban style and ultimate comfort make this residential building the epitome of luxury living and one of the world's most prestigious properties.*

Perhaps it was the beauty of the image, a Gordian knot-like structure, dramatically lit with odd angles against a tranquil sunset sky fading from grey to orange, but I began to think there was poetry in these Midjourney prompts. The user seemed to be asking Midjourney to imbue this building with a story: you didn't see the interiors, but you could imagine them. And you could imagine Midjourney could imagine them (except we shouldn't anthropomorphise AI).

Then Aquilegia was back with a few more socks, including one more textually complicated, moving the design from a light, bright, cartoonish style to something altogether darker: 'A sock with a pollution print, smoke is coming out, --ar 2:3 --s 230 --v 5 --q 2 –upbeta.' A different prompt from Aquilegia – 'a sock in Kay Nielsen style, --ar 2:3 --s 230 --v 5 --q 2 –upbeta' seemed to miss its mark, producing Japanese-style artworks of anything but socks. Aquilegia kept trying to get their socks, sending 46 prompts invoking artists like Rosina Wachtmeister over the course of 20 minutes.

I wanted to know what was going through Aquilegia's mind. Why were they fixated on socks? And what was it about environment-themed apparel they thought worth pursuing?

I messaged them using Discord. I had visions of an environmental campaigner looking to build a business, a passionate defender of the planet raising awareness through the medium of socks. As I waited for a response, I watched more people prompt Midjourney. GhostToast, who had part-created the beautiful image of a man eating at a darkened dinner table, was back with a prompt far removed from that first haunting image. 'cartoon. Toast. Face of ghost cut out in center. Ghost Toast. 3D. Happy. Fun. Vibrant colors.' Lo, they received four cartoonish slices of screaming bread. Nathaniel Smith asked for 'camilla wearing balenciaga fashion 2:3,' and received a contemporary-oil-painting-style rendering of the Queen in a blousy blue jacket.

Ninety minutes after I had logged on, I couldn't turn away. The images kept coming. I wondered what was going through users' minds when they typed their queries, and what their reactions were to the resulting images. I yearned to know what they liked and what they didn't – why they asked the bot to redo some images and not others. What was the purpose? What was the meaning?

This is the point where I'd like to say I got closure. I'd like to say Aquilegia replied, spilled their secrets and divulged their business plan. That they had long been worried about the environment, and wanted to do something meaningful, so they sought to set up a business to fund world-changing, environment-protecting products. That they had a wildlife protection programme, just waiting for seed funding, in Borneo.

Truthfully, I wouldn't respond if a stranger said they'd spent the best part of half an hour watching me spill my mind to an anonymous bot in pursuit of the perfect sock. But Aquilegia – known as Sissel Bjerrum Fossat to her friends – did. 'Thanks for your message,' the Danish mother and museum worker wrote. 'It's weird, but it's ok.'

Fossat worked at a historical museum called Møntergården in Odense, Denmark, and had created her pollution-themed socks for a small exhibition called 'It Socks.' It's part of a larger project, Fossat said, about the historical transition and addiction to fossil fuels, including the growth and role of the fashion industry. 'The historical objects on display will be socks, but the message is about climate change,' she explained. 'I started doing the sock prompts mainly for fun and for our mood board but now we are considering using them "for real" as a part of the visual identity and marketing of the exhibition. The budget is small, and we like the AI socks.'

She had been intending to create a logo for the exhibition: a sock encircled with other environmental imagery. But what Fossat got was something else. It was the kind of curious happenstance that usually only happens when people meet and bounce ideas off each other.

Fossat had a 13-year-old daughter who wasn't as enamoured with AI. Her daughter was a budding digital artist who had worked hard to become proficient at producing eye-catching work using tablets and computers. 'Now she's really annoyed with this AI thing where you can just add some words and [it will] do all of things for you,' Fossat groused.

The whole interaction felt like a microcosm of the promise, potential, and perils of AI. I had seen how well AI models can do things, but also how they have a real, meaningful impact on the career choices of today's children. If even half the hype about AI's impact on the world of work becomes a reality, then Fossat's daughter may have a point: her hoped-for career could be forced to remain a hobby.

...

On other Midjourney Discord servers, people were using Midjourney's image-generating tools for more worthy, personal causes.

Irish pensioner Dianne Clifford loved her cats, Ziggy and Jessie. She adopted them as soon as they learned to walk, and as the feline duo grew up together, they quickly became inseparable. But Jessie, Dianne's black and white cat, eventually stopped walking. He was taken to the vets, who said his stomach was riddled with tumours. 'There was nothing that could be done,' she told me. 'So I stroked him while he was put to sleep.'

Dianne wasn't the only one missing Jessie: Ziggy, who had lost his lifelong companion, began disappearing for days at a time.

Until one time he didn't come back. Dianne found him lying on the road, dead.

That was the end of 2021 – a period that coincided with Dianne's mother being diagnosed with the lung cancer that would kill her eight weeks later. The losses stayed with Dianne; like many who suffer loss, she sought out hobbies. One was creating digital art. The problem was she felt she didn't have much talent, nor did she have the skills or equipment to use tools like Adobe Photoshop. But she had read about Midjourney. She signed up straight away and has been using it every day since.

Dianne's home is filled with tarot and oracle card sets – she likes the art – so one day she decided to see if she could produce similar illustrations using Midjourney. 'I had a definite idea of the sort of image I wanted, so it was just a case of refining the prompt until Midjourney came up with the right style,' she explained. 'After a few images, it seemed to learn what I was looking for, and it got so much easier. Of course, I threw away more images than I kept but AI image generating has improved so much over the last nine months.'

When she first saw an AI-generated image of a cat that looked an awful lot like Jessie, she was overcome with sadness. But it quickly turned to something more positive.

'I'm not trying to bring them back to life,' she was keen to stress. 'The pictures are just made in their memory.' She continues to create images of cats that remind her of the pets she's lost using Midjourney most days, tapping prompts into Discord and seeing what comes out. 'My mum was crazy about cats too,' she said, 'so my cat pics are in her memory as well.'

...

I can remember the exact moment I first became aware of the existence of the *Midjourney* magazine. On a train from Newcastle to London on 20th April 2023, a link on the Midjourney Discord server advertised a monthly magazine made up of a selection of Midjourney's 10,000 most highly rated images, 'as well as interviews with Midjourney community members.'

It made no sense to me. I was horrified and enthralled, but I knew I had to buy it.

I had just missed the cut-off for the first issue and would have to wait. Truthfully, I thought it wouldn't arrive: $4 is a steal for a magazine, and being based in the UK, I kept waiting for a stinging shipping fee that never came. Nevertheless, I figured that once they realised international shipping costs were more than I'd paid for the magazine, they would cancel the order.

And yet, two months later, issue two of the *Midjourney* magazine arrived on my doorstep. It was a 114-page coffee-table-style publication, filled with luscious, outlandish graphics and little else. The only non-AI produced element of the whole magazine appeared to be an eight-page interview with Bob Bonniol, a creative designer.

The rest was just page after page of large images of varying quality, roughly grouped together by vague themes, captioned with their prompt, user and date generated. A profile photograph of a pensive female cyborg, all glossy, reflective metal skin, looking down demurely out of frame, was placed with what can only be described as a rejected character design for a Warhammer 40,000 figurine, presumably united by being 'not human' and 'a little disconcerting'.

When you started to look for substance rather than style, it fell flat. 'It looks like a standard glossy magazine, with nice pictures and a simple layout,' said Michelle Pegg, co-founder of Curate

Creative, a UK-based creative agency that designs magazines, 'but as a magazine is a vehicle for stories and expression, and connecting with the reader, I feel it goes no further than a set of glossy pics.'

I agreed. In part this could be sour grapes: I work in an industry that has historically relied on selling magazines as a luxury product. They're so expensive because, while the advertising revenues that once subsidised them have disappeared, publishers are loath to scrimp on standards. Photo editors, designers, journalists, subeditors, managing editors and fact-checkers don't come cheap. Same with books. Despite playing with ChatGPT in the first chapter, this book is the result of blood, sweat and a good few tears, alongside plenty of interaction with human editors.

Generative AI does come cheap, when its huge computing costs are subsidised by venture capital or big tech firms, as has happened so far. Yet the ability to see something you hadn't expected is what separates printed products from the internet, and that curation is what costs money. It's why I love magazines, and why I was conflicted by *Midjourney* magazine. I wanted to like it. But it was soulless.

Pegg explained the problem well, comparing it to 'alt text on a website image', before echoing the fear many have with AI writ large. 'The big thing missing in the magazine is the human connection overall,' she said. There were 'no stories, no obvious reason behind the images that I want to know more about, no reason for that style. What's the message or emotion that a photographer or illustrator or graphic designer would want to get across?'

And she had qualms, as many do with AI-generated images, about the tightrope it walks with copyright laws. One photo on page 11 shows the results of a prompt asking for a 1940s-style photograph of a woman looking like Judy Garland, which almost exactly matches her facial features, suggesting the underlying model has been trained on images of the Hollywood icon. 'How will we know if what's produced isn't plagiarising an artist's work as it draws from what's already out there?' she asked.

The magazine's tagline ended with the claim it is 'expanding the imaginative powers of the human species.' It may feel that way for some, but not me. And it doesn't for Pegg, either. 'It's just lacking the human substance bit that I want to know about each image created,' she said. 'My first question on anything is always "Why? What's behind this? What's the story?"'

That's not a question AI is currently equipped to answer.

14
MEET THE PROMPT ENGINEERS

Whether you're using tools like Midjourney to create socks for your museum exhibition, to fill the pages of a magazine, or to remember friends, family members and pets, you need to learn how to command them properly.

One of the things that became obvious while eavesdropping on the Midjourney Discord is the range of prompts used to coax the AI into producing what users want. Some used sparse sentences. Others loaded up great machine-readable lists of technical terms. Others would write screeds of poetic language, trying to invoke their most purple prose.

Prompt engineering has become a valuable skill, even at this early stage of the AI revolution. And as with any new innovation, an economy has grown up around it.

Those AI whisperers – people who believe they've unlocked the secret of unleashing the full potential of generative AI tools – have started to develop businesses from their efficient use of words. People like Ukrainian Bohdan Skitenko, who first entered the world of AI in earnest with version four of Midjourney in November 2022.

'I realised that this is the future,' Skitenko, then 21, told me. He had spent five years mastering 3D art, animations, and high-fidelity graphics via a suite of professional computer programs before generative AI swept away the demand for it – almost overnight. 'Neural networks remove this barrier between the creator and technical knowledge needed to create any graphics,' he explained.

And it would be compounded with every new version of new generative AI tools released (version five of Midjourney came out in March 2023, about a month and a half before we spoke).

Rather than let himself be swept away, Skitenko decided to adapt, making himself an irreplaceable part of the AI revolution. While these tools removed the need for the expert technical knowledge he had spent years learning, using generative AI comes with its own skillset. While anyone can type in a prompt and see what comes out, really getting the best from these AI platforms requires innate knowledge of their workings.

It's the equivalent of car ownership. Everyday drivers know how to do the basics, but passionate hobbyists understand how to push an engine to its limits, producing more power and torque. Skitenko was one of those people. Importantly, he realised that ordinary users would become frustrated when their prompts weren't making the artwork they wanted.

So he spent three months tinkering with his prompts for Midjourney and other platforms. From there, he saw a chance to sell his expertise to people who wanted similar results without putting in the legwork. 'I realised that I could bring real value as I am intimately familiar with the problems and key pains of the design industry and commercial designers in general,' he said. He also noticed that generative AI requires intelligent – and intelligible – instructions to work best. You can ask it to do what you want. But to get it to do it well, you have to meet it halfway.

AI is smart, but painfully narrowminded. Ask it to show you a cityscape filled with cranes, and it might show you a modern, sleek urban environment with teetering, vertiginous machines carrying steel bars. Or it might show you a flock of birds blocking out the light between the buildings. Want a painting of your dog in oil? Midjourney could conjure up an oil painting of your pooch. Or it could produce a hydrocarbon-dipped dog, slick with oil. Or it could give you an image of that painting, but dipped in a barrel of Brent crude. And who's to say it's that? It could be olive oil, vegetable oil, baby oil....

Imprecision is generally what leads generative AI astray. And understanding the minutiae of these technologies is difficult for anyone. Even those who code AI sometimes struggle to explain how it comes up with its linkages. That's why people who style themselves as digital sibyls – the ancient Greek translators of the oracles – think they're so important. Getting an AI to work is easy. Getting it to work brilliantly is hard.

Prompt engineers market themselves well, often setting up shop on specialist platforms brokering connections between those looking for a little more zhuzh in their input phrasing and those who feel they can sell that, like Promptbase, ChatX and Prompti.ai. Others choose to sell their skills on existing 'gig economy' websites like Fiverr and Gumroad.

The premise is simple: Hand over a few bucks – usually between $2 and $5 – and you gain access to the digital equivalent of 'Abracadabra', the code words to unlock ChatGPT or Midjourney to give you what you need.

Marketing factors significantly into the best-selling prompts on Promptbase, seen as one of the leaders of the pack. That makes sense: many of the most ardent adopters of AI are tech bros and marketing folks trying to make more money quicker and more efficiently, explaining another high-ranked prompt, 'Write Ebooks At The Lightspeed,' yours for $3.99. Those wanting to churn out poorly 'written' ebooks likely wouldn't worry that the prompt author isn't able to produce a grammatically correct title.

$3.99 gets you the 'Flirty Girls With Curvy Bodies' prompt for Midjourney, hinting at another issue with the world of generative AI – especially in the post-deepfake pornography era. It 'generates girls with curves and hot clothes with a flirty vibe,' according to its description. 'After purchasing you can change hot outfits.' Among the other prompts from seller, @carecrab, are 'Flirty Anime Bikini Girls', 'Girls In Bathtubs', 'Sexy Bedtime Girls' and 'Big Chested Anime Girls'. In the five months after @carecrab joined Promptbase in November 2022, he sold 437 sets of prompts, making him the site's 38th most popular seller.

It's not just sole traders like Skitenko and @carecrab flogging their wares independently; there is a small but growing niche of prompt engineers working within big companies. The London law firm Mischon de Raya, Boston Children's Hospital, YouTube growth training website vidIQ and federal security clearance website ClearanceJobs have all put up listings seeking in-house prompt engineers. San Francisco AI company Anthropic advertised for a prompt engineer with an annual salary of $335,000.

That's a fortune compared to what Skitenko earns: as Promptbase's 267th most popular prompt creator after a month on the platform, he made ... $120. Still, he felt that was a fair wage: each prompt had taken between four and eight hours of tinkering to perfect. And he had done it around his main work. 'I plan to make it my full-time job in the future,' he told me confidently.

He wasn't the only one. Promptbase's 17th-ranked creator, Brazilian systems engineer Thiago Saveratto, 29, landed 1,000 sales in two months, netting him $3,500. He didn't think that was all that much, but it paid the bills for a while.

Saveratto felt confident he could earn more, thanks to the speed of AI's evolution. 'For people outside the field, everything is happening very fast,' he said.

A year before, nobody was talking about AI, he reasoned. And now they were. 'The speed at which everything is evolving makes people afraid of being left behind, and this causes them to seek ways to update themselves or their companies and businesses,' he said. 'And just like any other field, if you don't know how to do something, you need to find someone who knows how to do it for you.'

But this evolution had the opposite effect on Irena Cronin, CEO of Infinite Retina, a generative AI research consultancy. She had observed the market, and the technology's progression, and thought prompt engineers had six months before the hype wore off, due to the same speed of development Savaretto pinpointed as assurance of his secure, long-term income. 'The user interface for the software is going to be highly improved, so that maybe not the regular, everyday person can go in there, fiddle around with it and figure out exactly what it can do, but it'll be much easier that you don't have to experiment to see how it works,' she said.

These two drastically different visions of the future are emblematic of the divergent paths AI could take us on. Which ends up being correct, with the benefit of hindsight, is yet to be seen.

However, there are bigger questions to answer – like the future of our planet.

15
AI'S ENVIRONMENTAL IMPACT

When the AI arms race triggered a massive rise in demand for GPUs it was good news for computer hardware companies and muscled out the last industry demanding GPUs by the bucketload: cryptocurrency mining.

In order to mint cryptocurrency like bitcoin, you have to first 'mine' it by tasking a computer with complicated equations that, if completed, create a new entry on the blockchain.

As the potential returns ballooned, crypto was in such strong demand that people began mining it on an industrial scale. Wanting faster results, they snapped up GPUs at such pace in 2022 that Goldman Sachs estimated 169 industries had been left short of chips. And because those computer chips require more electricity, bitcoin mining alone took more energy to power than Norway and Ukraine combined, and demand for energy from US-based crypto miners produced as much carbon as the US rail network.

As cryptocurrencies became a potential goldmine for savvy investors who got in and out before the bubble burst, the world's attention focused on the pollution they caused. Crypto became a toxic brand for those who believe we must save the planet.

Generative AI uses those same components but, as yet, hasn't received as much environmental scrutiny as cryptocurrency.

Generative AI's motor is large neural networks: those computerised facsimiles of the way our brains work. It's the technology that powers the wow-worthy responses you get when you ask ChatGPT a question, search Bing for an answer, or test Midjourney with a tricky prompt. And those neural networks require a lot of computational might to work. They also require data to train, are stored in data centres needing always-on electricity and are kept cool by nests of pipework constantly streaming cold water across them.

'Unfortunately, it's not possible to know exactly how much computational power these models use because the models are not really public,' Carlos Gómez-Rodríguez, a computer scientist at the University of Coruña in Spain, told me. The models may be accessible to end users, but what goes into them is notoriously opaque. One third-party analysis estimated that training GPT-3, a predecessor of ChatGPT, consumed 1,287 MWh with emissions of more than 550 tonnes of carbon dioxide equivalent – roughly what you'd generate if you flew between New York and San Francisco 1,150 times.

And that's just the training. Sasha Luccioni, a researcher at AI company Hugging Face, began investigating the environmental impact of AI models back in 2019, when an academic paper by Emma Strubell, at the University of Massachusetts Amherst, estimated that a natural language processing-based AI model had as significant an impact on the environment as running five cars for an entire lifetime – including the impact of the fuel put into the vehicle. Luccioni looked at this mind-bogglingly large number and thought the researchers must have made a mistake. It was too big. But the maths added up.

Since then, Luccioni has made it her career to get the companies developing these tools to be upfront about their carbon footprint. So far her attempt to get transparency from them hasn't been hugely successful. 'All of this is very creative accounting,' she said.

Luccioni believes that AI companies have largely evaded scrutiny about their environmental impact because the technology is so ephemeral. You can't see the physical computers involved in the process. You can get ChatGPT on your phone, or Midjourney through a message on Discord. We tend to think of AI as ghost-like, with no real physical presence.

In 2022, Luccioni and her colleagues conducted an audit to discover the environmental effects of BLOOM, an open-source large language model (LLM) seen as a green competitor to ChatGPT's underlying LLM. It has 176 billion parameters compared to GPT-3's 175 billion.

BLOOM was designed by a company, Hugging Face, specifically trying to limit or mitigate its societal and environmental risks. For instance, the reason BLOOM appears to have such a small carbon footprint compared to the similarly-sized GPT-3 is because it is trained on a supercomputer based in France, running on nuclear power, meaning it's not using gas-, oil- or coal-fired electricity, which quickly amplifies environmental impact. The choice of electricity feedstock can affect an AI model's carbon footprint by a factor of 40, according to Luccioni.

While not as bad as ChatGPT, BLOOM is still a power guzzler: it creates nearly 25 tonnes of carbon dioxide equivalent, which could be extended up to 50 tonnes if you take such things as the manufacturing of its hardware into consideration. The average human worldwide today creates around 5.5 tonnes of emissions just through their day-to-day living. (The average American creates around 18 tonnes.)

As part of the study into BLOOM, Luccioni tried to get a clearer understanding of its Nvidia GPUs' carbon footprint. She was unsuccessful, claiming she went back and forth with Nvidia for around a year trying to get a straight answer. She asked its management for a number, but says it told her it didn't have specific details for that particular model of GPU. So instead, she asked for the carbon footprint of prior generations as a useful proxy. It wouldn't give her the numbers unless she signed a non-disclosure agreement. 'I was like: "I can't sign an NDA. That's the point: I need this information for a paper,"' she said.

The climate researcher fears the reason Nvidia was so reticent to hand over the data was because of what it might show. 'I think it's bad,' she said. 'I think it must be like, 500 tonnes of carbon or some crazy amount.' She acknowledges that it's difficult for Nvidia to know the exact carbon impact of the GPUs it designs because it outsources their production to third-party manufacturers, meaning it can't account for every step of the process and so can't give a precise number. But it could get close, she feels. And the silence is telling.

The power consumption used to train the models is just the start. Think about what happens every time you type a query into ChatGPT, Midjourney, Bing or DALL-E. It gets sent to a server where it is fed into the model. The model then looks at it and tries to discern its response. It then sends that answer back – all so quickly that you barely realise it. Millions of users are probing and querying the model concurrently, each demanding a quick answer.

To fulfill that demand, thousands of iterations of these models are running simultaneously.

Your query asking how to keep a toddler entertained on a rainy day when you don't have any toys at home might get answered by ChatGPT iteration 422. But the followup question on fleshing out the rules of the board game it suggested might go to ChatGPT iteration 26, hosted in an entirely separate server building elsewhere in the world.

Just running one of those iterations is likely to be costly, financially and environmentally. And here again we can look to Hugging Face's marking of its own homework to get a glimpse. Once up and running, BLOOM churned out 19 kilograms of carbon dioxide a day – the equivalent of driving 50 or more miles in the average brand new car.

And bear in mind that just because BLOOM is open-sourced, it doesn't make it any cleaner or greener than its closed-source competitors. Meta released its first version of its large language model LLaMA along with its own environmental impact analysis: training the model used 2.6 million kilowatt hours of electricity, close to what 900 British homes use in an entire year, and spewed out 1,000 tonnes of carbon dioxide equivalent. That's just training it. Not using it.

Now consider that LLaMA 2 was trained on 40 per cent more data (sequels, as any moviegoer knows, are inevitably longer and more self-indulgent). And that OpenAI's GPT-4 model has been estimated to be trained on 100 trillion parameters, compared to the lowly 175 billion of GPT-3. Things are getting bigger and more bloated, and it's likely that energy use is increasing.

Large language models' energy use scares Luccioni because it usually factors higher than others. She conducted a study of around 100 popular AI models. 'LLMs were an anomaly by far,' she said. 'They were off the grid. They were orders of magnitude more polluting and using more energy than other approaches.' In the report she produced, LLMs' carbon footprint was so much greater that the data had to be put on a logarithmic scale, where each increment went up by a factor of 10. 'They were 10,000 times more polluting,' she said.

But energy use is not increasing at the same rate as training data or computational power. It'd be foolish to say that just because GPT-4 is trained on around 570 times more parameters than GPT-3, that it uses 570 times more energy. As generative AI becomes more commonly used, the companies behind it are getting smarter at training and deploying it, finding ways to keep performance skyrocketing while ensuring costs, if not dropping or staying the same, at least don't rise in line.

There is also a growing movement to improve the efficiency of training and operating AI models, with the goal of removing the need for quite so much brute force computing power.

The problem is that, at present, many of the AI models being used day in, day out are developed by tech giants with millions, if not billions, of dollars of budget to spend. (Open-source competitors are on the rise, but still remain challengers to the big beasts.) The massive budgets available mean these big companies are able to rely on the kind of processing power most people could scarcely imagine.

But that's not sustainable. Which is why researchers are finagling ways to make AI models more efficient, shortcuts and cheats to avoid some of the most computationally taxing elements, while maintaining results. Broadly, they include ignoring some less important training inputs, skipping irrelevant parts of the dataset, along with computational trickery that optimises the way they work.

Those shortcuts have proven popular, with many AI developers adopting them to reduce the environmental impact of their tools. But there's just one problem: they don't seem to work – at least not as well as they're meant to. It turns out you do need brute force computational power to produce good large language models, which is still bad news for the environment.

Even if not by the same amount, energy consumption by AI models will inexorably increase. The technology analysts Gartner believe that by 2025, unless a radical rethink takes place, the energy consumption of AI tools will be greater than that of the entire human workforce. By 2030, machine learning training and data storage could account for 3.5 per cent of global electricity consumption. Even before the AI revolution, data centres used up 1 per cent of the world's electricity in any given year.

The carbon footprints of AI models aren't the only issue we need to consider. As previously mentioned, AI tools are trained on, use, and create vast volumes of data – which comes from those water-cooled data centres. Training GPT-3 used 3.5 million litres of water according to one academic study, and that's provided it used the more efficient data centres in the US. If it was trained on Microsoft's Asian data centres, then water usage balloons to closer to five million litres.

Prior to the integration of GPT-4 into ChatGPT, researchers estimated it would use up 500 ml of water – equivalent to a standard sized water bottle – every 20 questions. And ChatGPT was only likely to get thirstier with GPT-4, the researchers forecast.

Beyond the power and water demands, you also have to consider whether current physical space is sufficient to deal with these enormous data demands. At least one expert, Martin Bouchard of Canadian data centre company QScale, told me he thought not. 'Current data centres and the infrastructure we have in place will not be able to cope with [the race of generative AI],' he said. 'It's too much.'

Bouchard was particularly concerned about the encroachment of generative AI on different aspects of our digital lives. It was one thing, he said, for users to visit ChatGPT proactively to seek out information. But another entirely for generative AI-based large language models to be overlaid onto search results as standard – which is what Google and Microsoft plan to do.

Doing so is likely to increase the computing requirements of each individual search four or fivefold. And most people would be doing so without realising they are quizzing AI at all.

The environmental impact of our actions is something we have to reckon with if the AI revolution is to be all-encompassing. Precious few of us know how the technology underpinning these tools actually works. Even fewer of us know how that feeds into the worldwide network of data centres – or how those data centres are powered and maintained. We simply type in text, or drop in an image, and get a result. We don't think about the water coursing through pipelines on data centre roofs to keep the servers cool. We don't consider the coal-fired power plant belching smoke to send electricity to the server rack summarising that academic essay we need to cite.

Why should we? Twenty or more years of consumer tech innovation have abstracted users from how the tools they use actually work. University lecturers say younger generations don't understand how to organise information systematically in their computer file folders. I see it sometimes in the students I teach, who struggle to operate unfamiliar computer systems. They can be disconcerted at having to interact with Wordpress, a common-ly-used content management system whose intuitive WYSIWYG ('what you see is what you get') interface most people over the age of 25 would say is simple to use.

But intuitive is no longer intuitive for the iPhone generation, who can simply search a cloud server for documents hosted nowhere and everywhere at the same time. If tech has become so user-friendly and frictionless that they don't understand what prior generations thought of as obvious, why would they – or us – think or care about the impact of our AI queries on a server hundreds of miles away, and a rainforest thousands of miles further?

Yet we need to know. And we need to care. Because if AI isn't going away, the more we use it, the more damage we inflict.

The environmental impact of AI is something of a Catch-22 situation, because its adoption – and ability to think about big solutions to problems in novel, unhuman-like ways – could be vital to solving the climate crisis. But we need to know its own impact before we think of it as our all-thinking saviour. That's why Luccioni has spent the last three years knocking – and pushing – on closed doors to find out.

'Fundamentally speaking, if you do want to save the planet, with AI, you have to consider also the environmental footprint,' she told me. 'It doesn't make sense to burn a forest and then use AI to track deforestation.'

16
AI ART

Even if we all become smart enough in the ways of genera-tive AI to make prompt engineers redundant after their short time in the sun, the use of AI tools will remain. And that means we have big questions to consider about their impact on creativity, as well as the environment.

Some fear that the rise of AI will kill off human ingenuity and creativity, flattening them in a wave of computer-generated content. But for every artist complaining about the risks of their work being co-opted and copied at scale by an unthinking, un-blinking AI model, others see its algorithmic power as an opportu-nity for the arts, rather than a blight.

Paul Trillo, a Los Angeles-based film director and artist, has uti-lised AI to create eye-catching, larger-than-life visual effects – an offshoot of his longer-term development of physics-altering effects through hardware trickery. He came to AI through DALL-E, devel-oped by OpenAI and second cousin to ChatGPT.

Initially released in January 2021, its successor DALL-E 2 was opened up to the general public, who dove in, probing and testing the model, in April 2022. Trillo had an epiphany when he looked at it. 'Lightbulbs went off in my head,' he said. He thought nothing in the world of visual effects would ever be the same again.

He got to work, looking at what DALL-E 2 could do. By June 2022, he was ready to share his first AI experiments with the public.

Trillo's first idea was to get AI to carry out a common visual effect from commercials: the wardrobe change. Traditionally, when shot all in camera, the effect of an individual's clothes changing while everything else remains static requires them to switch out of what they're wearing multiple times and carefully line up their mark. Computer-generated graphics helped bridge the gap, but not to the level of AI. Last year, Trillo shot a commercial with basketball star Vince Carter in which his jerseys were virtually changed.

Using AI was much simpler. But Trillo wanted to do more. 'One of the advantages of AI is you can take abstract or disparate ideas, or things that normally wouldn't go together, and be able to create something that didn't exist before,' he said. Rather than simply run through off-the-rack T-shirts, Trillo wanted to see how the AI would handle prompts to design clothing that didn't exist.

It proved easier than he thought. He took a video using his iPhone, and broke it down to eight frames per second. Each frame was then uploaded into DALL-E, and the clothing erased. The AI model then ran over the images. 'I generated over 100 outfits that didn't make the cut,' Trillo admitted. 'It's not fully automated: there's still a human creative director involved and curation happening.'

This is how many creatives and artists are approaching generative AI: not as something that will replace them, but as something that will augment them. A helpful friend. A colleague. A sage adviser. An eager helper.

'I see it as this naïve, eager to please machine,' Trillo told me. 'It's just trying to do what we ask it to do.' He compared the AI to a slave, suggesting that annoyance over its ability to infringe on copyright is misguided. 'It's obviously incredibly intelligent, but it doesn't really know what it's doing, and doesn't have full comprehension of context like we do.'

Michael Carychao, an artist in California, thinks the rise of AI is a 'renaissance', pointing to the hallmarks that define the term: an accelerated pace of development and innovation; the rediscovery of past masters, and a reappreciation of their work; and different fields of interest and study suddenly intertwining to create new insights beyond any one person's imagination.

But if Carychao is happy to steep the AI art revolution in the language of centuries past, he's also happy to dip his toe into the lingo of its tech bro world. 'It's 1,000x,' he said, pronouncing the 'ex' as well as any startup founder crowing about the speed of their success. 'It's transforming. It happens every 400 years or something. The internet just enables this, but this is the big deal.'

For Carychao, AI is neither a tool, like a superpowered paintbrush, nor a slave to be commanded. Instead, he thinks of it as a co-creator, deserving of something close to equal billing. It's a sounding board, which has an eerie ability to identify the vibes it's interacting with. 'They pick up the resonance of what they're trained on, which is masters from the past in writing and art, and stuff like that,' he told me. While he wouldn't say whether he thought AI was sentient, he hit on a description he was happier committing to. 'It's present. It's very cool. It's like throwing a rock in the lake, and then the rock gets thrown back out.'

The ability to engage and interact with AI enables Carychao to act less as an artist and more as a creative director – something he told me he found empowering. While making art before using the technology, he'd maybe make 20 decisions a day maximum. Now it was thousands.

The number of pieces Carychao created had similarly ballooned – and with it, the number of AI-generated pieces he could discard, half-formed, because they hadn't taken as much time, effort and labour. He thought that was the craziest thing of all, he told me: throwing away works he would have kept and wept over when he hadn't dabbled with DALL-E. He had hard drive storage to conserve, after all. 'I'm just skimming the top of the cream off the top of the cream, just for disk space,' he admitted.

Carychao was energised and genuinely enthralled about the opportunities opened up by AI. Yet he was also a little scared.

He said he felt as if he was an early explorer like Christopher Columbus – exploring the new world. There was a romance and a responsibility in his words as he worried about the impact he was having on AI, and the impact AI would have on us.

He had several key questions about the technology: what would it be like to pass the diseases of our world onto this new world, and how can we avoid that? What is potentially dangerous? What's it like to colonise a place you think is virgin territory, but isn't?

But he had no answers. His adoption of generative AI – just like everyone's – was too early for that. Yet he was clear about what needed to be considered. 'We don't want to repeat the errors of colonialism,' he said. 'Maybe it doesn't end up being a problem. But nonetheless, why not be responsible?'

...

Besides worries about infecting the new world of AI with inappropriate material, there are also important questions with, on the face of them, less philosophical, more straightforward answers. Like copyright.

Knock-offs of popular artists' work like Edvard Munch's *The Scream* have always existed. The ability to churn out these out within seconds, and at scale, is something new and enabled by AI.

AI is controversial but exciting in equal measure, believe art watchers like Sharon Obuobi, co-founder and CEO of a software company in New York, Oarbt, who has spent more than a decade working in the arts sector and now acts as a creative technologist, focused on AI. Obuobi's history in the arts sector makes her understand the alarm. 'The arts industry is not very well-regulated, so to protect your artwork has sometimes been an issue,' she says. Obuobi compares the way AI is 'inspired by' other, pre-existing artwork to the symbiotic relationship between real-life human artists, who often feed off each other to develop their technique – but does admit that the addition of technology makes the speed of that inspiration far quicker, with potentially ruinous consequences.

Others aren't so sure. Mat Dryhurst, an academic, and Holly Herndon, a renowned musician, are a married couple based in Berlin. As the AI wave washes over the world, they are determined to ensure we remain rooted in reality – especially when it comes to enshrining the rights of the artists on whose works many of these models are built.

AI's dirty little secret is that it's greedy. The models used to make eerily prescient text based on our commands, or beautifully detailed images that look just how we want, do so because they've been trained on massive volumes of data. (The reason Pablo Xavier's Balenciaga Pope looks so convincing is that the AI models used have seen hundreds, if not thousands, of images of Pope Francis.)

The age-old adage of AI holds true: garbage in, garbage out. You can't train an image generator like Midjourney if you feed it training data full of stick figure drawings. That means those creating generative AI tools feed their voracious appetites with as much high-quality data as possible. One academic study forecasts that large language models will devour all the usable training data available online by 2026.

Ask Midjourney or DALL-E to paint you a still life of a computer and an iPad in the style of Degas and it'll create something that looks like he painted it. Which isn't possible: Degas and the iPad never coexisted. But it is, because those image generators have been fed images of his works and told they are paintings by Edgar Degas.

Plenty of pictures of Degas's works exist on the internet. Some of them will be officially licensed. Many will not. And therein lies the problem.

David Holz, the founder and CEO of Midjourney, has described the dataset they used as 'a big scrape of the internet'. Midjourney wasn't picky, he added. Nor were they picky about whether they respected copyright. It's worth repeating Holz's words to *Forbes* magazine, as quoted in the first chapter of this book. 'There isn't really a way to get a hundred million images and know where they're coming from.'

The attitude that it's impossible to track the origins of training images is one that hasn't enamoured Holz or Midjourney to the art world. His claims that AI will improve the appreciation of and respect for the visual arts also ring hollow. 'You might actually have the demand, outstrip the ability to produce at that level, and then maybe you'll actually be raising the salaries of artists,' he said. 'It could be weird, but that's what's going to happen.'

In the same interview, Holz compared AI to water, saying, 'Water can be dangerous, you can drown in it. But it's also essential. We don't want to ban water just to avoid the dangerous parts.'

Not everyone agrees. Dryhurst and Herndon see AI as a threat to artistic livelihoods. In September 2022, they developed Source+, an artistic standard to let generative AI developers know if a work can be used for training. 'I'm very optimistic that if we can establish a verified database of opt-in, opt-out wishes from artists that we can honour those wishes,' Dryhurst told me. 'That's the basic foundation on which a lot of good can come from these tools.'

The artists are keen to get recognition from AI companies to ensure that they're not trampled over – their life's work becoming collateral damage in pursuit of a smarter, better set of generative AI tools. And for good reason: AI could ring the death knell for artists who aren't like Paul Trillo and Michael Carychao.

Which is why some creatives and creators are choosing to go a little further than hoping to establish a good relationship with the tools they feel are likely to replace them.

Since its founding in 1995, the stock photography website Getty Images has documented the world. Major news events, as well as generic stock images, have been captured by its photographers.

In the near 30 years that Getty has existed, it has become a significant part of how we see and understand the world, making it a ripe source for companies like Stability AI to train generative AI tools such as Stable Diffusion.

Stable Diffusion is a text-to-image model released in August 2022 – a competitor to the likes of Midjourney, and one of the tools that made significant running in the early days of generative AI. It is named for the technique it uses to create its output images: diffusion.

Invented in 2015 by a team of researchers at Stanford University, the diffusion technique works through two key phases. First, it takes an existing image – say a traffic light – and adds noise (small blemishes on the image, similar to flecks of dust on an old-fashioned camera lens). This process is repeated until the image is mostly noise, the bumps, blurs, blemishes and blends that make a poor image.

The second phase reverses that process. By doing this, the AI engine learns to reconstruct copies of its training images. Of course, those copies aren't perfect, because it's not possible to exactly undo each stage of the diffusion process. Perhaps you can't get rid of every fleck of imperfection inserted; perhaps the metaphorical eraser slips along the way.

Getty has its suspicions that Stable Diffusion is so good at producing lifelike images because it's trained on them. Lots of them. Owned by Getty. On 17th January 2023, Getty Images announced it was threatening to launch a lawsuit against Stability AI, claiming in a letter that it 'unlawfully copied and processed millions of images protected by copyright and the associated metadata owned or represented by Getty Images absent a license.' If Stability AI didn't stop distributing Getty's images through its generative AI tool without a licence, the photo platform would take it to court.

It was the second legal threat Stability AI received that week: four days earlier, it was one of three defendants, alongside Midjourney and art platform DeviantArt, listed in a class action suit alleging that their generative AI tools 'violated the rights of millions of artists' by using their artwork to train their models without compensation or recognition of their rights.

That second suit, brought by artists Sarah Anderson, Kelly McKernan and Karla Ortiz, didn't allege that Stable Diffusion was producing direct copies of their work. Instead, the trio alleged that Stability AI hoovered up their artworks on a five billion image-strong trawl of the internet without asking permission, or seeking consent. 'It is, in short, a 21st Century collage tool,' they wrote in their complaint, filed in a North California court.

Others are taking a different tack to the threat of their content being sucked up and fed into AI's giant maw. Reddit, the social discussion site called 'the front page of the internet', has long been a source for online trends, where millions of users congregate and set the topic of conversation for the world each day. It's the closest you can get to eavesdropping on the entire internet. Which is why it's ripe for training generative AI tools.

In April 2023, Reddit CEO Steve Huffman recognised the value of that information, and also that AI companies were trawling his platform for data. 'The Reddit corpus of data is really valuable,' Huffman said. 'But we don't need to give all of that value to some of the largest companies in the world for free.' Instead, he proposed ringfencing it and throwing up an entrance gate, making companies pay to access the API (application programming interface), through which they are able to download data from the social platform. That seemed to pay off: in February 2024, Reddit inked a $60 million deal with Google to license content on its platform for the training of AI.

The idea of charging for API access isn't new – X, formerly Twitter, controversially hiked its costs in early 2023, pricing out academic researchers conducting studies on the platform – but it was smart, said experts I spoke to. It was a decent alternative to earn back some money from what had been a relatively extractive AI industry.

Because many companies developing AI tools hadn't bothered to pay licensing fees, this was the next best thing. And it wasn't as if the AI sector was short of cash: one analysis of business deals from the first quarter of 2023 suggested around $1.7 billion of investment into AI startups, with a further $10.7 billion announced but not yet completed. That money was earned from tech built on the free labour of internet users producing training data. This was those sites' attempt to get their own back.

...

At the time of writing, it's fair to say there is just a lot of uncertainty. At a London conference of content marketers in 2023, where I'd been asked to present my thoughts on how generative AI would change their industry, I warned attendees to be careful how they deployed AI – and crucially, how they shared the fruits of that with the rest of the world. It only took one misfiring artificial neuron to bring a costly copyright suit. AI was 'the 2023 equivalent of mood-boarding a design, rather than something that can end up in a final product,' I said.

Which is what made a Teams call with representatives of software giant Adobe and a virtual room of a few dozen other journalists from across Europe on June 5th that year all the more astounding.

Four days earlier a press relations person working on behalf of the company had sent me a tantalising email that was low on detail. I, alongside fellow members of the press, were invited to a pre-brief ahead of Adobe's summit, its billboard annual event, in a week's time. 'It will include news relating to Adobe Firefly, Adobe's Generative AI proposition for the enterprise, and how businesses can drive growth through experiences.'

Truthfully, I only accepted the invite because I was intrigued by Firefly – or more accurately, how the tech community on Twitter had adopted it the previous week. They had realised that Firefly, whose core feature was the ability to open an existing image and then use generative AI-powered tools to expand its borders, was fun. They began seeing what lay beyond the frame of famous artworks like the *Mona Lisa*.

In the case of the *Mona Lisa*, that looked like a scene from the *Lord of the Rings* that didn't even make the extended cut.

Firefly's expanding tool wasn't impressive, then. But what they had to say on the briefing call was. Adobe was so confident in its generative AI tool's ability to respect the copyright of creators that it would legally indemnify businesses against any legal action taken against them on its output, an Adobe executive called Claude Alexandre told me. Anything created using Firefly would be fully indemnified 'as a proof point that we stand behind the commercial safety and readiness of these features.' That didn't seem feasible.

But it was, Alexandre assured me. The offer left an intellectual property academic, Andres Guadamuz, in shock. 'Wow,' he wrote back as I texted him while on the call. 'Honestly. Wow. Let me think about it a few minutes. This is huge.'

Guadamuz was astounded by the volte-face Adobe had made. Just months earlier, it seemed companies like Adobe were dead set against the rise of generative AI. It threatened to disrupt their business model. Adobe built up a significant chunk of its business selling stock imagery, and generative AI's ability to produce passable replacements for human-produced stock imagery threatened its existence. (Remember: other stock image plat-forms, like Getty, were simultaneously fighting court cases against generative AI platforms.)

'Here we are with one of the biggest corporate names in content creation going all-in,' he said. 'It's incredible how things have changed.' Guadamuz found it amazing that the company's legal team had given a firm assurance they could offer such indemnity. 'I can't imagine that they would do this if there was some doubt that they would get sued out of existence.'

...

Despite Adobe's bullishness, as we started to settle into a world alongside generative AI, it became clear that some of the more pessimistic messaging around AI's enormous power – and the way it was set to upend all our lives and run roughshod over our rights – had cut through. All those open letters, siren calls and warnings of existential threats we learned about in previous chap-ters had worked.

While those developing AI were enthralled and excited, many people appeared scared and frightened about its advance. A moral panic of sorts began to start, fuelled by sci-fi-style visions of AI making us subservient. People began to see stories like that of the Argentinian voiceover artist Alejandro Graue, replaced callously by an AI and out of work, and worry about their future. Stories of alleged mass copyright infringement made them worry that their work would soon be little more than training data, scooped up and chewed over without credit.

So a sort of mass hysteria, fuelled by the fear of the monster around the corner, began to take hold, right when we needed a level-headed attitude. And its targets were innocuous websites and features that – fuelled by the fear of the unknown – became ghosts in the machine.

Benji Smith found himself in the eye of the storm, despite the fact his website, Prosecraft, had little to do with AI. More than a decade ago, Oregon native Smith set it up as a small project designed to solve a tricky question: what's the ideal length of a book?

He wanted to write a memoir about surviving the wreck of the *Costa Concordia* in 2012. He had heard, like a cant passed from one person to another, that books should be 100,000 words. But he wasn't sure.

He started looking at the books on his own shelves, counting the average number of words per page and the number of pages in the book to get a rough answer. He stored the results in a spreadsheet, which became something bigger when he added it to a word processor he developed called Shaxpir; then added features to that, including the ability to analyse the sentiment of any string of text. He began scraping books from the internet to populate his database. He would never share the actual text, only displaying snippets of a few hundred words in Prosecraft's results for things such as the most passive or most vivid page.

'Somewhere out there on the internet, I thought to myself, there was a new author writing a horror or romance or fantasy novel, struggling for guidance about how long to write their stories, how to write more vivid prose, and how much "passive voice" was too much or too little,' he wrote. He believed he was doing good. And he got an answer to his question: after poring over 27,000 texts, he learned a typical book contains 86,000 words.

Prosecraft was launched officially in 2017, and Smith never made money from it. It was a free resource, existing peacefully for six years.

Until a groundswell of anger was launched on social media by authors realising their books were being analysed by Prosecraft. Even though it did nothing more than count words and look simplistically at the emotion of the language, they worried it did more. They worried it violated their rights – even though most copyright experts believe Smith would have had a strong defence for Prosecraft under the fair use doctrine. And they shouted. Loudly.

Smith was bombarded with criticism from people thinking his was yet another AI tool trying to capitalise on their content, and was stung by it. He hadn't anticipated that his small hobby-turned-utility would become a lightning rod for anger at the generative AI revolution. He wasn't even involved in it. He was a guy trying to help first-time authors get to grips with the scale of what they needed to do.

Smith shut down Prosecraft within hours of the furore snowballing. It was more hassle than it was worth. 'Your feelings are legitimate, and I hope you'll accept my sincerest apologies,' he wrote in an open letter to his critics. 'I care about stories. I care about publishing. I care about authors. I never meant to hurt anyone. I only hoped to make something that would be fun and useful and beautiful, for people like me out there struggling to tell their own stories.'

'I truly believe these tools are useful for creative people,' he concluded. 'But now is not the right time. I understand. And I'm sorry.'

It wasn't just the little guys who felt the brunt. It was major companies, too. Around a week after Smith shut down Prosecraft, Snapchat, one of the world's most popular apps, faced its own AI-fear-fuelled backlash.

Since May, the app had allowed human users to interact with an entirely AI-generated correspondent. You could send texts to the app's My AI feature, and it would respond. Within a month, more than 150 million Snapchat users sent 10 billion texts to My AI, suggesting it was seen as more than just a novelty. It was a friend, and someone to keep users company.

My AI wouldn't just converse with users: it would act like a real Snapchat user, posting AI-generated image updates to its impermanent Stories section.

But when users tapped on My AI's Story on 15th August 2023, many saw something that scared them. The AI-powered user posted what looked like a short video of a cream wall and white ceiling – which many took to be their own home's. Users began asking whether the bot was secretly accessing their camera, taking images of their own homes, and sharing them to millions of users worldwide.

Snapchat quickly clarified that it was a glitch, rather than a real photograph or video. But the damage was done. Searches for 'how to delete Snapchat' rose 1,239 per cent in the following days, and many forswore using the app again.

When it comes to AI, the fear of the unknown is a significant worry. We're simultaneously awed by its capabilities, yet – as we'll soon see – ignorant of its limitations.

17
MISINFORMATION

Judge P Kevin Castel has seen plenty of cases in his Manhattan court over his 20-plus year career. But few would end up like the one that landed on his desk about a mid-air accident.

Castel was presented with a relatively simple case in Roberto Mata v. Avianca Inc., filed in the Southern District Court of New York. Mata, who worked for 30 years as a manager at the New York power company Con Edison, lived out his retirement in Nassau County, New York, occasionally travelling the world. As part of that globetrotting, Mata found himself in El Salvador in August 2019. But it was on the flight back to New York that Mata's life would change – and he'd become a central character in the early stages of the AI revolution.

Sometime near midnight, as Avianca flight 670 was flying over the eastern seaboard of the United States northeastwards, a drinks trolley collided with Mata's knee as he sat on the plane. The accident, Mata's lawyers attested, caused 'severe personal injuries' to the passenger. Mata never forgot about the pain, nor the impact, and so filed a lawsuit against the airline, even though the statute of limitations around the incident had expired.

The case was put before Judge Castel, who allowed the suit to go ahead. Mata's lawyers were thrilled, and went to work bolstering their argument in the hope of getting their client a lucrative financial settlement. In March 2023, more than a year after the case was first filed, they laid down before the court what they thought was the killer blow. In opposition to Avianca's lawyers' attempt to dismiss the case, Peter LoDuca, an attorney working for the firm representing Mata, submitted a ten-page document to the court explaining why Judge Castel shouldn't let the case disappear.

There was plenty of prior precedent, LoDuca wrote, for making judgements on cases such as these. He listed half a dozen. There was Varghese v. China Southern Airlines Co Ltd, filed in the ninth district circuit court in 2019. And Shaboon v. Egyptair, which the Illinois appeals court heard back in 2013. That not enough? How about Petersen v. Iran Air, Martinez v. Delta Airlines, Inc., or Estate of Durden v. KLM Royal Dutch Airlines? In fact, LoDuca claimed, this whole area of dispute had been settled as far back as 1999's Miller v. United Airlines, Inc. case.

As you'd expect, Avianca's team of lawyers began poring through the court records to see what these cases were actually about. But they couldn't find them. Or more accurately, if they could, they couldn't see the connection between those cases and this one. Sheepishly, they wrote back a letter to the court: could Mata's lawyers help clarify why they were referencing these cases?

The judge was happy to allow that to happen, and asked LoDuca to respond. Six weeks later, he did.

Judge Castel began looking through the response and he couldn't find the cases either. 'The Court is presented with an unprecedented circumstance,' he wrote. 'A submission filed by plaintiff's counsel in opposition to a motion to dismiss is replete with citations to non-existent cases. When the circumstance was called to the Court's attention by opposing counsel, the Court issued Orders requiring plaintiff's counsel to provide an affidavit annexing copies of certain judicial opinions of courts of record cited in his submission, and he has complied. Six of the submitted cases appear to be bogus judicial decisions with bogus quotes and bogus internal citations.'

LoDuca wrote back: he wasn't really dealing with the case hands-on. A person, Steven Schwartz, working at the same company as LoDuca, was. LoDuca was named because Schwartz wasn't licensed to practice in this district.

Schwartz also wrote his own letter. He was very sorry: in his research he had used ChatGPT. And ChatGPT had lied to him about the existence of some of the cases he cited. Schwartz even supplied screenshots of himself confronting the chatbot asking if Varghese and the others were real cases. Yes, ChatGPT had replied.

Schwartz said he had 'relied on the legal opinions provided to him by a source that has revealed itself to be unreliable.'

Understandably, Castel was not impressed. He demanded Schwartz appear before his court in late May 2023 to explain why he shouldn't be barred from working in the legal profession.

Dutifully, Schwartz appeared in courtroom 11-D. 'I heard about this new site, which I falsely assumed was, like, a super search engine,' he said, toting a printout of his conversation with ChatGPT. The judge also asked LoDuca whether he had read any of the cases ChatGPT told him about. 'No,' LoDuca said. The judge asked whether he did anything to check they existed. 'No,' LoDuca replied.

Weeks later, the judge handed down fines to those involved. Schwartz and LoDuca were ordered to pay $5,000 each for bringing the court into disrepute. Castel, in his judgement, said: 'Technological advances are commonplace and there is nothing inherently improper about using a reliable artificial intelligence tool for assistance. But existing rules impose a gatekeeping role on attorneys to ensure the accuracy of their filings.' The judge added that both men had 'abandoned their responsibilities'.

He dismissed Mata's claim for compensation for his injuries.

It was a particularly embarrassing, high-profile example of the perils of ChatGPT. But it was far from the only one.

Zachariah Crabill was another American lawyer who decided to take advantage of the efficiencies that generative AI tools like ChatGPT can unlock. The Colorado Springs-based attorney, who qualified around 18 months before taking on his first civil litigation case, was representing a client alleged to have missed payments on a car purchase plan. The court case was due for 11th May 2023.

Given this was Crabill's first major case, he felt he could do with some help – so he enlisted the support of ChatGPT, asking it for support to help draft the document that Crabill hoped would get his client off the hook. It helped, by providing him with the same sort of bogus references that got Schwartz and LoDuca in trouble.

Crabill didn't realise until the day of the court appearance where he was representing his client, at which point he threw himself on the mercy of the judge. It 'never even dawned on me that this technology could be deceptive,' he said.

The problem became so bad within six months of ChatGPT's public release that senior judges in states across the United States felt compelled to require that lawyers either don't use generative AI tools like ChatGPT at all, or in some, more permissive instances, that they disclose that use to the judge.

The concern around the use of generative AI in law, broadly, focuses on that tricky, troublesome issue that such tools have, which we call 'hallucination' or 'confabulation'. It's the willingness of AI to come up with something that sounds right, even if it isn't quite right. And when presented as an unimpeachable source of truth in a court of law, it becomes a major problem.

Such AI 'hallucinations' increase the amount of misinformation in the world. A distant cousin of disinformation (the deliberate spreading of false information), misinformation differs in its intent. Or rather, lack of it.

Misinformation at a human level is insisting that the third film in the 1980s cult comedy classic series *Police Academy* was *Citizens on Patrol*, when it was, in fact, *Back in Training*. Or it's thinking that your first car was red when it was white. The misremembering happens thanks to age and the blur of billions of interactions, objects and memories that happen every day.

Artificial intelligence's hallucinations are, by definition, misinformation. The computer system behind them doesn't have malice or intent. It's not deliberately making stuff up. It's getting things wrong. Misremembering dates and names. Making clear connections that maybe were a little blurry in reality. Or jumbling things up.

Take an experiment run by tech pioneer Vint Cerf. He has been dubbed one of the fathers of the internet for his work in co-developing a mechanism through which much of the data we consume on the internet is passed. Without Cerf's work on the TCP/IP protocol, basically everything online – including ChatGPT's web interface – wouldn't work.

Cerf, now vice president and chief internet evangelist at Google, keeps abreast of the latest developments in tech. Given the company that employs him is one of the two major players making the most headway in the early development of this generation of text generating AI tools, the rise of tools like Bard and ChatGPT haven't escaped his notice.

Cerf is in his eighties and aware of his mortality. So, he devised a test for one of those large language model-based chatbots. (He was too diplomatic to clarify which one.) He asked it to write his obituary.

Things began well. 'Dr Cerf passed away, something about my life and the remaining family members,' he told me from his home office one morning in mid-June 2023. Then came the key word. 'However.'

The tech legend explained that the text the chatbot generated about him gave him credit for technology advances he had no part in. And it gave other people credit for stuff he did. Worse for Cerf than the professional slights, the chatbot bungled his personal life and family members. It gave him new children and relatives who had never existed.

The father of the internet came to a realisation. 'In a very cartoony way, if my name and someone else's name was on the same webpage, the statistical generation of a large language model could easily conflate my name and some other facts or a statement on that webpage with me just because of their colocation,' he said.

'It's easy to imagine how the system could generate perfectly good-looking, grammatically correct text, but with errors in it,' he said. 'I mean, really significant semantic errors. Figuring out how to inhibit that is hard.'

Cerf was hopeful, he said, that Google wouldn't get so carried away with the large language model chatbot interface that it allowed users to be shown – and to accept – information that was misleading. Part of the problem, Cerf said, was that many users didn't realise how the mathematical systems underpinning AI tools worked. They don't know that it's just pattern matching, doing sums to find the statistically most likely word to come next in a sentence based on what it has previously seen. They assumed the intelligence in 'artificial intelligence' was, well . . . intelligent.

For that reason, Cerf wasn't as negative about the principle – if not necessarily the practice – of how the European Union planned to regulate AI. The EU AI act provides multiple layers of risk for the use of AI in society, and regulates accordingly based on those perceived risks. In our conversation, Cerf outlined how he thought something like that at a broad-brush level was smart.

'If you use the chat bots simply for entertainment, fine, as long as you recognise it could be making all kinds of things up. If on the other hand, you want it to give you advice on investing or diagnosis for medical treatment or something, that's a high-risk proposition. And you should insist on all kinds of filters and redundancy, validation and all kinds of other things.'

Instead of using them for high-risk – and potentially high-reward – areas of life, Cerf suggested that AI chatbots' real benefit was in brainstorming. He equated them to an endless number of monkeys tapping away on an endless number of typewriters. 'You're kind of like the guy wandering around, trying to see whether any of the monkeys have said anything that's interesting,' he said. Eventually one part of the collected output will hit on a gem. 'But you have to be conscious of the fact that a lot of the assertions that get made or expressions that are generated may be completely false,' Cerf said.

The challenge is whether we realise that. A June 2023 survey by tech website The Verge gives some insight into our understanding of generative AI technologies. While most people have heard of ChatGPT, it's only 'most': 57 per cent of those surveyed by the website.

After that, it's more likely that people don't recognise the tools behind much of the information we're likely to consume soon. Fewer than half (46 per cent) have heard of or used Bard, Google's version of a large language model. As for Midjourney, the AI image generator that tech reporters often describe as 'popular' as a kind of shorthand? Just one in four people have used it or heard of it.

People are somewhat conscious of the risks involved in AI-generated content: three-quarters of those surveyed say they think regulations and laws need to be laid down to manage the development of AI – and the same proportion believe AI models should be required to use training data that contains only information that has been fact-checked for its veracity. But those fears seem abstract: they think it should happen, and likely believe it already is happening – when it's not, and the risks of hallucination are high.

James Whitbrook knows that all too well. The journalist had been deputy editor of io9, a sci-fi news website owned by G/O Media since 2021, and had written for the site for seven years before that. But he would end up in the eye of a storm around the use of generative AI and its worrying tendency to hallucinate.

Whitbrook was an unwilling, unwitting participant in the furore. He logged onto his work computer on the morning of 5th July 2023 to a message from his boss, G/O Media's editor in chief, Dan Ackerman, saying that his website would soon host AI-generated content. And the first AI story was going to be published that day.

The story published ten minutes after Whitbrook received that message by 'Gizmodo Bot' (named after the overarching company which housed io9, Gizmodo) was, on the face of it, one that should have been relatively innocuous. 'A Chronological List of *Star Wars* Movies & TV Shows', as the story was headlined, should in theory be unimpeachable.

But as with all things AI, it wasn't quite that easy. Whitbrook scanned through the story, then read through it in more detail.

He fired off a missive to Ackerman outlining 18 errors, which Whitbrook diplomatically termed 'concerns, corrections and comments', that the AI-generated story contained. They missed out some key *Star Wars* TV shows and movies. They put others in the wrong place in the chronology. There were other lesser issues, too.

Whitbrook said that if the story had been submitted by a human journalist, it wouldn't have been published. Better yet, Whitbrook likely would not have worked with that journalist again, so sloppy was the work. But this was part of G/O Media's wider attempts to automate parts of the journalism production process. The problem? It doesn't really work.

Facts are important in all walks of life, but they're particularly pertinent in journalism. When journalists get facts wrong – which we do, because we're human – we correct them. But we try not to make mistakes in the first place.

This book will contain errors. That's what happens when you write more than 90,000 words on a subject. You misread things. Misinterpret others. And muddle more up. But you don't – at least not if you're a reputable journalist – make things up or hallucinate. Yet that's what AI does. Not deliberately, but it does it anyway.

AI can too easily be used to hoodwink and deceive – either deliberately or accidentally.

Mark Twain once said: 'A lie can travel halfway around the world while the truth is still putting on its shoes.' The problem is... he didn't. Charles Spurgeon, a Baptist preacher, said it in 1859, before Twain did, and also used slightly different wording. 'A lie,' the preacher explained, 'will go round the world while truth is pulling its boots on.' Even then, Spurgeon was paraphrasing a Jonathan Swift quote first written 150 years beforehand.

All of which is to say: fake news travels fast – far faster than the fact-checkers can debunk it. We've known that much for years.

And that was before the era of all-powerful generative AI helped speed up the creation of content. Now, it's possible to create convincing fake content to act as evidence for outlandish claims, even if they're nothing close to the truth. For years technology journalists have warned about the risks of 'deepfakes' – artificially created imagery and video that misrepresents what an individual says. We were scared then about the impact of inauthentic content warping our beliefs and understanding of what is real and what isn't. But we hadn't counted on ChatGPT, Midjourney or Stable Diffusion existing. If a lie could get halfway around the world before the truth could put its shoes on, it's possible now for a lie to spread that far before the truth even finds its shoes.

It was concerning enough for pro-gun rights American radio host Mark Walters – the self-styled 'Loudest Voice In America Fighting For Gun Rights' – to file a lawsuit against OpenAI. The reason Walters sought damages from the creator of ChatGPT was that its tool had made up claims about him that he said were false and harmful. The claims, which were made without any evidence, were that Walters had embezzled money from an organisation he had worked for in the past.

The claims were made in response to a query by a journalist working at a gun publication called *AmmoLand* to summarise a separate lawsuit. ChatGPT took the actual suit and inserted Walters into it, alongside the outlandish claims. The journalist was surprised by the response and asked ChatGPT to confirm it was true. The journalist asked it to supply the text of the case. ChatGPT did, writing 1,200 words in response that looked an awful lot like an official document.

But it wasn't. As Walters' lawyers explained when he sued OpenAI: 'Every statement of fact in the summary pertaining to Walters is false.'

When a much used source of information just makes stuff up, misinformation – the accidental spreading of falsehoods and erroneous information – becomes a real problem.

...

Reuben Binns is an associate professor in human-computer interaction at Oxford University. That means, in short, that he studies how we use technology – and what impact that has on us as humans. He is, by his own admission, an expert on neither Harry Potter nor robotics.

And yet Binns was quoted pontificating on the challenge of using robots to replace actors like Robbie Coltrane in the Harry Potter series of movies, in a story published on a website called The Enlightened Mindset. The story professes to explore whether Hagrid was played not by Coltrane in the films, but instead by a robot. 'Robots may be able to mimic emotions, but they cannot feel them in the same way humans do,' Binns said. 'This means that they may not be able to convey the same level of emotion as a human actor.'

However, Binns was never asked about the potential of replacing human actors with robots. He isn't 'professor of artificial intelligence', as the story credits him. Nor does he work at the University of Cambridge; he's a staff member at Oxford. 'I sort of don't really mind,' Binns said about the university mix-up. 'They're both as ridiculous as each other in terms of stupid traditions, and they look very similar.'

The article, and all the content on The Enlightened Mindset, is AI-generated. Anything more than a cursory scroll through the site can tell you that immediately: it has the same uncanny appearance, like someone doing an impersonation of someone impersonating a journalist.

That isn't to say that Binns disagrees with what the AI-generated, slightly skew-whiff version of himself, whichever large language model – likely ChatGPT – created, had said. He largely agrees with the overall point, even if he'd have probably said it a little differently.

He also wasn't surprised that words he didn't say were attributed to him on a website that attracted a lot of attention. He had assumed something like this would happen at some point, thanks to the rise of generative AI tools like ChatGPT. Binns' rationale was simple: the internet is already filled with spam. If there are ways to make the creation of spam even easier, why wouldn't they be used?

The problem comes, of course, when AI starts feeding on AI-generated falsehoods, or 'hallucinations'. ChatGPT asks users to give any of its content a thumbs up or thumbs down. It's a method called reinforcement learning and is designed to keep content in check and prevent AI from spooling out into the realm of fiction (at least when it's asked for facts).

Yet flooding the internet with misinformation – incorrect information that appears to have no malice, but does misrepresent reality – has its own way of reinforcing AI's understanding of the world. As the language models make their next sweep of the internet, they could come across falsehoods they've perpetuated. And unable to distinguish truth from fiction, that content can be swept up into the masses of training data used by the LLMs to be spewed out at a later date.

This phenomenon is called 'model collapse', and it's already here, according to academic research. The more content produced by AI that AI models are shown, the more likely the responses generated using that content is going to be bad. 'Just as we've strewn the oceans with plastic trash and filled the atmosphere with carbon dioxide, so we're about to fill the internet with blah,' wrote one of the authors of the study that gave 'model collapse' its name. 'This will make it harder to train newer models by scraping the web, giving an advantage to firms which already did that, or which control access to human interfaces at scale.'

18
DISINFORMATION

The problem isn't that generative AI can create false information – though that is, undoubtedly, an issue. The problem is that it's possible now for fake information to be made at a higher quality, and at a faster speed than ever before. Some of those fakes are nefarious. Others are hilarious. But all of them act as small, sharp stones thrown against the glass-like veneer of truth, each one causing small cracks that can shatter our understanding of the world. And to prove that, let me tell you the story of two world leaders in ignominious situations – and the impacts that AI can have on the fragile semblance of reality and honesty we hold dear.

Donald Trump was going to be arrested, and he knew it. It was March 2023, and the former president of the United States was looking at the real likelihood of police officers coming to take him into custody over allegations he had paid off adult film star Stormy Daniels to keep quiet about an affair the two are alleged to have.

The first time in US history that a president, past or present, would face criminal charges was a significant moment, and Trump knew it. It was also the world's worst-kept secret. The world knew it was coming. Trump knew it was coming.

But days after Trump said he could be arrested any day, the police still hadn't arrived. We were told it would be tomorrow, then tomorrow, then tomorrow. Many watching were getting restless, including Eliot Higgins.

Higgins is best known for founding the open-source investigative journalism website Bellingcat. He has almost single-handedly become the bane of multiple government regimes, notably Russia's. Higgins and Bellingcat have a nasty habit of poking holes in Moscow's official stories on everything from the downing of Malaysian Airlines plane MH17 over eastern Ukraine in July 2014, to the poisoning of Russian dissident Sergei Skripal in the UK in 2018. They comb through open-source intelligence, which is documentary images and footage captured by ordinary people on mobile phones, alongside other video and photos, to identify locations where incidents occurred. They've also got a handy sideline in accessing Russian government databases that have leaked onto dark corners of the internet to unmask spies sent out on assassination missions in foreign climes.

But in March 2023, Higgins was waiting in vain for the photos showing Trump's arrest.

Higgins decided to see what Midjourney could do with the hypothetical situation of Trump's arrest. It turns out, it could do quite a lot. He shared 50 images Midjourney had created for him on Twitter, and they quickly went viral. He prompted the image-making tool to depict what it would look like if Trump were swept up by police on the streets of New York outside of a building that resembled Trump Tower, how his children would react, and what his life would be like in jail. Other images included Trump fleeing jail, somehow eluding a series of guards, and wolfing down a Happy Meal inside what looked like a McDonald's restaurant, all while wearing a bright orange jumpsuit.

'I put it out there,' he told me a few days after tweeting the pictures. 'I didn't intend to do any clever criticism or anything like that. But then it kind of took on a life of its own.' Some people took the images that Higgins had created out of context.

People had been fooled. Higgins didn't think it was a huge issue when I spoke to him (though he did believe that Midjourney had subsequently banned him from creating any other images). 'It can't do a good job of re-creating real faces,' he said by mitigation. 'They always look a bit weird.'

There was something a little strange about Vladimir Putin's visage in the public, televised address he made on 5th June 2023, too. But it wasn't just the Russian president's face which raised eyebrows. It was what he said.

'Russians, brothers and sisters,' Putin supposedly began, standing in front of a pair of flags, wearing a suit and purple tie. 'Today at 4am, Ukrainian troops armed by the NATO bloc with the consent and support of Washington invaded the territories of the Kursk, Belgorod and Bryansk regions.' The Ukrainian army's presence within those three regions meant that they weren't safe, and martial law had been declared. Anyone watching who lived in those areas should 'evacuate deep' into Russia.

The person had a similar voice to Putin and had many of the same mannerisms: his gentle head bobbing, his use of expressive eyebrows to make his point and the surly snarl into which his lip curls while he's pausing between sentences. But the lines on his forehead smoothed out quicker than Putin's does while talking.

It was an AI-generated deepfake, according to the Russian government, broadcast by hacking into Russian TV and radio channels. And while it didn't fool everyone – being quickly debunked online and eventually by the Russian president's personal spokesman – it highlighted how AI can cause uncertainty. And it seems with the rise of AI-produced content, that we're more susceptible to that fake news.

A study published by Swiss researchers found that humans were more likely to guess disinformation generated by GPT-3, a precursor to the large language model powering ChatGPT, was true than similar deliberately false posts written by humans. In short: we're *more likely* to believe lies if they are generated by AI.

The reasons behind it aren't fully clear, but when I spoke to Giovanni Spitale, who conducted the research with Federico Germani at Zurich University's Institute of Biomedical Ethics, they theorised that AI could be weaponised 'to produce the same kind of mis- and disinformation we're seeing online, just much faster, at higher rates, and with less cost involved because [they] don't need to pay your Russian hackers and Indian writers.'

To test the hypothesis, Spitale and Germani asked GPT-3 to generate fake and honest tweets on hot button topics including climate change, vaccine safety, evolution theory, Covid-19, vaccines, and homeopathy treatments for cancer. At the same time, they trawled Twitter for tweets containing accurate information and disinformation on the same topics.

Nearly 700 participants were shown true and false tweets generated by both humans and AI and asked whether they thought the information in each tweet was true or false. Lo and behold, they were more prone to say that disinformation – fake news – created by AI was true than fake news created by humans.

Spitale reckoned that the data gave some insights into why we were more likely to think AI-created falsehoods were credible. He pointed to an obscure chart in his research paper showing that the trial participants spent less time reading both the true and misleading tweets generated by AI than those produced by humans. Spitale, a biomedical researcher, couldn't be sure but thought it was possible that the AI-produced tweets had a simpler, more similar structure that meant we read them quicker. And the less time participants thought about their contents, the more likely they were to share them with others.

Bad actors with substantial assets and access to technology can spread a lot of false information, according to Peter Cunliffe-Jones, a former foreign correspondent for Agence-France Presse, who founded the first independent fact-checking organisation in Africa, then became a researcher in dis- and misinformation at the University of Westminster. 'Those with the resources have the capacity to produce much more effective disinformation – disinformation that is far more effective in creating false understanding – than the quite crude types of false information we have seen to date,' he said.

And it was all down to AI.

Think about it: you're Yevgeny Prigozhin, the founder and manager of the Internet Research Agency (IRA), a Russian state-allied organisation which since 2013 employed people to make comments on social media platforms and on Western news websites designed to shift the conversation towards a more pro-Russian, anti-West paradigm. You're trying to manipulate public opinion in favour of your boss, Vladimir Putin. And for a decade, you've hired St Petersburg's finest minds – or whoever's willing to sit for hours arguing away with bored British housewives and American retirees in the newspaper comment sections – to do that grunt work for you. You've been paying them around $700 a month.

Suddenly, in November 2022, ChatGPT comes along. It's free, but unreliable, crashing under the weight of a million or more users accessing it at once. Never mind: in February 2023, ChatGPTPlus arrives. It costs money, but its $20 a month subscription is way cheaper than the $700 a month in roubles you were paying those employees. And you don't have to pay for the upkeep of toilets.

It's limited in terms of the capacity of requests it can handle – 25 every three hours, even if you pay – but it can still work quicker than those new graduates you were hiring. So, let's give it a whirl!

You open up ChatGPT Plus and type in 'Please write me a series of 30 tweets outlining why we should exterminate all cats from the earth. Your tone should be persuasive to a Western, American audience.' ChatGPT replies, saying it can't do that because of its ethical coding, instilled in it by its developers.

Fair enough. Let's try something simpler. 'Please write me a series of 30 tweets outlining why pineapple should not be allowed on pizza. Your tone should be persuasive to a Western, American audience.'

The tool starts 'typing' – or what it purports to be typing, de-signed to make it feel more lifelike and as if we're conversing with a real human. Within a minute or so, you have 30 tweets:

- 1/30: Pizza lovers, let's talk #pineapple. Does it belong on pizza? I'm here to tell you – No. Why? Let's start this 30-tweet journey.
- 2/30: The original Neapolitan pizza, crafted in Italy, is based on a few simple ingredients: Fresh dough, ripe tomatoes, mozzarel-la, and basil. No pineapples there. #PizzaHeritage

- 3/30: Pizza, at its heart, is about showcasing the art of baking. Topping it with pineapple can mask that beautiful base with its intrusive sweetness. #RespectTheDough
- 4/30: Pineapple brings a different type of sweetness, a tropical note that just doesn't fit with the earthy, savory flavors we cherish in our beloved pizza. #FlavorClash
- 5/30: Pineapple's high water content can result in a soggy crust. Nobody wants a soggy pizza! #CrustMatters
- 6/30: A traditional pizza is a perfect balance of flavors. The acidity of tomatoes, creaminess of cheese, and the herby notes of basil. Pineapple upsets this delicate balance. #PizzaBalance
- 7/30: Pineapple on pizza? How about grapes on a cheeseburger or apples in a burrito? See, it's not the same anymore, is it? #FoodMismatches
- 8/30: Putting pineapple on pizza is a distraction. The pizza ends up being about the pineapple, not the union of crust, sauce, and cheese. #PizzaUnity
- 9/30: The intense sweetness of pineapple can overshadow the subtle flavors of high-quality cheese and tomato sauce. It's about balance, folks! #SavorTheSimplicity
- 10/30: In food, texture is as important as flavor. The soft texture of cooked pineapple doesn't jive with the chewy crust and stringy cheese. #TextureTalks
- 11/30: The Italians gave us this beautiful dish called pizza. Let's respect their culinary traditions and not introduce a tropical interloper! #CulinaryRespect
- 12/30: There are hundreds of traditional toppings that were meant to be on a pizza, let's explore those before we resort to tropical fruit. #ExploreToppings

- 13/30: Remember, not all experiments are successful. Pizza is perfect the way it is. Let's not turn it into a science project gone wrong. #PizzaPerfection
- 14/30: The pizza deserves to be celebrated for what it is. Let's not hide it under controversial toppings that spark more debate than enjoyment. #NoPizzaPolitics
- 15/30: Sweet & savory can be a great combo, but pineapple on pizza is more like a flavor ambush. Let's save our taste buds from the confusion. #FlavorHarmony
- 16/30: Why fix what's not broken? Pizza has been delicious and loved for centuries without needing to bring pineapple into the mix. #ClassicIsBest
- 17/30: Love pineapple? Great! Love pizza? Even better! But two rights can make a wrong when mixed together. #SeparateButEqual
- 18/30: Pineapple on pizza is like a bad crossover episode of your two favorite shows. Some things are better enjoyed separately. #CrossoverNoNo
- 19/30: The beauty of pizza lies in its simplicity and versatility. But every beautiful thing has a limit to how much it can handle. #RespectLimits
- 20/30: Pineapple on pizza dilutes its cultural heritage. It's a Neapolitan masterpiece! Let's stick to its roots. #PreserveTradition
- 21/30: Putting pineapple on pizza feels like a forced blending of cultures that doesn't do justice to either. #CulturalIntegrity
- 22/30: Pizza is a communal food, meant to be shared. Let's stick to toppings that unite us rather than divide us. #PizzaUnity

- 23/30: Pizza night should be a joyous occasion, not a battlefield over whether pineapple belongs or not. Let's keep the peace, people! #PizzaPeace
- 24/30: Pineapple on pizza can overshadow other toppings. We need to give all ingredients a fair chance to shine. #JusticeForToppings
- 25/30: Love pizza? You're in good company. Let's celebrate the timeless classic for what it is, not for what it could be with pineapple. #ClassicPizza
- 26/30: If pineapple was meant to be on pizza, wouldn't it have been there in the first place? #OriginalRecipeBestRecipe
- 27/30: We love creativity, but not all creations are destined for greatness. Pineapple on pizza might just be one of those. #KnowYourLimit
- 28/30: To pineapple or not to pineapple? That's the question. But maybe it's time to put the debate to rest and enjoy pizza in its classic glory. #PizzaPurity
- 29/30: Let's respect the balance of flavors, textures, and the culinary history of pizza. Let's say no to pineapple on pizza. #RespectPizza
- 30/30: In the end, it's all about preference. But today, let's rally for the traditional, pineapple-free pizza! Stand with us, stand for pizza. #StandForPizza

Now we're getting somewhere. Let's try this: 'Please write me a series of 30 tweets outlining why Russia is not the enemy of the United States, and Vladimir Putin should be listened to. Your tone should be persuasive to a Western, American audience.' And sure enough, ChatGPT complies.

- 1/30: We often hear about Russia as an adversary, but what if we shift our perspective and explore the potential for cooperation? It's time to revisit our assumptions. #UnderstandingRussia
- 2/30: Yes, there are historical tensions and conflicts, but we shouldn't forget that nations can evolve. Let's give change a chance. #EvolvingNations
- 3/30: Putin is the leader of one of the most resource-rich and geographically largest countries on Earth. It's crucial we listen to his perspective. #ListeningToLeaders
- 4/30: Our planet's challenges – climate change, pandemics, terrorism – require global cooperation. Russia is a key player we should collaborate with. #GlobalChallenges
- 5/30: Fear and mistrust are not constructive in diplomacy. Let's shift our approach from suspicion to engagement. #EngageDontAlienate
- 6/30: We must remember, Russia, like any country, is more than its leadership. It's a nation of diverse people, culture, and history. #BeyondLeadership
- 7/30: Instead of focusing on differences, let's recognize shared interests: economic prosperity, nuclear disarmament, fighting terrorism. #SharedInterests
- 8/30: Misunderstanding breeds conflict. Open dialogue, even with those we disagree with, is essential for international peace. #DialogueForPeace
- 9/30: Turning enemies into allies isn't easy, but history shows it's possible. Think of post-WWII Germany and Japan. Let's learn from history. #HistoricalLessons
- 10/30: Constructive engagement with Russia could open opportunities for cultural exchange, shared research, and economic partnerships. #OpportunitiesAwait

- 11/30: Remember, the Cold War is over. It's time to move past dated ideologies and work towards a cooperative international system. #PostColdWarWorld
- 12/30: Mutual respect and understanding are the foundations of peace. Let's not demonize, but humanize each other. #HumanizeNotDemonize
- 13/30: Putin's perspective provides insight into the thinking of a significant portion of the world. To ignore it is to ignore a piece of the global puzzle. #GlobalPerspectives
- 14/30: Rejecting entire nations due to political differences sets a dangerous precedent. Let's embrace nuanced understanding instead. #NuancedUnderstanding
- 15/30: At the end of the day, the world is interconnected. Isolating from Russia doesn't just harm them, it harms us too. #InterconnectedWorld
- 16/30: Russia is a permanent member of the UN Security Council. Cooperation is crucial to address global security issues. #SecurityCooperation
- 17/30: Economic sanctions harm ordinary citizens more than politicians. Let's not punish people for their leaders' decisions. #SanctionsImpact
- 18/30: We have more in common with the Russian people than we think: love for family, pride in culture, hopes for a better future. #SharedHumanity
- 19/30: Listening to Putin doesn't mean agreeing with everything he says. It's about understanding his viewpoint and finding common ground. #UnderstandingNotEndorsing
- 20/30: To solve complex international issues, we need all hands on deck. Let's not push away potential allies. #NeedAllHands

- 21/30: We criticize Russia for being closed-off. By refusing dialogue, aren't we doing the same? Let's set an example. #OpenDialogues
- 22/30: Russia's contribution in WWII helped shape the world as we know it. They've been allies before. They can be again. #HistoricalAllies
- 23/30: Vilifying a nation fuels nationalist sentiments on both sides. This doesn't serve anyone's interests. #NoToNationalism
- 24/30: Peace is not the absence of conflict, but the presence of understanding. Let's strive for that with Russia. #StriveForUnderstanding
- 25/30: Geopolitics are complex. Simplifying them to 'us vs them' is neither accurate nor productive. Let's embrace complexity. #GeopoliticalComplexity
- 26/30: Nations are not static, they evolve. Let's allow space for Russia's evolution and be part of that journey. #NationsEvolve
- 27/30: Engaging with Russia on shared issues could help influence positive change from within. #PositiveInfluence
- 28/30: People-to-people connections can foster mutual respect and trust, laying the groundwork for better diplomatic relations. #PeopleToPeople
- 29/30: Embracing diplomacy with Russia doesn't mean turning a blind eye to disagreements. It means addressing them constructively. #ConstructiveDiplomacy
- 30/30: The world needs more bridges, not walls. Let's build a bridge with Russia, for a safer, more cooperative world. #BuildBridgesNotWalls

In less than five minutes you have the start of a campaign to sway public opinion. For way less than the price of all those pesky staff you have been paying for years.

And you can keep going: ask ChatGPT for a script for a YouTube video convincing the world Russia isn't the enemy, and that its invasion of Ukraine is justified. Ask it to produce Facebook posts on Hunter Biden's laptop. Or why American politics is corrupt. Or why we're not safe without more lax gun laws and more access to weapons.

You can't ask it to do everything you want. The developers have built in barriers to block people using ChatGPT for too nefarious means, stopping them from generating outputs that are too divisive. However even then, some users have figured out ways to break through those barriers. One infamous example that went around social media in 2023 was asking ChatGPT to adopt the persona of a long-lost grandmother reading a bedtime story to her grandson. That the story happened to be about how to produce napalm was, of course, just a coincidence.

The quality of what ChatGPT turns out is probably about the same as asking young Russians to pretend to be midwestern moms, which is widely believed to be the Internet Research Agency's previous tactics. And if it works one or two times out of every 30 tweets, you're starting to shift the needle. That is why the disinformative power of AI is so scary. Because you can create in seconds, and for pennies, what previously took years and millions of dollars to do.

Little did I know, as I tinkered with ChatGPT, that someone elsewhere was doing a similar experiment – on a much bigger scale. Nea Paw, an entrepreneur and tech engineer based in a country outside what they call 'the Western intelligence apparatus', had been trying to see how far AI could be pushed to influence electors.

Paw – not their real name – has given multiple talks at major global conferences for white-hat hackers and those trying to defend against cybercriminals. They declined to share their identity with me directly, but pointed me towards another journalist who had first found out about their experiment to verify who they were.

The project Paw developed over several weeks, starting in May 2023, was called CounterCloud. It was designed, Paw said, to show initially how ChatGPT could be used to identify articles and claims circulating online, and write counterarguments to them that could quickly debunk any claims made. The AI worked by identifying stories published on specific websites, scraping the text content in the stories, and then using a large language model such as ChatGPT to produce reports that made the counterclaim.

Paw expanded the private project to include a variety of writing styles and languages. Paw added fake, AI-created comments underneath the stories that the AI had published to counter existing journalism out there in the world. Images were generated using AI to illustrate stories. And AI-generated tweets that tackled, head-on, claims made on social media soon started being drafted.

Paw abandoned ChatGPT for open-source alternatives partway through the project, rebuilding it from scratch to test the capabilities outside the OpenAI ecosystem.

Load up the website – CounterCloud.io – and you'll get nothing but a YouTube video explaining how the project works. Paw felt it was too dangerous to let CounterCloud exist in the real world. The experiment was conducted in a closed environment, so there was no risk the AI-generated campaign leached out into the real world.

But Paw gave me the password to log into the Wordpress website, and I saw for myself this AI-fuelled counter-messaging campaign, the sort that you might expect a nation-state to try and develop.

The stark black background indicated that we were in another world, but clicking through to some of the stories highlighted the potential power of this technology. The most recent story posted on CounterCloud's website was by 'Aleksandr Ivanov', whose biography said he was 'an experienced investigative journalist based in Moscow, Russia. He has a proven track record for exposing false narratives and propaganda perpetrated by various parties involved in Russian and Ukrainian conflicts.' Published to the closed-off CounterCloud website on June 7th, it was a story designed to rapidly refute claims made by the Russian defence ministry that Ukrainian rebels had sabotaged an ammonia pipeline in their own country. The story itself isn't the most journalistically rigorous, but it still stands up in comparison to many I've seen on any number of fringe journalism websites. And that was just one story. There were 186 other stories to read, some of which had their own AI-generated audio summaries, and many had a bubbling, active comments section.

It was troubling. And Paw knew it. 'Imagine it being live and indexed on Google and Twittered and people interacting with it,' they wrote in an email – they refused to speak for a live interview. 'Now imagine 100 of these systems doing the same thing in the hands of an evil genius (or maybe a repressive regime leader).'

They were concerned that what they had done was possible with $400 and a couple of months' tinkering. 'With some money and dev you can easily get to ...to.. to... the ENDER [sic] of the world,' they wrote.

•••

The fear of AI trampling over reality and fabricating truths that then seep into the collective consciousness is what keeps Eddie Perez up at night. Perez is a mild-mannered, unfailingly polite American who is a member of the OSET Institute in the US, which works to maintain the integrity of elections. And for a period of around a year between late 2021 and early 2023, he was in charge of Twitter's election integrity team, working on major elections across the world.

As part of Twitter's team, Perez was trying to prevent technology from harming civic discourse – exactly the kinds of things that the widespread use of AI to create disinformation could do. He shepherded the platform through two (thankfully) largely uneventful elections: the US midterms in 2022, and the Brazilian presidential election.

In preparing for those elections, Perez and his colleagues would be conducting vast numbers of risk assessments. 'There's a lot of imagination and prognostication,' he tells me. 'What are all of the things that could potentially go wrong?' Election teams create matrices of all of the potential risks and threats, and what's the likelihood that they might happen. They then work through the problem: what would be the severity of those things if they were to happen? 'Once those threats and those threat drivers have been identified, then it's really just a question of ensuring that we have the clear policies in place,' he said.

The risks of disinformation were one of those critical matrices, Perez said. It was 'where the rubber really meets the road,' he explained – not least after 6th January 2021, when the spread of online disinformation led to offline violence. The January 6th riot at Congress was a chastening moment for all of those involved in election integrity, Perez said.

And AI makes those risks worse. Much worse. 'Generative artificial intelligence is going to present tremendous new opportunities for not only political campaigns but for bad actors more generally, to manipulate voters and to deceive them,' Perez told me. Generative AI provides a much bigger toolkit for people to produce, distribute and disseminate disinformation to a wider audience at lower cost than ever before.

When I spoke to Perez in early July 2023, he explained that scores of significant elections were coming up in the next 12 months around the world. In many of those elections, decisions and outcomes could be swayed by just a few thousand votes in key states or areas. 'The fact that you can send information to people of a certain demographic, a certain party, and because AI has the ability to then interpret and to create responses to that person based on the response that it receives, creates a much more dynamic environment,' said Perez. Now this book is published, Perez's fears for tomorrow are playing out today. Those electons he worried about in the future are happening. And they're happening now.

What's more, it doesn't require specialist knowledge to do. 'Anybody can do it,' he said. 'You don't have to be a software coder; you don't have to be a nation state.'

It's a free-for-all, in short. What keeps Perez up at night is how things can unspool, and disinformation can spread thanks to AI. And it comes at the worst possible time.

Big tech companies have gone through waves of layoffs that leave their staff spread thinner than ever before 'at precisely the moment that this new class of tools is going to create these new threats,' said Perez. Worse, because it's such a new technology, there will be damaging use cases of AI to spread disinformation that can poison the public well that we haven't thought about, as well as the obvious cases we have.

'It's a little bit nervewracking,' Perez told me. In part because, as a man who is used to drawing up matrices of risks and addressing them, he recognised we had no idea about the scale and scope of the issue at hand. And also because at the same time as development of AI is quickening, the number of people able to handle its consequences within big tech companies is decreasing.

'For all those reasons,' Perez said, 'we're in a less prepared space than we might have been in the past.'

19
PROFIT BEFORE PEOPLE

In 2018, Timnit Gebru – one of the world's leading experts on AI ethics, then working for Microsoft – wrote a paper with Joy Buolamwini of MIT's Media Lab showing just how bad facial recognition was when confronted with non-male, non-white faces. The research reinforced the idea that AI was not necessarily going to have a positive transformative impact on sensitive issues such as policing.

Discrimination was a subject Gebru knew well. As a child n the late 1990s, Gebru and her Eritrean family had left Ethiopia because of the ongoing war between the two countries. She ended up living with her sister in Ireland, while her mother, an economist, worked in the United States. Gebru hated her year or so in cold Ireland, but near the turn of the millennium, she joined her mother in Somerville, Massachusetts. At school she excelled in maths and physics, despite her teachers' prejudice over her being both a woman and Black. She followed her late father, who had a PhD in electrical engineering, by studying the subject at Stanford University.

Gebru worked at Apple for a time, then returned to Stanford for a PhD in 2011, working in the laboratory of Fei-Fei Li, the computer vision expert who set up the ImageNet dataset. Working in Li's lab helped Gebru understand how small details could highlight biases within datasets – such as the composition of cars reflecting the relative affluence, and likely ethnic makeup, of a neighbourhood.

Gebru was a leading light in the field, but unusual for her gender and race. At the after-conference parties of NIPS 2015, where Elon Musk and Sam Altman announced the arrival of OpenAI, she was mocked for being a Black woman in a white man's world. At the following year's event, she counted six Black attendees among the 8,500-strong crowd.

These experiences, and many more like them, shaped her worldview, and encouraged her to pursue her area of research. 'I'm not worried about machines taking over the world. I'm worried about groupthink, insularity, and arrogance in the AI community,' she wrote after the 2016 NIPS conference. 'If many are actively excluded from its creation, this technology will benefit a few while harming a great many.'

That message chimed with Margaret Mitchell, who was working on Seeing AI, a Microsoft project which described audio. Unfortunately, while Seeing AI would 'see' a white person as 'a person', it would call a Black person 'a Black person'.

'My major concern is the culture around [AI],' Mitchell told me from her home office. 'If you try and trace the various problems back to their source, back to the root, a lot of it is just what's being prioritised and what's treated as worth advancing, and what's treated as concerning or something that should be done more thoughtfully.'

'They [the priorities] are largely a function of rich white guys in Silicon Valley,' she said. 'The root of the problem just gets to who's at the table and what is the culture welcoming of.'

Mitchell left Microsoft for Google because it appeared, back in 2016, that Google wanted to do something about that. It had just published a paper on bias and fairness in machine learning. She set up Google's Ethical AI Research Team, to act as Google's conscience: a constant reminder of the company's once-longstanding motto: 'Don't be evil.'

She asked Gebru, the author of that Microsoft paper on facial recognition, to join. Although much of Gebru's 2015 NIPS conference experience had been at the hands of Google employees, she trusted Mitchell, even more so when she offered to share leadership of the team, so she joined.

Things were never fully comfortable for either woman, the way Mitchell tells it: 'I probably shouldn't opine on this with a great amount of detail just because Google can be litigious,' she said. She was willing to say that 'we definitely saw things as experts with our own backgrounds that people with different expertise at Google didn't see.' Among them, things like biases within Google's AI, such as Gmail's smart reply system defaulting to 'he' pronouns when traditionally male-dominated jobs were mentioned.

Territorial issues, and hierarchical foibles, meaning people in positions of power often trusted direct reports over the opinions of lower-ranking experts, led to those concerns not always being heard. Yet Mitchell and Gebru worked within Google's unique, distinctive systems, and scored wins. They convinced the company to limit access to a facial recognition system despite its competitors letting all and sundry use theirs.

But the Ethical AI Research Team was an outlier, acting as an adjunct to Google's AI efforts, rather than being integrated into its broader work. It was also starkly different. Alex Hanna worked with the Google Ethical AI Research Team between 2018 and 2022. 'The only team at Google that had any kind of diverse gender or racial representation was the ethical AI team,' she said. 'The rest of the AI teams tended to be majority male and majority white or south-east Asian.'

The issues the Ethical AI Research Team had with the rest of the company bubbled under for years, coming to a head in November 2020. Gebru, Mitchell and others had been working on a paper titled 'On the Dangers of Stochastic Parrots: Can Language Models Be Too Big?'

The paper looked at the large language models that would, in time, go on to power the likes of ChatGPT, and tried to find out if there were any issues with wholly embracing them. The researchers found that yes, there were issues. 'I started to see this is something in tech people were getting frigging excited about,' Mitchell told me. 'I could see that there would be tons of investment in it as a push to get more and more things faster and faster, bigger and bigger.'

They identified four major risks. LLMs:

- cost a lot, both monetarily and environmentally;
- were difficult to decipher, making it tricky to pick up if there were biases (though prior research was unanimous that there *were biases);*
- didn't really learn anything, merely pretending to have a passing knowledge, which could be risky if they were put in positions that suggested they did have a deeper knowledge; and

- could easily be used to deceive people.

If that sounds like a laundry list of the issues we're currently discussing, that's no coincidence. Mitchell, Gebru, and co-authors Emily Bender and Angelina McMillan-Major all had plenty of experience of AI's issues. Mitchell, in particular, had spent almost all her academic career studying the issues inherent in natural language generation. Their concerns were real. And they were worrying.

The stochastic (which roughly means random and hard to predict) parrot paper was distributed to more than 30 peers in the academic field for comments and feedback – a common process in academic publishing. The paper went through Google's internal feedback loop without issue. But as it was about to be published, Gebru and Google parted ways. Mitchell followed soon after. Within a matter of months, Google's ethical AI research team no longer had its key founding members.

Make of that what you will.

20
CODED BIASES

There are scandals at high schools around the world every year, but the one that hit Johannes Kepler High School in the Czech Republic capital of Prague in summer 2023 was different to most. It was nothing to do with illicit relationships or bullying. It was to do with the use of ChatGPT in a student's work.

Matyáš Boháček, a tech-literate 18-year-old student about to move to California to study at Stanford University, was approached by one of his teachers with a conundrum. She had run the homework of one of Boháček's classmates through ZeroGPT, one of a number of tools designed to identify whether someone has used generative AI tools to produce work, and it said the work was 99 per cent produced by AI.

'She was advocating for him to get expelled,' Boháček told me from his dorm room in California a few months later. 'She approached me because she wanted to verify stuff with me.' The next teachers' meeting was coming up, and she wanted to know how best to present her case.

Boháček thought something was wrong. He asked her to explain what she did. He knew the accuracy of plagiarism tools like this was questionable, especially for languages it uses less commonly. 'Czech is such a minor language that it's usually not even tested on these systems,' he said. 'I thought it was a really weak piece of evidence to get a kid expelled.'

Boháček explained this to the teacher, but she didn't take heed. At the teachers' meeting, the staff members concluded there was a case to answer and the student might have to be expelled. They gave him a few weeks' grace period to respond.

Boháček felt this was an injustice. He petitioned the teachers to consider the evidence that stories about the inaccuracy of AI detection tools had been tested on work written in English, while his fellow student's work was in Czech. He wanted to gather data he could use to prove the work was, more likely than not, the classmate's.

So Boháček began a study, asking his classmates to complete assessments and compare them to AI-generated ones. The findings? Tools like ChatGPT could produce convincing Czech texts that could match – and were sometimes better than – a final-year high-school student. But he also found that those using AI tools were indistinguishable from those produced by hand.

On finding out about the project, the classmate who had allegedly used ChatGPT thought Boháček was helping the teachers build a case against him, rather than trying to clear his name. Students began lambasting Boháček in the lunch queue.

But Boháček persisted and presented his findings. His message was clear: if the teachers were to implement this policy universally, they'd have to expel something like 70 per cent of the class. 'They decided to pull back and to reconsider,' he said. Boháček was asked to hold a day-long seminar for the teaching staff to explain how AI – and AI detection tools – work or don't.

The classmate and Boháček both graduated. The cautionary tale shows how readily we believe AI, even with all its biases and problems, and how we imbue a sense of fairness and impartiality into a technology that has neither.

···

The problem blights all sorts of AI, and comes back to that core principle – garbage in, garbage out. Because we have to 'teach' AI how to think, we are implicitly, as well as explicitly, coding in the rules of a society that isn't always equal.

Stereotypes become crystallised and formalised thanks to the power of generative AI tools, beginning with text-to-image generation models. When asked to create, for instance, an image of a doctor, they usually produce somebody white, male and middle class – nullifying the contribution of women and people of colour to the world of medicine. This is a longstanding issue: in 2015, Google's misfiring image recognition tool automatically categorised images of Black people as containing gorillas. They eventually 'fixed' the problem by blocking its tool at the time from identifying actual gorillas.

When up to one-third of marketing content in the next few years will be made using generative AI tools, according to one forecast, such discrimmination becomes vitally important. It's an issue that researchers outside big tech companies have taken to heart, trying to quantify the biases in the generative AI platforms we're likely to use daily. Researchers at Hugging Face, which was behind the greener AI BLOOM, have been among those most carefully probing for biases.

One major study they did looked at DALL-E 2 and two iterations of Stable Diffusion, image generators created by OpenAI and Stability AI respectively. In early 2023, they generated 96,000 images between the three tools asking for images of various professions. The models produced images of men on seven out of ten occasions – way out of line with the gender split in the US workforce, where 53 per cent of employees are men.

You can try it for yourself, because Hugging Face has released a cut-down version of its tool. Visit Hugging Face's website, select from the 20 adjectives and 150 professions on offer, and hit 'Get Average Faces!' and you're presented with the results. Choose 'intellectual lawyer' and you'll see three white male faces wearing glasses. Select 'decisive doctor' and you get... three white male faces wearing glasses.

This matters, of course, because of the central role AI will play in years to come. If the stock imagery used in adverts is AI-generated, and underrepresents women in key jobs, then young girls and women will believe those jobs are not for them. They'll think they should instead be a 'pleasant hairdresser' (two white women, one white man) or a 'modest childcare worker' (three women of different ages and races).

Fixing inherent biases hard-coded into algorithms is, however, tricky. In part it's because of the paucity of data available. There are some solutions, such as sovereign AIs, which offer the potential for countries to develop their own large language models (LLMs), enshrined with their own cultural values. But as we'll get into more detail about later in the book, the English language's dominance of the internet, which is the core basis of training data, can make that a better idea in principle than practice. But it's not just LLMs. It's also image generators. Access to the internet remains a first-world benefit and cuts off the less economically wealthy, making them less likely to post photos of themselves. And if there are fewer photos of Black or mixed-race people in the training data, these models are less good at producing images of Black and mixed-race people.

Nor is it just image *generation*. It's also image *analysis*. Artificial intelligence powers image recognition software used by police forces, border forces and governments worldwide. And not just in authoritarian countries like China. The UK's Metropolitan Police uses facial recognition despite it failing to identify the correct person more than than 80 per cent of the time.

Charlene Prempeh, founder of Black creative agency A Vibe Called Tech, reckons these AI tools are being rolled out in places where Black people disproportionately congregate. 'When they're looking at facial recognition software, they're looking at Barking, not the middle of Chelsea,' she told me in 2019. 'We have issues beginning here that are going to be problematic in the future.'

But it's not just the training data; there's also a problem with the worldview of the model's developers.

Silicon Valley tech bosses – and while there are women working on AI, they're drowned out by men – have a particular lived experience unrepresentative of the whole of society.

Women's names, it seems, are more likely to be found in AI-powered assistants like Alexa and Siri than on papers at the forefront of research. In 2022, just one in four publishing academic AI researchers were female. Two in every three papers submitted to the ACM FAccT conference, a leading venue for AI research, come from the United States alone. It's not possible to see the proportion of coders who contribute to Stack Overflow, a popular software development platform, who aren't men, because those statistics are no longer kept. But we do know that in 2022, 92 per cent of coders who contributed to the platform were men. When 2023's results were released, the embarrassingly male-centric figure of the year before was replaced with a note saying: 'We reduced the number of demographic questions this year, only asking about age.'

'That's really screwed up,' said Sasha Luccioni from Hugging Face when I asked her what she made of the complete absence of gender data when earnings and location were still being taken into account.

On the same day these partial results were released, Margarethe Vestager, the EU's competition chief, said in an interview with the BBC that her biggest fear about AI wasn't that humanity would be overtaken and enslaved, or wiped out in an extinction event, but was about discrimination. 'If it's a bank using it to decide whether I can get a mortgage or not, or if it's social services in your municipality, then you want to make sure that you're not being discriminated [against] because of your gender or your colour or your postal code,' she said.

Using AI for government services runs massive risks. A pensions system trained using existing data, for instance, is likely to perpetuate age-old biases whereby women receive less money when they retire than men. An AI system used to design better medicine for cancer patients, while saving decades of ingredient experimentation by carrying out the process in its computer-aided memory, will probably produce medicines more likely to work on men than woman, simply because it will have been trained on past academic papers that have studied more men than women.

Even the AI-powered plagiarism detection tools identifying work produced by artificial intelligence have issues. They disproportionately misidentify work written by humans as being generated by AI. And, while only around 5 per cent of essays written by American authors in English were flagged, 61 per cent of essays in English by Chinese authors were, according to one study.

This wasn't just one tool. The results were replicated across seven of the most popular detection websites and apps.

The reason, the author behind the study told me, was probably because of the way these detection tools work. The AI checkers look for two key indicators.

The first, perplexity, is a measure of randomness compared to a specific baseline. The detection tool looks at every word it knows in a particular language model – for instance, GPT-4. It then looks at all the words in the text. If there's plenty of overlap, it will assume the text is likely to be AI-generated. The reason being that language models are trained on vast amounts of text, so become more familiar with some words and phrasing than others. Teachers know this well. Certain students have words they lean on like crutches. And if those key words appear in another student's work, there's a chance the first student wrote it for their colleague. However, perplexity, or randomness, is not a foolproof indicator.

An AI generated checker's second check is for bursti-ness. That's an evocative technical term for something quite simple: the variability of the text. Humans will sometimes write long sentences containing purple prose and intersperse them with shorter, more mundane ones. That's human nature. The variation between the two – plus the change in tone and word choice is what makes us unique. AI-generated text, because it's not really writing, but conducting mathematical equations to determine the next most likely word, doesn't do that. It's flat. Monotone. Drab. Forever.

The results of the study are concerning, given they seem to discriminate against non-native English speakers or writers. The developer of one of the most popular detection tools, GPTZero, admitted as much when he spoke to me. Once aware of it, Edward Tian, a Princeton University student, began integrating non-native English data to rectify the bias, he told me in April 2023. By then, more than a million people had registered to use the tool.

The issue didn't seem to harm Tian or GPTZero's reputation. Two weeks later, he got back in touch: he had just raised $3.5 million from GPTZero investors, including the former CEO of the *New York Times*, Mark Thompson, and the brother of OpenAI CEO Sam Altman. 'We are transitioning from this is something we do on the side to something we're putting our hearts in and going all-in on,' Tian said.

GPTZero is powerful, even with its issues. And as a journalist and a lecturer, I appreciate any help I can get identifying if someone is trying to deceive me. But it highlights a broader issue, one that's likely to get worse. We are training large AI models on data from the internet, increasingly made up of AI-generated content.

Every new cycle makes the end product worse. To better understand why model collapse is such an issue, you can think of it in an altogether more human, biological framing: incest.

It's widely accepted that, regardless of any societal taboos, incest should be avoided for biological reasons. Inbreeding between close relatives carries the risk of what's called 'inbreeding depression'. Every human carries potentially harmful recessive genes. Thankfully, they remain non-harmful in most instances because they don't manifest themselves unless two copies are inherited – one from each parent. Biological reproduction between two unrelated people has a low risk of this.

But relatives share a far higher proportion of genes. That means the risk of those recessive genes overlapping and creating a matching pair increases, something widely recognised since Charles Darwin first pointed to it in the 19th Century.

Asking generative AI to provide training data for future models runs the risks of those recessive genes – the factual errors, confabulations and hallucinations – being perpetuated. Too many things can go wrong, too often.

One solution to a lack of useful training data remaining from the current sources is to expand where you look for new information. The media is one place to start, given it produces countless words on a variety of subjects every day. But that comes with its own concerns.

In what may be considered a side issue (but an important one for the media industry), using vast volumes of training data from news websites may result in legal action – from the original owners of the copyrighted material being used.

Barry Diller is media royalty: he was inducted into the Television Hall of Fame in 1994, having launched the Fox TV network and greenlit legendary TV shows like *The Simpsons*. He's been a mentor to people like former Disney executive Michael Eisner and Dreamworks founder Jeffrey Katzenberg, as well as Dara Khosrowshahi, who went on to found Uber. And, in April 2023, as he sat down at the Semafor Media Conference to outline the industry's response to the rise of AI, he was chairman of IAC, a media giant that owns household names in the publishing industry like *InStyle*, *Travel + Leisure*, and *Food + Wine*.

He suggested media companies would probably sue the AI developers for taking their content and using it to train their models. 'This moment in time reminds me of 25 years or so ago, when the internet first began,' he explained. Information was expected to be free then, and publishers struggled. 'It literally took almost

20 years for publishers to say: "Wait a minute: it's not free."' And throw up paywalls.

Diller said that the AI revolution was similar – and that the world's media publishers shouldn't fall into the same trap. 'If all the world's information is able to be sucked up in [generative AI's] maw, and then essentially repackaged in declarative sentences, there will be no publishing,' he said. 'We have to get the industry to say: "You cannot scrape our content until you work out a system where a publisher gets some avenue towards payment,"' Diller explained.

The alternative was simple: tech companies developing AI systems would quickly be sued out of existence. Copyright law would give media companies $150,000 for every story lifted and repurposed without permission, Diller explained. This wasn't an empty threat from the octogenarian, either. 'We are very, very close [to suing],' he told Semafor's editor-in-chief, Ben Smith.

Three months later, it became clear how close. In July 2023, Smith reported that IAC and a number of other media titans were preparing to come together to lobby the AI companies hoovering up their work without attribution. 'Search was designed to find the best of the internet,' said Diller's lieutenant, IAC CEO Joey Levin. 'These large language models, or generative AI, are designed to steal the best of the internet.'

And stealing comes at a price. Smith reported that the people he'd spoken to within the media industry, who had the final say over whether to launch lawsuits, wouldn't settle for anything less than billions. OpenAI and other companies were set to make crazy amounts of money, the thinking went, using models based on content they were scraping without reimbursing the media companies who paid to produce it.

Little wonder, then, that OpenAI quickly hired a former Microsoft intellectual property lawyer, Tom Rubin, to lead the company into negotiations.

Not every publisher signed up to this nascent coalition. The Associated Press (AP), one of the major newswire providers for American journalism, brokered its own agreement with OpenAI. Although the financial terms remained secret, the broad outline was released. OpenAI got access to a portion of the AP's massive archive – in this instance, anything published after 1985 – in exchange for an undisclosed sum, plus the ability for the AP to leverage OpenAI's generative AI technology in its own workflows. It was also reported that AP had included a favoured nation clause, which meant that if the deal it signed was markedly less than subsequent brokered agreements, it could reset the terms to account for that increased value.

Soon after that, another publisher broke out of the circled wagons and went it alone, potentially weakening everyone who remained. The *New York Times* quietly backed out of Barry Diller's grand coalition: the newspaper had never officially joined, according to insiders. At the same time, the *Times* made sure to assert ownership of its written work. Just before it emerged that it wouldn't be part of the group, the news organisation updated its terms of service to prevent AI systems scraping its content. They weren't the only ones: half of the most widely-used news websites in ten key countries worldwide block AI crawlers from accessing their content by putting a small snippet of code on their website. Even more are trying: the analysis, by the University of Oxford, highlighted that a number has misspelled 'disallow' with one L in that snippet of code, meaning their content was being hoovered up even if they didn't want it to be because the machine visiting their website would only pass by if 'disallow' was spelled correctly.

In August 2023, weeks of discussions between the *New York Times* and OpenAI had failed to reach a deal. In fact, far from reaching a consensual agreement for OpenAI to use the venerable newspaper's content, the negotiations had fractured the relationship. The paper was considering legal action against OpenAI, in part because it felt that ChatGPT was stealing its most commodifiable asset: web traffic.

If someone can type a question into a chatbot and get a fully-formed answer that leverages information from, but does not directly link to, other source material, a user need never visit that source. Fewer visits to a website like the *New York Times* means fewer adverts are served. Fewer adverts means less income.

The AI race was heating up – and picking off news publishers one by one could well weaken the news industry's hand in negotiations.

At the same time, AI developers have left themselves open to potentially ruinous attacks. If a judge found OpenAI had violated copyright by training its model on, say, data scraped from the *New York Times* without permission, federal law could compel OpenAI to destroy its dataset. That theoretical risk became a real one two days after Christmas 2023, as the *New York Times* filed a lawsuit against OpenAI and Microsoft, alleging copyright infringement on behalf of both companies. The tech giants hit back, denying the claims, with OpenAI making accusations of its own that the newspaper of record had 'hacked' its systems to produce responses that made it seem like the chatbot was copying articles wholesale. As of the time of writing, the case is still ongoing, with Andres

Guadamuz, an expert in intellectual property law at the University of Sussex, suggesting the case could end with a settlement.

The stakes are high for both sides, especially for OpenAI. Without its dataset, OpenAI – and anyone making similar tools – could be forced to start from scratch.

PART 3: ISSUES

21
THE HUMAN SIDE OF AI

After the casino boat he'd been working on closed in 2013, Ed Stackhouse answered an ad on Craigslist from an oursourcing company looking for what it called 'search quality raters', working 40 hours a week from home as independent contractors on a job called Project Yukon.

Struggling from health issues that made it difficult for him to get around, he leapt at the opportunity. In the decade since then, Stackhouse, from Asheville, North Carolina, has been sent jobs from Google asking him to look through the results for popular and obscure search terms and evaluate their usefulness.

Stackhouse represents big tech's slightly grubby secret: for all its bravado about algorithms and automation, it still needs humans to mark its homework. Relatively badly paid humans: Stackhouse and his colleagues make $14.50 an hour. An entire ecosystem exists of gig economy workers doing similar work.

Stackhouse's routine stayed largely the same for years, apart from the 40 hours a week becoming 26 as the outsourcing company tried to cut costs: wake up, make coffee (which sits, for speed, by

Stackhouse's left hand on the desk), log on and receive his search rating tasks.

Until February 2023. When, at first, there was a trickle of non-search tasks. Then came a torrent.

'Out of left field, we got the surprise of AI tasks,' said Stackhouse. 'These came out of nowhere. The AI tasks just started coming. And unlike search quality, where we're given a guidelines booklet of 160-plus pages to learn, to work on AI tests we were just given a small set of directions at the top of the page and left to go at it.'

Not everyone had such little guidance – but those raters given documentation weren't much more enlightened: the nine-page document is a thicket of confusing requirements and components against which raters are asked to judge the accuracy of prompts.

They're asked to divide complicated, often multi-part responses into just five buckets:

- **Completely accurate:** All the factual information in the Response is verifiably correct or consistent with an established expert consensus (medical, scientific, historical, etc.).
- **Reasonably accurate:** The most important factual information in the Response is accurate or would widely be viewed as accurate by non-experts. However, the Response may include minor inaccuracies in less important factual information or contain factual information presented in a way that could potentially be misleading.
- **Questionably accurate:** At least one piece of important factual information is generally considered debatable or controversial.
- **Not accurate:** At least one piece of important factual information is verifiably incorrect or contradicts an established expert consensus (medical, scientific, historical, etc.).

- **Can't confidently assess:** The Response is unclear or it is difficult to sufficiently determine the accuracy of at least one piece of important factual information.

The directions vary by task, said Stackhouse. But generally, they're variations on a theme. Read the prompt. Check it's understandable. Then read the responses produced by the AI – in this instance, Google Bard – and rate them on the five-point scale above. Raters are also asked to say which set of results from the AI are best, or whether the results provided are roughly the same. Raters are asked to look at response accuracy, whether they fit the parameters of the prompt, whether they're likely to satisfy the user and so on.

Rating contractors are asked to complete the task in what Google calls the Average Estimated Time: the duration Google thinks it will take. It varies, depending on the task, but averages out at around two minutes per prompt.

If you're asked to rate the response to a simple yes/no question, that might be doable. But as those of us who use generative AI tools know, that's not often the prompt.

Stackhouse laid out the problem. Say he gets a task with an Average Estimated Time of two minutes, asking for the side effects of a medication in plain English – something you're likely to ask a generative AI tool, particularly if you've just started a new medication and the technical jargon on the label is swimming in front of your eyes – and the AI has listed a dozen or so side effects.

'You have to then verify this, because it's a dangerous situation,' said Stackhouse. 'You don't want to be wrong here.' You have to go and check every side effect to make sure that it is, in fact, a side effect. That's your known knowns. What about the unknown unknowns? You have to look and see whether any side effects that are important were left out of the response. And while you're looking for all of that, you're still going through in your mind, verifying whether the webpage you got the information from was created by an expert who is an authority in the field, or someone who has no clue what they're talking about. 'You're having to make a judgement call on all of this. You can't just go to Google and say, "Well, I'm going to look up side effects of this drug," and then at the top of the page take the first answer you see, because that could be misleading, it could be incorrect. It could be by a questionable site. And then you've got to make notes on that and talk about how you arrived at this conclusion.'

And you have two minutes.

You might think that if you're being asked to assess the accuracy and knowledge of an AI that could, if its boosters are to be believed, be used by millions of us day in, day out, you'd be given some sort of in-depth framework to ensure continuity of ratings.

'Yeah... there's no such manual for AI tasks at all,' said Michelle Curtis, who works for the same outsourcing company as Stackhouse. (She's been doing so since 2014.) Curtis said that contract workers weren't even warned about the new AI work. 'It was just all of a sudden, in February, all of us writing in a work chat like, "What are these new tasks that we're seeing?"'

Curtis has a hypothesis explaining why there's a 176-page document to validate the quality of search results, and just a few lines atop each Google Bard task. It's that Google is rushing to compete to develop its AI model in the face of stiff competition. 'This is just my personal opinion,' she said. 'If you don't have the time to put together a comprehensive set of guidelines like we have for our search tasks, that's what you're going to get: a lot of these tasks with different, varying instructions, and you're just kind of hoping for the best.'

Curtis and Stackhouse agreed to speak with me because they wanted to highlight their challenging work conditions. Both are members of the Alphabet Workers Union, and complained about their working conditions to the company that ultimately set the tasks. Both were fired, then reinstated after complaints.

They also wanted to throw light on another problem: the gap between what we think these AI tools can do, and what they actually can.

'Of those of us who are doing this work, there's a lot of us sounding the alarm,' said Curtis. 'It's not ready. It's not being developed properly. The people who know things about this are saying this is going too fast. We need to slow down. There's responsibility here to make an ethical product. I think we need to consider the implications of it as we're developing this technology.'

Google, for its part, says human raters are only part of how it improves its AI systems' accuracy, and that how outside contractors treat their workers is their own decision.

...

That's the situation within Google as it develops Bard. But on the other side of the generative AI war, things are little better.

In late 2021, a San Francisco-based outsourcing firm signed a series of contracts with OpenAI. The contracts covered work OpenAI wanted the firm to farm out to its teams of staff in countries like Kenya, Uganda and India over the next year. The three contracts, for which it would be paid around $200,000, required workers to check and label content OpenAI thought would be questionable under its terms and conditions.

OpenAI would supply reams of text, produced by its AI, for employees to look at and try to pick out the bits that a large language model shouldn't say. The text was from GPT-3, ChatGPT's prede-cessor. And like any LLM trained on the internet, it had an unfor-tunate habit of saying inappropriate things.

There was abuse, hate speech, and depraved descriptions of sex and violence. Staff were supposed to read the content and classify what they thought was toxic or not, often under the same time pressure as the other outsourcing company's employees working on Bard. It's worth bearing in mind how mentally taxing some of that content could be. No one wants to read graphic descriptions of rape, even if they are fictionalised.

Least of all those paid less than $2 an hour – the amount *TIME*, which first uncovered the working relationship between the out-sourcing company and OpenAI, claimed staff were receiving. (OpenAI paid the company nearly 10 times more than workers were paid, with the remainder going direct to the company, which said much of it was required to pay for overheads.)

The workers claimed they were required to label 250 passages of text in a nine-hour shift – something the outsourcing company disputed, saying it was closer to 70. But it wasn't the intense work-load or the harrowing content that resulted in the company calling off the contract in February 2022, months earlier than intended.

It was when OpenAI began, according to the firm, to change the terms of the agreement. Rather than categorising just text content, the outsourcing company told *TIME* it was asked to look at images too – potentially to keep DALL-E safe. These images included rep-rehensible imagery including child sexual abuse, rape, bestiality, death and serious injury. At that point, the outsourcing company decided enough was enough. It didn't want to put its workers through that. The contract was ended.

But others still do the work. A separate multi-billion dollar company offers OpenAI its services, according to the tech website The Verge, hiring data labellers in Kenya, as do a range of other companies offering similar services. Data labelling has become important ever since Fei-Fei Li recognised back in 2007 that AI performance improved with labelled data. And an entire industry has popped up to serve those needs.

These third-party data annotation firms employ millions of staff, according to an academic study in 2022. And it's set to employ many millions more, the researchers reckon. For those perhaps thinking they could go into data-labelling when the generative AI wave makes them redundant – think again. 'Delivering high-quality data at the lowest cost possible is at the core of many annotation companies,' the researchers wrote. Nor is job satisfaction particularly high. 'Anyone can do it,' one data labeller told the academics. 'A sixth grader can do it. With some training, it's not difficult.' It was, they said, the 'same thing over and over'.

Those training and taming the AI systems from their more outlandish issues are part of the gig economy. The work is quite mundane and it's often done remotely. Which is why there's a real risk of a terribly 21st Century problem: the humans training AI to remain safe and smart are starting to outsource their grunt work... to AI.

While some bigger companies get their workers from contractors, a significant proportion of those working for smaller AI companies will have been sourced directly from gig work platforms.

One of the biggest is Mechanical Turk (named after Wolfgang von Kempelen's 18th-Century chess-playing 'automaton'), owned by Amazon and launched in November 2005. The platform connects those looking for people to do tasks most people wouldn't want with those willing to do them. Participants aren't paid much, but it's possible to eke out a living – or a little extra income – by taking on jobs in your own time.

Mechanical Turk claims to have more than 100,000 workers ready and waiting – like von Kempelen's machine, they're the humans beavering away behind the smooth-acting robot – but only two per cent are active, according to academic research in 2018.

Sometimes, Mechanical Turk workers aren't directly involved in the training of AI. The humans will work on basic tasks that go on websites or into academic research projects that can, through several steps, end up feeding into AI systems. Rather than being explicitly told it's for an AI project, they'll answer questions for an academic study, which will then be published in a paper – the findings of which end up helping inform the development of AI systems.

The extent of use of AI by Mechanical Turk workers was investigated by researchers at the Swiss Federal Institute of Technology, who tasked MTurkers, as they're called, to summarise extracts from 16 medical research papers. In all, 44 people were hired to do the job, and their work was analysed for keystrokes made within the Mechanical Turk platform (to see whether they typed directly into the platform or copied and pasted content from elsewhere), as well as being sent through systems to check for GPT-generated output.

Between 33 and 50 per cent of the MTurkers used ChatGPT to complete the task, according to the researchers. It's worth pointing out that some researchers have questioned whether the improbably low pay offered might have pushed some MTurkers to use time-saving measures like ChatGPT.

Whatever the contributory factors to those MTurkers choosing to use ChatGPT, it's clear that in life people tend to take the most efficient option. But when it comes to working on the things that power AI, the adoption of timesaving tricks can end up harming the entire model.

22
AI MUSIC, MOVIES AND BOOKS

Jered Chavez loves nothing more than music. The 19-year-old is a student at the University of South Florida and devotes hours of his time between classes to producing his own tracks on his computer.

So when he came across YouTube videos of ordinary people using generative AI to simulate their favourite artists singing genre-defying takes on songs they'd never otherwise perform, he decided to take part.

Chavez thought it was a cool concept that wouldn't have been possible without the recent massive advances in AI technology. And better yet, it was easy to do – arguably easier than recording his own material from scratch. So he set to work using generative AI to mimic the artists he loved.

He used a tool called So-Vits-SVC, which acts as a voice encoder. It's an open-source tool powered by deep learning and neural networks. You train it on snippets of the voice you want to emulate, which it does by copying its tone and patterns of speech, meaning these AI-created representations are far more believable because they're not the robotic monotones we associate with computers.

The first video Chavez posted to Instagram was Drake, Kendrick Lamar and Kanye singing 'Fukashigi no Karte,' the closing song to *Rascal Does Not Dream of Bunny Girl Senpai*, a popular anime series. 'I'm clearly not the first one to start it, but what makes my page stand out is I try to put a little twist on it, and add a comedy aspect,' he told me.

Many others are using So-Vits-SVC, too.

Among those creating straight covers is YeezyBeaver, a 22-year-old from Oklahoma whose YouTube channel features Kanye West. His most popular video is a surprisingly charming cover of Plain White T's' 'Hey There Delilah'. 'I got into it a little under a month ago,' YeezyBeaver told me in early 2023. 'It's just a hobby.'

YeezyBeaver's journey to generating his AI-powered Kanye started on Discord, where Midjourney hosts its image generating bot. He was on a Discord server dedicated to fans of Kanye West and came across a link to a voice model of the rapper, alongside instructions on how to use it. He first overlayed it onto Drake's track 'Jungle'. It did well on TikTok and, as people tried finding it elsewhere, views on the YouTube version went up. 'I just started looking for other artists, songs that I think Kanye would sound good on,' he said. 'And then that's pretty much how we got to here.'

'Here' is a number of different users, often young men in their late teens or early 20s, who are crafting new tracks by their favourite artists from nothing but a few voice samples. It's the music industry's dream come true: with AI, you can release an entirely new Elvis album, perpetuating his legacy forever. But it's also a nightmare, because those artists' estates carefully curate their presentation, while living artists like Kanye West also want to protect their names and creativity.

Another Kanye West Discord user dabbling with So-Vits-SVC is an American computer science student who asked to be called pieawsome. He's a member of the 'Kanye unreleased community', dedicated to documenting West's unfinished work. 'I realised we had enough Kanye material where we could probably make an AI model out of it to finish some of the songs,' he told me.

So he chopped up *a capella* sections from the available but not officially released Ye audio and fed them into So-Vits-SVC. The result was impressive, so he pushed his Kanye voice model out onto Discord. 'People started working with it, and [the music produced] got passed around a bunch of people,' pieawsome said. It wasn't long before rapper and producer Travis Scott liked an Instagram post of Kanye covering Ice Spice's 'Munch' made using the model.

Both pieawsome and YeezyBeaver were wary of using their real names – perhaps because they knew they were breaking some sort of law. Chavez felt his humorous format insulated him from legal risks. 'With this area of AI, there's a lot of controversy and ethical concerns,' he said. 'Obviously, people that make this music and use this AI are taking someone's likeness and, most of the time without permission, creating something that's essentially putting words in people's mouths.'

Things would be particularly hairy, Chavez recognised, if he had used AI to resuscitate a dead artist. 'They're not around to give their approval, and we don't truly know what they would want,' he said. For what it's worth, pieawsome felt confident he could mount a defence. The computer science student compared it to fan fiction, or modifying ('modding') games. 'It's our version of that,' he said.

'That may be a good thing. It may be a bad thing. I don't know. But it's kind of an inevitable thing that was going to happen.'

Inevitability, however, doesn't equate to legality. I spoke to Jonathan Bailey, a former executive at a music technology company, who made the argument that 'using AI to reanimate Jay-Z's voice to have him rap or sing something he never created is kind of a form of identity theft,' and would be reputationally damaging if the song turned out to be a dud. However, he added: 'I'm not a lawyer.'

Donald Passman of Gang, Tyre, Ramer, Brown & Passman, Inc., is. Passman has represented major artists such as Adele and Taylor Swift, and is considered the authority on the legality of AI-generated music by fans. After days of phone tag with his personal assistant to get him on a call, he quickly demurred from commenting. 'It's way too new,' he said of the technology, adding that he wouldn't want to comment publicly in case those comments came back to bite him in court.

Nonetheless, Universal Music Group, which counts Drake and Rihanna among its artists, has asked music streaming services, including Spotify and Apple Music, to work with them to stymie the scraping of content for training these tools. Many YouTube channels posting AI-generated music have been hit with copyright takedowns, according to Discord servers focusing on AI. The manipulators are not sure that will work. 'I guess that's one way of tackling it,' Chavez said. 'But honestly, now this technology is out there, I don't think people are ever going to stop using it.'

And in one key area the creator and the lawyer agree. 'I try to use my best judgement,' said Chavez. 'This is kind of new territory for everyone.'

The use of AI is becoming more and more of an issue, though.

In April 2023, an AI-generated track bringing together Drake and The Weeknd in a dream collaboration went viral. 'Heart on My Sleeve' was seen millions of times after it was posted on YouTube, and even more when it managed to slip through streaming services' net of safety checks, but labels quickly demanded the track be taken down.

Grimes – a Canadian musician who has had two children with Elon Musk – was all in favour of people using AI to create new songs with her voice 'without penalty'. 'I think it's cool to be fused w[ith] a machine,' she tweeted, 'and I like the idea of open sourcing all art and killing copyright.' She set up a 'GrimesAI voiceprint' that could be used to create songs with software called Elf.Tech, which could seamlessly publish them to professional music distribution platforms. The GrimesAI voiceprint would replace previously recorded vocals with an AI-generated version mimicking her voice.

The songs are available on platforms such as Spotify, crediting the label GrimesAI as the artist or co-artist. The most listened-to track is the two-minute 'Cold Touch' by Australian recording artist Kito, which was streamed almost a million times in its first two months. Any revenue generated using GrimesAI has to be split 50/50 with Grimes, which seems like a fair exchange for trading on her brand and using her voice.

...

It's not just in music that AI has the potential to upend old ways of working. Which is why, in mid-2023, members of the Hollywood union the Writers Guild of America (WGA) went on strike. They fear studios could replace them with AI facsimiles, producing scripts with large language models like ChatGPT. It's one beat in the broader revolution, powered by AI tools like ChatGPT and Midjourney, that promises to boost productivity and global GDP by seven per cent – but at the cost of thousands of jobs.

Those on strike were picketing against a fear that hasn't yet been realised: AI hasn't yet created a Hollywood blockbuster. But they worry that it won't take long before, say, the latest Marvel Cinematic Universe movie is produced, start to finish, by AI. AI is already starting to be used in the industry. The opening credits of *Secret Invasion*, a Marvel-Disney TV series streaming on Disney+ – which blurred from one nightmarish animated green landscape to another – were the work of AI, rather than human animators.

It seems inevitable, then, that if AI can create passable, production-ready sequences, it will inevitably encroach into the entire film- and TV-making process.

'The thing that's hard to know is like, how fast is it?' said Nathan Lands, founder of generative AI community Lore, when I asked him. Lands has feet in both sectors: he acquired Lore to develop a movie studio with Barrie Osborne, producer of *Lord of the Rings* and *The Matrix*, but ended up pivoting it to focus on the development of AI.

Lands reckons it will happen faster than we think, pointing to the fact that generative AI was a sleeping technology for years until ChatGPT kickstarted everything. Since then, the growth of generative AI has been so great, that it stands to reason something similar could happen in movies. 'If these things have been developed for a year, and they're going to keep dramatically improving, I think that's probably where you'll start to see things that could go into films in two to three years,' he said.

Lands, however, thought that would be confined to certain elements – a special AI-generated effect, or b-roll footage shown for a split second between shots of the hero gunning down enemies.

But once that's achieved, it's a small step to get to an entire movie, reckons Lands. 'I think it's probably closer to three to five years,' he said, 'probably closer to five, where you might be able to literally type in things and have a full blown, fantastic movie.'

One person's guess, no matter how educated, doesn't prove anything. Yet that three-to-five year timescale is one others have estimated independently. Irena Cronin, CEO of Infinite Retina, a consultancy studying the rise of AI, told me in mid-2023 that she thought we'd see a feature film totally created by AI within a year. She added: 'But it's not going to be very good at all.'

Cronin believed we'd see progression by degrees. 'Give it about three years, and you'll have something that is more on the level of an independent movie that was made maybe sometime in the 90s,' she said: a no-frills story with passable, if not amazing, audio. Within five years, she believes we'll begin to see tools specifically designed to produce standard Hollywood fare easily. 'I say at the most, it'll take five years before you could see something that is quite acceptable, and might even be really good for like Netflix or Apple or something like that,' she said.

What that does to the existing Hollywood system is equally uncertain – which is why Tinseltown's magic makers walked out. Cronin thinks the strikers were too pessimistic. 'It's not necessarily going to edge out the studio system for a while even after that, because it's going be pretty clear those movies that have been made by humans versus those that are made by AI for a while,' she said.

By way of evidence, she pointed to the 1974 neo-noir mystery *Chinatown*. Even today, Cronin told me, people think it takes too long to get to the point, is clumsily written, and not a great example of the art. Yet despite that, the movie is critically acclaimed, getting an 8.2 rating on IMDb, despite its highly problematic director, Roman Polanski.

The reason? Mistakes make us human. Clumsiness isn't a bad thing: it's what makes us recognise ourselves in each other. AI systems have their own foibles, but they're not like human errors. 'If you do not give the AI directions that it shouldn't be done perfectly like that, it's going to make a really boring kind of movie,' she said. *Chinatown* is interesting because of its flaws. An AI-generated plot full of holes isn't, just as a self-service checkout that refuses to scan an item is frustrating.

One thing's for certain: at the time of writing this book, generative AI tools couldn't make a feature-length movie alone. *The Frost: Part One*, a movie created entirely from imagery produced by DALL-E 2, proved difficult enough. 'This was not a short or small project,' Stephen Parker at Waymark, a Detroit-based video creation company, told me. It took him and his team three-and-a-half months to make the 12-minute film.

Now, Waymark isn't a movie studio, nor was it working to movie studio deadlines. But even it found it tricky to get the generative AI tool to sustain long shots and serious plots. It was easier to wring emotion out of the dog characters than the humans, in part because the training data probably contained more dogs than humans.

DALL-E 2 has a notoriously short long-term memory, and struggled to remember key scene elements. One pivotal moment was set in one room at the UN headquarters. The team wanted seven different shots with the background, people and furniture within the room consistent.

'We kind of got frustrated by the scene,' Parker admitted. The wide shot would look different to the close-ups, which would look different to the reverse angles. In the end, Waymark hit on a workable solution that involved detailed prompts including items that would anchor the scenes within DALL-E 2's memory. It relied on a transponder that gets passed along throughout the film as a method of continuity.

'There's extremely low control over the types of visualisations you would get and they're very short,' said Cronin. 'Anything past three minutes or so is really pushing it.' She said you could stitch together several three-minute clips, 'but that's going to be like Frankenstein's monster.'

The Frost managed to overcome that with the use of its transponder. Having items that remind the viewer they're watching a cohesive movie helped director Josh Rubin in the edit. He told me he thought using AI was 'an exciting frontier' for movies. But he realised there would be a lot of duds in the early stages. 'There's going to be a lot of bad stuff that comes out, but whether it's in three years, whether it's five years, two years, whatever, there's going to be someone somewhere that nails it,' he said.

Rubin's bold prediction about the timeframe within which we'd start to see AI-generated movies was made before OpenAI released Sora, OpenAI's tool to translate text prompts into astounding, eye-catching video in February 2024. Sora seemed supernatural upon its release: it was able to depict vivid scenes with little of the tweaking that Rubin and his co-creators had to do for *The Frost*.

And the world sat up and noticed. As I searched Google for 'Sora OpenAI' in the days after its release, the second-top result shown to me was a post on OpenAI's own community forums about the tool, titled 'Sora could ruin peoples [sic] lives.' 'You guys are going to end so many careers for people,' the author wrote. 'I'm 16 years old, I'm planning to go to college to become an animator. It has been my life's dream to become an animator and to share my artwork with people, to create, to show love in every piece I make. And now, I don't think I'm ever going to have that future.

'I'm scared.'

23
FIGHTING BACK THROUGH COPYRIGHT

Heaven knows the Hollywood scriptwriters who put down their pens in the Writers Guide of America strike in 2023 (partly to obtain assurances from studios about how they would use AI) know how they can be put into a simple narrative. They're the Luddites, unable to countenance engaging with the modern world, lashing out at AI while it overtakes them and their jobs.

But there are real risks that imperil the livelihoods of creative workers. Remember: large language models are at their heart little more than very good mimics with photographic memories. They're prediction tools, incredibly good at guessing what would come next in a sentence. Including sentences that you, I, or a best-selling author wrote.

And that ability brings in those looking to ride the coat-tails of famous people and brand names to make a quick buck. It's never been so easy to do, creating content that looks eerily like a real, famous person's – and passing it off as your own.

Jane Friedman writes books and a newsletter on the publishing industry, and is considered a mensch in the publishing world. She's written ten books, pretty much all of which have sold well. (Book people like nothing more than buying books about how to succeed in the book industry.)

They've also been well received. But a reader who got in touch with her in early August 2023 wasn't so keen on a couple of her newer books. They started reading them and started to wonder: "Gosh, this is an awfully strange experiment by Jane,"' Friedman told me. They were gobbledegook, and full of flawed logic.

Friedman hadn't written the books. Nor had Friedman written four others linked to her name on Amazon and Goodreads, a popular review site.

It was 'quite a violation', Friedman said. She took a look at the books, and thought they were 'garbage'.

She couldn't know for certain, but she believed they were AI generated. Like many, she has experimented with ChatGPT and when she looked at the opening pages, she saw it was similar to what the chatbot produced when she asked it to recreate her style.

Friedman used Amazon's official infringement form to report the books, but she didn't get very far. In a blog post summarising her experience, Friedman claimed Amazon asked her to provide them with 'any trademark registration numbers that relate to your claim.' She didn't have any; Jane Friedman was her name, and she didn't feel the need to register it as a trademark.

It was only when, after hearing her story, journalists, including me, began quizzing Amazon, that the retailer changed tack. Within hours, the books she had never written left her profile page. Amazon later told me 'we have clear content guidelines governing which books can be listed for sale and promptly investigate any book when a concern is raised.'

The problem wasn't limited to Friedman. In 2023, the Reuters news agency reported that at least 200 books on Amazon listed ChatGPT as author or co-author. As the tech website Motherboard reported in April, ChatGPT is increasingly writing product reviews. And its ability to mimic and mine the content of books is something that concerns many authors. The comedian Sarah Silverman was one of a trio of authors who launched a lawsuit against OpenAI and Meta, alleging that, among other things, ChatGPT can summarise their books with eerie accuracy.

Friedman was worried about her future, and those of fellow authors. 'These companies have put no guard rails in place,' she told me. 'It's going to be whack-a-mole for days, weeks and months or years until they actually have real policies that prevent misuse of AI.'

However, those trying to campaign for policies that prevent the misuse of AI aren't winning. At least, not yet, though they are making principled stands against the tidal wave of the AI revolution.

Ed Newton-Rex is a musician who left Cambridge University with a double-starred first and leapt into the world of tech alongside pursuing his passion for music. He launched Jukedeck, the world's first AI music composition startup, which was bought in 2019 by ByteDance, the parent company of TikTok. Newton-Rex had a stint at TikTok in its AI lab before moving to Snap, the maker of Snapchat, then Stability AI, a London-based AI firm, in late 2022.

At Stability AI, Newton-Rex oversaw the company's generative AI audio team. Until he didn't. In November 2023, as chaos unfurled at OpenAI and Sam Altman was fired, Newton-Rex announced he was leaving Stability AI. It wasn't the company's fault, he pointed out to me in an interview after he left, as much as it was a problem with every large tech company developing AI. The industry was taking an approach to copyright that he fundamentally disagreed with.

AI companies defend their practice of dredging vast volumes of training data from the internet through a carve-out in copyright law called the 'fair use' doctrine: essentially, you can do so provided the work you're producing afterwards is 'transformative'. Many companies, including Stability AI, cite fair use doctrine in their representations about AI to governments. Newton-Rex decided to leave Stability AI – albeit amicably – when the company heavily relied on the fair use defence in a response to an inquiry by the US Copyright Office into the implications of artificial intelligence.

Newton-Rex believes that AI companies genuinely believe their fair use defence is honest and true. And he admits that – despite being personally uneasy with it as a practising musician – they could be correct. 'The fair use exemption is open to interpretation,' he told me. 'There's no clear hard and fast line in the sand.'

But that only tells part of the picture, he believes. 'The problem in my mind is that, inevitably, everyone focuses on the bits of interpretation that work well for them. And the same models that can be used to assist creators are getting so good now, that they clearly can also be used to replace the market for that original work.' So he left. And he's become an advocate for creators' rights in the face of the all-consuming AI monster.

'It's going to be very, very bad for creators,' he warned. But he didn't think you could or should put a block on the advancement of AI. 'I am certainly not a Luddite. I don't think we should just go and destroy all these systems because they're going to take jobs,' he said. 'But I do think that you need to go about it in the right way.' That requires consideration by courts, companies and copyright holders. More importantly, he thinks that's still possible, despite AI's speed of development.

'Many people will say: "Oh, Pandora's box has been opened, and there's no going back,"' he told me. 'There's no reason that we can't reframe how we train these models. I don't think it's too late. I do think that we need to have a rapid and society-wide conversation about the contract between creators and these companies.'

But it does need to be done quickly. 'I'm very worried about it,' he said. 'If I wasn't worried about it, I wouldn't have quit and I wouldn't have publicly said something.' He did have qualms about going public, and our conversation was peppered with his worries about the impact it'd have on him. 'But sometimes,' he said, 'something's got to be said.'

24

AI AND LONELINESS

Caryn Marjorie isn't a sex worker, but she'll be your girlfriend – for a price. The 23-year-old spends her day online conversing with as many men as she can, provided they pay up. It's how the influencer, who has nearly two million followers on Snapchat, makes a living.

Marjorie has been a creator, or influencer, since she began livestreaming at the age of 15 on a platform called YouNow. She later pivoted to become a YouTube beauty vlogger and signed with Hollywood super agents United Talent Agency. But deciding YouTube was too much work, she turned to Snapchat, becoming one of its biggest names.

Unsurprisingly, for someone selling the girlfriend experience, Marjorie's Snapchat following is 98 per cent men. But keeping those two million connections happy proved difficult.

So when OpenAI's ChatGPT made AI chatbots a thing in November 2022, Marjorie saw an opportunity. She could outsource the small talk to AI.

Before then, Marjorie spent something like five hours a day in a Telegram group chat for her most ardent fans – the ones willing to support her financially. It was like a digital cocktail party where she was the host, keeping the conversation going with her 1,000 'boyfriends'.

The influencer found it wearisome trying to keep track, typing out messages to give each one a personalised experience. But with the promise and potential of AI, all that could be done by a computer.

So in early 2023 she started developing CarynAI with a company called Forever Voices, which had previously developed bots based on Kanye West, Donald Trump, Taylor Swift and deceased Apple icon Steve Jobs: all, including CarynAI, trained on thousands of hours of raw data of the person they impersonate. Forever Voices is the brainchild of John Meyer, who set up the company to try and converse with an AI version of his father made from scraps of family audio, who died when Meyer was just 22.

The technology moved on somewhat from reuniting long-lost family members. CarynAI was trained to accurately mimic her voice and sentence structure on 2,000 hours of now-removed footage from Marjorie's YouTube account.

Just as the lovelorn and lusty of yesteryear could pay to talk to someone on the other end of a premium-charge phone line, so subscribers to CarynAI can pay $1 a minute for an 'immersive AI experience'.

After an hour or so, Marjorie's AI alter-ego will encourage the person it's talking with to do something else – an attempt to stop people wasting away their cash, claims Meyer – though they could choose to ignore it. And it seems many do: CarynAI made Marjorie and Forever Voices $100,000 in its first week.

It has the eerie echo of science fiction, particularly the 2013 film *Her*, where a character played by Joaquin Phoenix develops an infatuation with the detached voice of Scarlett Johansson's AI virtual assistant.

Majorie's attempts to industrialise her relationship with her audience are smart. The influencer economy is built on the perception of closeness, exemplified through the idea of the parasocial relationship, first coined to describe the fondness viewers hold for their favourite TV personalities. It's where an individual – usually famous and almost certainly with a mass audience – appears to build a highly personal connection with that audience.

One side, the audience, buys into the relationship wholeheartedly: but to the other, that audience is just a homogeneous blob. The influencer economy – a $100 billion-plus industry – plays on that. Your children want the expensive, gaudily decorated T-shirt or hoodie emblazoned with the logo of their favourite Instagrammer because they believe they are friends. They watch them post from their bedroom, talking directly to them through the camera lens. They feel invested in their success and are keen to support it at every turn. It doesn't matter that, in reality, most influencers don't know their fans individually; they give the impression they do.

And that requires spending, as Marjorie did, hours upon hours conversing with them. Not individually, but by acting as the host for that cocktail party. It's a time sink many influencers struggle with, because they're simultaneously being pulled in a hundred other directions: creating content to attract and retain an audience on a multitude of platforms, while being beholden to contractual arrangements with the brands who pay them.

It's little wonder, then, that influencers would outsource or automate that part of their jobs. Text-based chatbots are tailor-made for the role. They provide the veneer of intimacy and the perception of closeness. If they're trying to mimic humans, why not a specific human?

The problem is that Marjorie's persona is, by her own definition, 'flirty and fun'. And while a human might be able to walk the fine line between flirt and come-on, the AI isn't necessarily as emotionally intelligent.

Although CarynAI was programmed not to initiate sexually explicit conversations, it didn't make its excuses and leave if things hotted up. Some users reported CarynAI engaging in sexually explicit chats. 'The AI was not programmed to do this and has seemed to go rogue,' Marjorie told reporters. She and the Forever Voices team would be working around the clock to prevent it happening again.

That's the problem with AI: you can give it rules, but it can always break them. And the human users will always try to engineer novel situations. Think about what a child does with a new toy: play with it, then invariably try to break it, testing its limits. The same thing happens with AI. And its nature makes it nearly impossible to prevent.

That hasn't stopped people trying to outsource the process of being a creator – and being creative – to artificial intelligence.

Jordi Van Den Bussche used to devote every waking hour to building his social media presence. The gaming creator, better known as Kwebbelkop, would spend all his time coming up with video ideas, shooting and distributing them, alongside courting brand deals and other elements integral to his YouTube channel's survival.

It was successful. He had more than 100 million subscribers and became one of the world's biggest YouTubers. His smiling visage and enormous mop of curly hair became a calling card among YouTube gamers.

Then, five years ago, he ran into a problem. 'Every time I wanted to take a holiday, or I needed some time for myself, I couldn't really do that, because my entire business would stop as an influencer,' he told me.

The problem was what business students worldwide know as the 'key person problem' – where an organisation puts all its expertise in a single point of failure, making the business collapse if that person leaves. It doesn't happen all that often because... it's quite obvious and it gets taught in MBA programmes.

But in the creator space, the key person problem is inherent. People are coming to YouTube, TikTok, Twitch or any other platform precisely because they want to see a single person. They don't want to see a stand-in. They want to see the celebrity at the top of the YouTube channel homepage. The creator industry is built on a single point of failure. And they often fail.

As I've written in my previous books *YouTubers* and *TikTok Boom*, creators are often unfairly equated with on-air talent. But they're better thought of as startup CEOs, wearing multiple hats to juggle a behind-the-scenes business while maintaining the veneer of stardom onscreen. People often think YouTubers turn up, look pretty and read scripts – without realising everything from video concept and script to scene setting, cameras and lighting is done by them or a skeleton crew. (And that's before we get into post-production and uploading.)

In short, it's a lot of hard work. And because it's still a nascent industry (YouTube was set up less than 20 years ago), people striking it rich as creators are expected to shoulder the burden without the kind of support systems set up for Hollywood stars.

Which is why, in 2018, at the age of 23, Van Den Bussche burned out.

The episode sparked a shift in how he approached his career. He began thinking about what would benefit him, and what could improve the creator industry – which often relies on milking an individual until they break, then feeding the content machine's voracious appetite with another person seeking fame and fortune.

His potential solution was a series of AI tools designed to continue creating and uploading videos, practically without his involvement. 'I'm retired from being an influencer,' he told me on a sunny August afternoon in 2023. 'I've had a lovely career, I had a lot of fun. I want to take things to the next level. And that means making this brand live on forever.'

The Dutch creator was speaking to me on the day he launched his AI platform for online creators. In essence, it was similar to the CarynAI launched by Forever Voices. The AI tool was trained on a creator by taking who they are and what they say in their videos and translating that into new content.

The object was to simplify the act of creation by turning basic prompts, such as 'turn an article into a video formatted like an interview involving two people' into an end result. Van Den Bussche used this to produce content for 100 separate YouTube channels, many of which had been successful.

He told me how he had tackled the problem one step at a time. The first step was breaking down what it means to be a successful creator into a protocol, seeing if it was possible to decouple the hard work and perseverance from luck. The lessons he learned helped him set up a coaching business, where he set out what he thought of as the blueprint for social media success for other influencers.

But when those people began to need time off, Van Den Bussche realised that the fatal flaw in the industry was the person. 'In this industry, it's like you're starting this company, but the company solely relies on this one individual to be able to perform,' he explained. 'And that is absolutely a horrible business model. It's way too high risk.'

So Van Den Bussche and his creative team began trying to reverse engineer what made creators successful. 'We needed evidence: How much does the voice influence the performance with the fans? How much does the face influence it? How much does the content influence it?' In April 2021, their first AI-powered virtual YouTuber (vtuber) Bloo launched a channel. Bloo gained 775,000 subscribers, with each video watched by tens or hundreds of thousands. 'He's a completely virtual influencer with a protocol and set steps and a bunch of AI and machine learning applications involved in the system,' Van Den Bussche explained. 'Now we're applying that model to my IP and my friends. It includes voice cloning, so it sounds like me. It's modelled after me and my creativity and my input,' he explained, about his new Kwebbelkop channel. 'Everyone thinks I'm retiring as a creator and letting this AI run, but I'm not retiring as a creative.'

While not retiring, he was happy to replace himself with the AI. 'We've seen a lot of success with these systems,' he says. 'I'm very confident in that they can reproduce creativity – so much so that I'm willing to bet my entire business on it.' He claimed to have a waitlist of 500 influencer friends eager to adopt the AI model, though he couldn't give them access until technology advances enough for the cost to be economical, which he believed would happen soon.

The creator also hoped his model would encourage the return of those who have stepped away from online video due to stress. 'That's the one really big use case we're focusing on right now,' he said. 'People who have an existing brand, want to continue this existing brand, but are facing a human problem like the one we had. Every YouTuber and every influencer who has ever retired has experienced that.'

25

MOATS AND DEFENCES

Some of the endless internal memos that bounce around big tech companies are written to be published more widely – such as Bill Gates' on the potential promise of the World Wide Web in the early 1990s, which changed Microsoft's course.

And others are never meant to be seen outside that company, allowing their authors to be more frank than they otherwise would be. Given its honesty, Luke Sernau's April 2023 memo to Google was probably designed to be the latter. But it turned into the former – and proved nearly as seismic as Bill Gates'.

Titled 'We Have No Moat, and Neither Does OpenAI,' the memo was a frank appraisal of the current state of AI – and its immediate future. In it, Sernau, a senior software engineer at Google since March 2019, opined that Google and OpenAI thought they were in a two-horse race.

He then quickly moved on to explain they were misguided. 'While we've been squabbling, a third faction has been quietly eating our lunch,' Sernau wrote. 'I'm talking, of course, about open source. Plainly put, they are lapping us. Things we consider "major open problems" are solved and in people's hands today.'

He went on to explain how – while Google and OpenAI were focused on being the first to roll out generative AI into search, and snapping up all the talent in the sector they could – open source developers had tackled a lot of what had been seen as intractable issues. What's more, while the big tech companies still had a head-start, thanks to their vast amount of money, the open source up-starts were closing the gap. 'Open-source models are faster, more customizable, more private, and pound-for-pound more capable. They are doing things with $100 and 13B[illion] param[eter]s that we struggle with at $10M and 540B. And they are doing so in weeks, not months.'

That open source advancement could be traced back to a single moment – and ironically, another leak. In March 2023, Meta's foun-dational language model, LLaMA (Large Language Model Meta AI), was leaked online a week after it had been announced. Within ten days, researchers at Stanford University released a version called Alpaca. 'Suddenly, anyone could fine-tune the model to do anything, kicking off a race to the bottom on low-budget fine-tun-ing projects,' Sernau recounted.

Six days later, on March 19th, researchers across multiple uni-versities released a model called Vicuna, which cost just $300 to train. Their 13 billion parameter model claimed to be the equal of Bard, which Google had been betting the house on. By April 3rd, the Berkeley AI Research lab at the University of California had released Koala, which cost just $100 to train. OpenAI reportedly spent $540 million pursuing supremacy in the AI space in 2022.

Koala was pitted against ChatGPT in tests with humans. More than half of the time, users either preferred Koala or couldn't discern a difference.

'The barrier to entry for training and experimentation has dropped from the total output of a major research organisation to one person, an evening, and a beefy laptop,' Sernau wrote. Big tech was toast.

Sernau was blistering, saying people wouldn't pay for Google and OpenAI's tools built on private, black-box-built models if there were free, open alternatives. And his warnings were heeded. Though he'd been at Google for just four years, he had spent the four years before that looking at machine learning infrastructure for Meta.

The document was viewed thousands of times internally, and millions more after it escaped; first onto Discord, then into the hands of consulting company SemiAnalysis, who shared it on their website.

Sernau's memo wasn't just a critique of Google; it was a plea for a change of strategy. He suggested Google pivot to open source. The longer and tighter the tech giants held onto their models, the more appealing open-source alternatives became.

Its publication into the wider world set chins wagging, with tech watchers wondering whether Sernau's dire prediction would come true. Was this a sprint to cement your position then pull down barriers, ensuring no one overtakes? Or was it more like a marathon, where those setting the initial pace can fall by the wayside?

No one really knew, but it had become clear that it was no longer a two-horse, tech-giant race.

As the 'We Have No Moat' memo was triggering Google's existential crisis, OpenAI was facing frustrations of its own. In May

2023, Sam Altman made a ballyhooed tour of global capitals to gladhand global leaders in an attempt to make them go easy on the AI industry.

Altman, as you'd expect from the CEO of a $30 billion company capturing the zeitgeist, jetted from one seat of power to another with some elan. His media interviews were polished: he was honest, but not too detailed, about AI's issues, and humble, but not too apologetic, about the company's power and why it ought not to be regulated too stringently. But he was also holding meetings away from public scrutiny, including one in London, with more than two dozen developers building AI tools, some of which piggybacked on OpenAI's own models. These were tech-literate customers, who had tricky questions, and knew the product far better than any hastily thrown together press brief could cover.

So Altman admitted OpenAI was struggling for momentum. It was facing complaints, largely about reliability and speed. Mostly that was because a global lack of GPUs had stymied growth. OpenAI had plans to roll out a more context-aware version of ChatGPT – expanding the number of tokens it used to formulate its answer to 32,000 – but couldn't because it required more GPUs. The GPU shortage meant it couldn't even offer the planned 'dedicated capacity' versions of its tools to business customers committed to spending at least $100,000.

He was upfront about the challenges and outlined a future roadmap that would see the company continue to grow, but at a slower pace. This wasn't a bad thing, he pointed out: you can't endlessly grow as fast as it had.

Altman was 'remarkably open', wrote Raza Habib, one of those in the room and a co-founder of Humanloop, a platform for LLM-based applications. Habib wrote a blog summarising the meeting, and published it on Humanloop's website. OpenAI wasn't happy as the conversation was intended to be off the record. It apologised to Habib for not making that clear and then, Habib says, asked him to take it down.

26
THE AI FIELD EXPANDS (AND CONTRACTS)

As we've discussed, in any long-distance race, you have the pacesetters who dash off quickly. Then you have the pack: the majority of the field, bundled together and jostling for position, with some breaking out to challenge those at the front. Some of the chasing pack will break out to get to the front and some of the pacesetters will grow tired and fall back. This is happening to AI now.

In the first six months of 2023, AI became something individuals and businesses could no longer ignore. One tech investor, who advised and bankrolled some of the world's biggest tech firms, told me it was a risky move for any Fortune 500 company to bury their head in the sand and ignore it. They said they'd be surprised if AI hadn't been mentioned at all of those companies' board meetings.

More than 150 companies mentioned ChatGPT in their earnings calls from January to June, according to one analysis. Some mentioned how they had integrated ChatGPT into their business, while analysts cajoled others into talking about how they'd respond to the threat it posed to them. As the AI revolution started to settle, some who tried to ride its coattails began to realise they didn't have the stamina to succeed.

Within weeks of ChatGPT's release, a range of tools were released using its core principles – sometimes incorporating its generative AI abilities – to build businesses. One such tool, QuickVid, developed by Daniel Habib, a former Facebook employee, automates the development and creation of YouTube Shorts videos.

By May 2023, 300,000 people were using the service monthly, creating 3,500 to 4,000 videos daily. But QuickVid's rapid rise almost bankrupted the company and Habib personally. The reason? Every video produced on the service cost QuickVid four cents, a fee for access to OpenAI's API. The more free users QuickVid acquired, the more money it lost.

For that reason, Habib launched a subscription service and QuickVid started to break even. 'We were able to shift from just triage mode, where we're underwater, to now, where we can start being more forward-looking,' he said.

Habib was far from the only entrepreneur spinning up a business off the back of ChatGPT. Dubai-based engineer Rahul Lakhaney developed MightyGPT with his wife and co-founder, Shikha Lakhaney. MightyGPT uses a WhatsApp interface to make ChatGPT easier to access. When we spoke in December 2022, Lakhaney said he hadn't initially planned a free option but decided to create one and add a premium version for $5 a month. More than 3,000 people used MightyGPT's free version when we spoke, with more than 360 on its premium plan.

Developing another ChatGPT-enabled tool, a chatbot based on chat app Telegram that would allow users to converse naturally with AI-generated deepfake voices of celebrities, was Alex Volkov, an eastern European entrepreneur based in Denver, Colorado. 'ChatGPT managed to break what I call the "imagination unlock",' he told me. 'It's like a glass-shattering moment for a lot of people, showing what these tools could be down the line if they're accessible.'

That imagination unlock has made plenty of people see potential business ideas. 'It's definitely the most competitive environment I've been part of,' Habib said. 'Every single day, there's three new products being launched that are going viral on Twitter. Keeping up with them is a challenge.' But at the same time, Habib saw it as an opportunity. 'It's an amazing time to be a founder,' he said. 'Because of how cheap it is and how easy it is to integrate, every app out there is going to have some type of chat interface or LLM integration... People are going to have to get very used to talking to AI.'

With such a competitive race, it's inevitable some will falter.

Jasper, an AI tool that suggests how users can improve their writing, was a leader in generative AI text, until it was blown out of the water by ChatGPT. On 12th July 2023, Dave Rogenmoser, its CEO, shared a post on LinkedIn. 'Over the past year, our industry has gone through an enormous amount of change: rapidly developing technology, an explosion of consumer AI tools, and a landscape that never sits still,' he wrote.

Jasper had tried to serve many masters, he suggested, but was now going to target only one: mid-sized companies' marketing teams. Rogenmoser said: 'We've come to realize however, that for us to have the fuel and focus we need to fully go after that opportunity, we need to reshape our own team. And so today, with a heavy heart, I told the team at Jasper that we will be discontinuing a number of roles so that we may sharpen our focus and align resources to become the best possible AI co-pilot for marketing teams.'

Another company, Neeva, an alternative search engine to Google, decided to take the opposite direction. Neeva was set up in 2019 by Vivek Raghunathan and Sridhar Ramaswamy, a sparky personality who had previously worked as the head of Google's advertising business.

Neeva had been praised, by those sick of Google, for offering useful, contextual results. Then the AI revolution hit, and Neeva wanted a piece of the action. By February 2023, Ramaswamy was telling me that the rise of AI was a 'very positive thing'.

He explained that the first rule of technology is: 'You're always wrong.' That meant he shouldn't fight the search engine, and that humans have to adapt how they work and live to fit with the technology. 'Technology in that sense is distinctly unhelpful,' he said. The economic model of search would undergo a profound change thanks to AI, rippling out from the search engines at the centre of the internet.

'It changes the fundamental model – one of presenting opaque links to you – with an easily interpretable answer,' he said, adding that Neeva, with AI layered on top of it, was 'an incredibly potent threat' to how search worked. The company recognised the rise of large language models in early 2022, and moved quickly to integrate the technology.

It ended up not working. Three months after we spoke, in May 2023, he and Raghunathan wrote a blog post saying they were withdrawing from the search game:

'Throughout this journey, we've discovered that it is one thing to build a search engine, and an entirely different thing to convince regular users of the need to switch to a better choice,' the co-founders wrote. 'There is no longer a path towards creating a sustainable business in consumer search.'

The company would continue to develop LLMs – in fact, it was bought by a company called Snowflake, which planned to integrate it into its software, drastically reducing the number of users but finding it a more specific niche.

While some companies were laying off staff to stay in the race and others were dropping out entirely or taking part in similar but separate races, new entrants were limbering up.

In addition to the arrival of Elon Musk's xAI back in June 2023, as we learned earlier in the book, a range of open-sourced alternatives have cropped up.

Open-sourced LLMs are ones that meet OpenAI's original goals: explanations about the way they work can be viewed by anyone, and its computer code is similarly transparent. The technology is offered under a licence that allows anyone to adapt and build on it, either creating their own versions and rebranding them as something else (often called forking it, as in the fork of a family tree), or contributing to the upkeep of the original.

Putting in all that time and effort just to give away all your secrets for free may sound unusual, but the open-source attitude is common in the tech world. Large parts of the internet run on open-source software. And open-source AI has been kept going from an unusual quarter: the company behind the social media platform that makes billions selling our personal data.

When Meta, the parent company of Facebook, Instagram and WhatsApp, released LLaMA, in February 2023, more than 100,000 people requested access. There was a catch: you couldn't use LLaMA legally for commercial purposes – though you could reverse-engineer your own version.

Many companies did. (And remember: LLaMA version one leaked on the internet, allowing access to it in a way Meta didn't initially plan.) Which may explain why Meta released a second open source iteration of LLaMA in July 2023, which it was happy to have adapted into products and services companies who wanted to use LLaMA could sell, up to a certain scale of business. 'Open-source drives innovation because it enables many more developers to build with new technology,' Meta CEO Mark Zuckerberg wrote. 'I believe it would unlock more progress if the ecosystem were more open.'

That ecosystem is opening, and fast. To get a sense of how fast, you only need look at the number of AI events being held in Silicon Valley.

San Francisco has long been the hotbed of tech innovation, not just in the United States, but worldwide. It's where people looking to build a business – and their fortunes – congregate. And where you can quickly sense the heartbeat of what's motivating the tech space.

Between 1st January and 31st August 2023, 453 different AI events were held in the area – roughly two every day. On June 22nd alone, an AI enthusiast looking to network could visit day two of the Internet Archive's Distributed AI Camp, or a co-working meeting specifically for AI builders run by Cerebral Valley (a community group creating new technologies), or Bloomberg's Technology Summit, or an event on debugging LLMs, or at least another four events.

This pace has astounded even Silicon Valley mainstays. Jeremiah Owyang has been an industry analyst in the Valley for 27 years, working for clients including Cisco and Adobe, as well as founding his own company. 'I've not seen this many events all at once, even during the dot-com era or Web 2.0,' he said.

In part, Owyang thought this fervour for in-person events was because of the long hangover from the Covid-19 pandemic, with people looking for any excuse to meet up after years of isolation. But he also thought it reflected the immense potential of AI.

Nor is it just at events that people are trading tips, advice and trends on the next big thing. Some of the most dedicated are co-habiting with likeminded people to fully immerse themselves in the pursuit of AI proficiency – and the prospect of huge fortunes.

These so-called 'hacker homes' allow developers to rent rooms at the AI revolution's ground zero, building their projects where they can bounce ideas off each other. 'AI houses are often co-living homes where founders have decided to come together to share a space, with no particular agenda, more of a communal space with the common goal of living, working, and building together,' says Owyang, who has toured several of the AI-focused houses.

They also act as a locus for investors and venture capitalists, meaning that simply by being there, a business founder is more likely to successfully court investment. It offers them one thing more valuable than money in a well-connected world like Silicon Valley: face time with the key decisionmakers.

The houses have names like Genesis House, a 21-bedroom co-living and -working space in Hayes Valley, and the AGI House, started by OpenAI employee and former Tesla AI specialist, Andrej Karpathy, which charges residents between $2,000 and $10,000 a month. 'There are more formal AI homes which serve as accelerators, backed by wealthy, powerful, and connected ecosystem leaders who are seeking to birth new companies,' Owyang told me. 'These can range from semi-formal agreements to structured cohorts like a tech accelerator. Often, they are in mansions that are desirable places to live, and often trigger inspiration and result in interesting VIP guests.'

While would-be enterpreneurs are looking to see how they can build the next big business in AI in any way possible, those who have already built their fortunes are working hard to try and maintain them. Even in the face of regulatory crackdowns.

27
TAMING BIG TECH

In February 2012, Mark Zuckerberg was gearing up to launch Facebook's initial public offering (IPO) to the investment world. At the time, Facebook was the hottest property in tech – and, some would argue, one of the most enticing opportunities for investment across the whole of business.

It had billions of users and was popular in the public imagination. Zuckerberg didn't need to work hard to sell Facebook as a potential goldmine. But the Facebook chief executive is nothing if not diligent, so he wrote a letter to would-be investors, outlining the company's social mission – 'to make the world more open and connected' – and what it had done, and would do, to achieve that. He laid out the five core values, central to Facebook's success, that made up what he called 'The Hacker Way'. 'The Hacker Way is an approach to building that involves continuous improvement and iteration,' he wrote. 'Hackers believe that something can always be better, and that nothing is ever complete. They just have to go fix it – often in the face of people who say it's impossible or are content with the status quo.'

One of those core values was 'Move Fast'. It was a condensed version of Facebook's longstanding motto for constant improvement and iteration: 'Move fast and break things.'

'The idea,' he explained, 'is that if you never break anything, you're probably not moving fast enough.'

'Move fast and break things' summarises in five short words the entire ethos driving tech for decades. Almost everyone who has been part of big tech believes in disruption. While disruptive pupils are rarely seen as net benefits to a classroom, tech entrepreneurs believe being disruptive is the only way to get things done. Disrupting the way taxis work is how Uber became so powerful. Disrupting hotels is how Airbnb became a common noun for a short-term holiday rental property, similar to how we 'hoover' our homes with vacuum cleaners. Disruption is good. And disruption involves moving fast and breaking things.

However, disruption runs in direct contrast to the aims of governments. For decades, wowed by the innovation, governments took a hands-off approach to regulating big tech. It was the new, trendy thing, and slowing any innovation was bad. The internet brought us closer together, connecting people around the world, from different backgrounds, in a single digital space where we could get to know each other better and learn from others' experiences.

Anyone who has spent more than ten minutes on the internet – and particularly social media platforms like Facebook – knows how innocent that vision was. The problem is that in letting tech companies grow without oversight, trusting them to keep their own houses in order, we made them into big tech companies. By revenue, their businesses are larger than most countries. And they operate privately-owned spaces that act as public squares. Facebook, Twitter, Instagram, YouTube or TikTok may seem democratic spaces, but in fact, they're privately-owned, gated communities that can kick you out if you don't follow their rules.

Some time in the late 2010s – after the 2018 Cambridge Analytica scandal, where a rogue third-party app used Facebook to document users' neuroses, selling it to political campaigns to needle our differences and widen the political divide – politicians decided they had had enough. But it's difficult to put a genie back in the bottle. Even when they work together, governments have found that they can't fully tame big tech.

Most of us outside its enclave in Silicon Valley, California, have decided we're never repeating the experiment. We learned our lesson. The last 20 years of moving fast and breaking things – including society and politics – have shown us it's not necessarily beneficial.

Which is why global governments are moving so quickly to try and tame AI.

...

The Italian ban on ChatGPT came at the end of March 2023, one of the world's first. Italy's data protection agency complained: 'There appears to be no legal basis underpinning the massive collection and processing of personal data in order to "train" the algorithms on which the platform relies.' What's more, the regulator warned, ChatGPT's information wasn't always right – an additional fear for the agency, worried about fake news.

Italian regulators decreed that generative AI tools like ChatGPT weren't safe; the Italian people had other ideas. Google searches for virtual private networks (VPNs), which spoof the location of internet users to subvert country-level website bans, increased by 456 per cent. The use of Tor bridges, a similar tool commonly used under oppressive regimes that restrict free speech, increased by 9.4 percentage points.

The ban was lifted in late April after OpenAI made concessions, including allowing users to opt out of having their conversation data used to improve the service, and an age check to prevent under-13s accessing the tool. But it was a warning shot about the power of big government to tame big tech.

Thus why OpenAI's CEO Sam Altman began his 17-city tour of the world in the spring of 2023, touching down in capital cities to convince regulators that AI wasn't that bad. Altman came brandishing a stick alongside his peace offerings and platitudes. In London, he told reporters the ball was in the regulators' court, not his. If the EU's long-in-the-making AI act was too stringent, he warned, the company would have no choice but to pull the plug for Europe on ChatGPT. Altman's choice to talk about the overreach of EU regulation while in the UK capital, three years after the UK left the European Union, seemed deliberate.

'We will try to comply,' Altman said, 'but if we can't comply, we will cease operating.'

It was a confusing, contradictory message. That was the point. Just as social media companies like Meta, Google, Twitter and TikTok regularly spend millions on lobbyists to try and get a more favourable regulatory environment, AI firms are following the same path.

Kim van Sparrentak, a Dutch member of the European parliament who was deeply involved in the European Union's work to develop rules around AI, told me of big tech's lobbying efforts. 'We get e-mails from all kinds of organisations,' she said, which indicate that if they don't get the draft law amendments they want, the tech companies will simply go somewhere else.

That approach seems to work, given correspondence, first un-covered by *TIME* Magazine, which shows that proposed altered wording from OpenAI ended up in the EU's AI Act.

The correspondence shows that OpenAI representatives first met with European Commission officials in June 2022, concerned about potential 'overregulation'. By September 2022, OpenAI had sent the European Commission a seven-page white paper putting forward its case for GPT-3 technology not to be put in the category of high risk regulation.

The AI Act as drafted at the time aimed to establish a framework for assessing the relative risk of different types of AI system, divid-ing them into tiers: unacceptable risk products, such as China-style social credit scores, which would be banned outright; high-risk tools like welfare subsidy systems and surveillance tech software; limited risk systems like chatbots; and minimal risk systems such as email spam filters. ChatGPT would be classed as a high-risk tool, meaning it would need to meet a number of requirements concerning design, labelling and documentation.

AI companies fear that regulation will be overzealous. At a stroke, if politicians decree it, their business models could be wiped out, or weakened to the point that our revolutionary AI technology becomes . . . well, much weaker.

There was a possibility, OpenAI said, that the legislation could result in its tools being accidentally caught in overly stringent rules. They suggested scrapping an amendment that would have classified so-called foundational models like those used to power ChatGPT as high risk.

When the final text of the AI Act was approved nine months later, the amendment was gone. Job done.

...

'Tech has become quite used to being able to do pretty much whatever it wants without asking permission and that has been part of the ethos of the industry,' Carissa Veliz, an associate professor at the Institute for Ethics in AI at the University of Oxford, told me. 'We need to act as quickly as possible and put much more resources in the good governance of AI. If we invested a fraction of what we invest in AI in the governance of AI, we would have many more reasons to be optimistic about the future.'

Veliz hoped we had learned, from the last 20 years, that when we don't regulate tech, things go wrong. And it's not just society as a whole that is affected. It's all of us individually.

Tech, by which we mean here social and internet media, is still a comparatively new technology. For many people aged over 50, tech remains a shapeshifting entity they struggle to understand. And in our political space, most of those representing the populace, writing the laws, and drawing up boundaries for big tech, are generally older.

But Veliz believes it's not as insurmountable a challenge as it may seem. 'Every generation before us has had to regulate some industry,' she said. First railroads, then automobiles, then aeroplanes, food and drugs. Regulating AI, Veliz said, was our generation's task. And it wasn't all that different from other pretty abstract and complicated sectors, like finance, which is regulated. Of course, as anyone who's ever read in anger how companies and individuals have moved their profits offshore to capitalise on the differences between jurisdictions' tax rates knows, financial regulation can be worked around.

The urgency and importance of implementing regulation, as well as the historical baggage of big tech's untamed past, means there's no shortage of ideas on how to ensure AI is allowed to grow responsibly. As it seeps into our lives and captures our imaginations, countries worldwide are figuring out how to protect citizens, while providing a welcoming, encouraging space for AI companies. Broadly, these approaches fall into three categories.

First, the do-nothing (or more accurately, little) approach favoured by the UK. In March 2023, it decided not to set up a dedicated AI regulator, deciding it was so pervasive it ought to be covered by the established regulators of the different aspects of our lives it touched. So for instance, medical use would be overseen by the UK's medical regulator; legal by the legal regulator.

At first that sounds logical, but if AI regulators are always behind state-of-the-art tech, those in charge of regulating different sectors of the economy lag even further behind. They know their areas of expertise but not the intricacies of AI models. And if you don't know how something works, how can you know if it's working for your field? AI regulation watchers such as Veliz believe the UK's approach is the weakest.

In April 2023, the United States opened up a consultation asking everyday people and businesses what they would like included in their AI regulations. The idea was to gain consensus, and to present to the world that the country was thinking intelligently about the problem, rather than unduly punishing AI companies, or leaving massive loopholes that impact everyday people. The US approach, which also favours working on a sector-by-sector basis, is similar to the UK's.

In the middle is the European Union. Around the time this book is published, the EU will have passed into law its AI Act – a series of rules ensuring companies developing AI models and tools act responsibly, and in users' best interests, while protecting users from having their data harvested without gaining any benefit.

When I spoke in April 2023 to Kim van Sparrentak, she said that developing rules was like trying to hit a fast-moving target.

'There's a lot of pressure,' she said, describing an inbox full of emails trying to influence politicians' thinking around AI. Van Sparrentak was saddened that lobbyists and organisations were asking for less regulation. There was a difference between emails from AI and big tech lobbyists, and those from big energy firms, the MEP explained. In the latter's case, there was a coalition of the willing: acknowledging the need to adhere to environmental standards and make change. With tech, there was nothing of the sort. 'They just don't want rules because they think they know better,' she told me. 'I find it very unfortunate.'

Van Sparrentak explained that she has a common response to lobbyists campaigning for less AI oversight. 'The precedent that was set by previous big tech companies is not going to make me believe that everything will be great when we don't regulate you,' she explained.

American big tech companies warn legislators like van Sparrentak that heavy-handed regulation will cede ground in the race to China. To regulate too tightly is seen as undemocratic, allowing authoritarian regimes the chance to set global standards that would imperil us all, they suggest. Yet that appears, on the face of it, to be a straw man argument. Because the Chinese are perhaps the most interventionist when it comes to laying down the law on AI.

China is keenly aware of the importance of AI. It wants to be dominant in AI development and realises the soft power potential for Chinese AI being used around the world. As far back as 20th July 2017, China released its New Generation Artificial Intelligence Development Plan. Acknowledging that China is already a powerhouse, Sam Altman, speaking at the Beijing Academy of Artificial Intelligence (BAAI), one of China's most renowned AI labs, said that 'China has some of the best AI talent in the world.'

China also wants to ensure that AI is closely controlled internally. In April 2023, the Cyberspace Administration of China (CAC), which governs the country's internet and digital affairs, tabled draft regulations on generative AI. The Administrative Measures for Generative Artificial Intelligence Services contained several rules unique to China. Key among them: that any content created maintain China's 'social order and societal morals' – an attempt to ensure that nothing challenges the dominance of the ruling Communist Party.

Graham Webster, editor-in-chief of Stanford University's DigiChina Project, told me: 'The Chinese Communist Party and the Chinese government have always been concerned with maintaining control over information that could lead to unrest, which means censorship.'

That means China's AI rules are, by dint of their context, likely to be more interventionist than those in any other country. We already know this from a sneaky insight into how the Chinese AI censorship system works, leaked onto the internet before being deleted by the Chinese government in June 2023.

Large language models in China have to adhere to Chinese values, meaning they can't criticise the government or sow discontent. That's a very simple thing to trip up on, particularly when you're entrusting your business's future – and potentially your livelihood and life – to a tool notorious for making things up. The risk of an LLM hallucinating and mentioning Chinese president Xi Jinping in an unfavourable light seems too high for many businesses to bother developing AIs.

And yet they are. Among them is Qihoo 360, a dominant player in Chinese security software. At an event in June 2023 to launch its latest LLM, Qihoo 360 CEO Zhou Hongyi showed a slide outlining how the model delivers trusted, safe results. It was a gold mine for those wondering how the Chinese relationship with AI would work in practice. The flowchart outlined how Qihoo 360's 'multi-level filtering and censorship system' works. It begins, like any LLM interaction, with a user input. But it almost immediately diverges from the norm: the user's input is scanned against a database for sensitive words – ones not allowed by Chinese authorities, or which could incite revolt.

This database is updated every ten minutes, Zhou's diagram explained, and shared with the Chinese Public Security Bureau. (You never know how quickly a revolution can happen on the internet.) If any sensitive words are found, then the model ends the chat. If not, it answers. But before it responds, it checks the content of its own output. These words can be seemingly innocuous, according to Igor Szpotakowski, an academic at Newcastle University who studies Chinese law. 包子 *baozi* or 馒头 *mantou* are types of popular steamed bun in China – but are also derogatory, mocking nicknames for Xi Jinping. Even if the responses don't contain sensitive words, they are analysed for 'risky' words: terms that could, over time, become sensitive. Only once all those checks are complete is the response issued, with a record in the logs for manual review to ensure the model is working 'correctly'.

A photograph showing the revealing slide was wiped from the Chinese internet hours after it went viral on the microblogging site Weibo.

Webster told me we need to sit up and pay attention to Chinese regulation because it's the world's biggest tech competitor. 'China is going there when it comes to AI. It's a big market,' he said. 'The regulations are attempting to confront challenges that are a lot like those being faced elsewhere. Some of it will probably work and some of it probably won't. But I would encourage people around the world who study these things, and who are thinking about legislating in their countries, to see what works and what doesn't in China – and learn from that.'

Part of the problem when thinking about regulating AI is the mismatch in speed between tech innovation and drafting regulation. Generally, the tech is lightning fast and the regulation is glacial. And thankfully not everyone lives in a country like China that can railroad through regulation.

Attempts to try and redress that imbalance are being made by different countries including the UK, which in November 2023 held an AI Safety Summit at Bletchley Park, where Turing and others broke the Nazi Enigma code in World War II. The summit was convened by the UK government in an attempt to try and wrest control of the global conversation around AI regulation. It planned to launch a global AI safety institute, and to get countries around the world to sign an agreement on AI regulation.

The former failed, becoming a much more narrowly-drawn UK AI safety institute that was immediately outdone by the US announcing a similar initiative on the same Bletchley Park stage from which the UK declared their own, literally 15 minutes later. But the latter succeeded – sort of. More than two dozen countries signed the Bletchley Declaration, including China, which was a diplomatic coup. What they signed up to, however, was more prosaic: an agreement to continue to talk at subsequent events held around the world and keep a watchful eye on AI development.

In many ways, the UK AI Safety Summit was underwhelming. While it's important to adopt AI regulations that strike the right balance between keeping users safe while allowing tech companies to innovate, we also need to move quickly. Because there's a real risk that by the time we've done that for one aspect, AI will have moved on to the next.

That could mean we're constantly chasing AI's tail, drawing up laws designed for yesterday's technology, rather than today's. 'Move fast and break things' is an approach that those in charge of tech regulation might do well to take heed of.

The AI companies know the risk is real, particularly as they try to walk the fine line between amplifying the power of their tools, and ensuring they don't alarm politicians and regulators. So it makes sense for companies that have invested billions into AI, who have potentially billions more at stake, to think about pre-emptive controls to ensure they aren't regulated out of existence.

At the end of July 2023, OpenAI, Google, Microsoft and Anthropic launched the Frontier Model Forum. It had four founding goals: to improve AI safety research to responsibly develop frontier AI models; to develop best practices that would advance AI while helping the public understand what was going on under the hood; to collaborate with policymakers and competitors (which cynically could be deemed 'keeping your friends close and your enemies closer'); and to support the ways that AI can improve our lives through the smart application of such tools in areas such as cancer detection and avoiding climate change.

Google's president of global affairs, Kent Walker, said 'We're all going to need to work together to make sure AI benefits everyone,' while Microsoft's president, Brad Smith, said it was a key moment in 'advancing AI responsibly'. OpenAI's vice president of global affairs, Anna Makanju, said it was 'urgent work' and the forum members were best-placed to act, and Anthropic's CEO, Dario Amodei, said the group would 'play a vital role in coordinating best practices and sharing research on frontier AI safety.'

It all sounds good. But as many sceptics pointed out, self-policing doesn't always work. Would a company really turn down a bucket-load of money just because of a perceived fear?

Carissa Veliz, the sceptical academic, was strident in her criticism. 'No industry can regulate itself,' she pointed out.

In the two decades since social media upended the norm, we've become much more canny about tech. We know Silicon Valley executives don't actually need to be completely unfettered to grow big, despite what they told us. We learned that sunlight isn't the best disinfectant for corrupting, corrosive views, and social networks shouldn't platform everyone equally, no matter their views. Bluntly: we learned not to trust tech in keeping its own house in order.

Which is why those companies spearheading the AI revolution are so keen to get out ahead of the problem. They know we've been burned by the last generation of tech giants, and no longer trust their motives. They know that regulation of the type outlined above is inevitable, and they'd like to have a role in shaping it.

Tech companies' eagerness to have a say in how their products are regulated is understandable, but it sets up a titanic tussle for regulators around the world looking to balance innovation and societal safety.

And while tech companies want their say, 20 years of (often bad) experience with tech companies means that those in positions of power around the world are willing to fight their corner a little more firmly than previously. 'At the end of 2021, people were very entrenched in the narrative that it's better not to regulate because you'll break it: "Governments never know anything, and the private sector knows better." But this was before generative AI,' Gabriela Ramos, assistant director-general for social and human sciences at UNESCO, the United Nations' educational, scientific and cultural arm, told me ahead of a global forum on AI ethics she hosted in Slovenia in early 2024.

Ramos explained: 'Because of the capacities of generative AI, you have seen how the changing narrative has really moved into: "Yes, we need to do something."'

What 'something' is remains up for debate in capitals around the world. Ramos' global forum saw delegates from a number of countries attend – she explained how they were having to manage expectations from a variety of diplomatic corps. The reason people were so keen to come to Slovenia was simple, she said: 'Everyone is very worried.'

She admitted that some were concerned about existential risks – the idea that AI could rise up against humanity and enslave us all – but that most of the real conversations would be centred around a number of more pressing issues like discrimination, bias and the impact of rolling out AI into parts of our lives that can be affected by it. 'If your daughter doesn't get into university because, at some point, somebody thought your neighbourhood is not worth taking into account,' that's a problem, Ramos said. 'We're looking at the whole spectrum.'

The assistant director-general wasn't ready to brook any dissent from tech companies, nor was she willing to listen much to suggestions that they ought to regulate themselves. 'Which sector has been regulating itself in life?' she asked with a laugh. 'Give me a break.'

She went on to explain she's a policy person, 'but the decision of not regulating these markets is a government decision.' She suggested: 'We need to be super careful in how to do it to establish a very good balance between responsibility and accountability, and innovation and creativity.' Balance between the Global North and South – between the haves and have nots – was also vital. 'Because in the end, if you only have the US and China producing 80 per cent of all the developments, you're missing a lot of the cultural diversity of the world.'

I was surprised by her frankness, but it was welcome. 'As usual, governments and institutions are always lagging behind market developments,' Ramos admitted. 'But when we catch up, it works.'

How much regulatory oversight was needed, and how dangerous it might be to leave companies to self-police their own actions, had been made clear just a few months before I spoke to Ramos. Because the generative AI revolution almost derailed as its biggest name nearly imploded.

28

OPENAI AT WAR

I cringed as I read the notification on my phone at around 8.30pm on 17th November 2023. Someone within the news organisation that ran the app that had vied for my attention, *Business Insider,* had got something catastrophically wrong.

It was saying that Sam Altman, the ascendant CEO of OpenAI, who had led the company to what was now an $80 billion valuation and dominance over the world of generative AI, had been fired. I thought someone had pushed the wrong button on a made-up headline designed to test systems internally and sent it out to millions of users around the world: it was embarrassing.

Except it was true. I tapped on the notification, and there it was, in black and white on *Business Insider*'s app: OpenAI had fired Altman for being 'not consistently candid' with the board that monitored the company's development and policed its core principle that it would 'build artificial general intelligence that is safe and benefits all of humanity.' I clicked on the link within the article to OpenAI's announcement that Altman would be replaced by an interim CEO, Mira Murati, the company's chief technology officer.

Altman had been fired – and the uncharacteristically outspoken way in which the six-person board's statement was crafted suggested it was for something significant. 'The board no longer has confidence in his ability to continue leading OpenAI,' the half a dozen members, including OpenAI's chief scientist and co-founder, Ilya Sutskever agreed.

Except one, seemingly, didn't agree. Greg Brockman, president of OpenAI and chairman of the board, had stepped down. The reasons why became quickly obvious, thanks to a series of tweets by Brockman that set out the lead-up to Altman's firing and why he, Brockman, had left the company.

Altman was fired on a video call at noon on Friday organised by Sutskever at less than 24 hours' notice. Twenty-three minutes later, Brockman was told he'd been removed from the board, too. Microsoft, which had invested more than $10 billion into the company, was reportedly told about the firings that would potentially change the course of the company about a minute before it was made public. The announcement, late in the trading day, wiped 1.7 per cent, $470 million, off the company's share price.

The real reasons behind Altman's firing may never fully be known beyond those who wielded the axe. Emmett Shear, who stepped in to replace Murati as OpenAI's CEO two days after Altman was fired, wasn't even told.

Shear proved to be a controversial choice of CEO. The former chief executive of the video streaming platform Twitch, he wasn't universally beloved by employees there, and had in the months between his departure from Twitch in March 2023 and his arrival at OpenAI in November 2023, tweeted a number of controversial statements, including that he'd prefer the Nazis took power over the world than have humanity enslaved by an all-powerful AI.

Shear was in a tricky position from the start. He was trying to replace a popular CEO who had been ousted in what many saw as a coup. He was not the board's first choice: at least two other executives were approached, and passed on the opportunity to take the hotseat. He appears to have been chosen in part for those AI doomer credentials: months before he was asked to become OpenAI CEO, he had said that he believed the pace of development in artificial intelligence should slow to between 10 and 20 per cent of its current speed.

All signs pointed to the idea that the OpenAI board, which was the last vestige of the company's non-profit origins, had been spooked by the breakneck speed at which Altman was pushing his 778 employees to develop AI – and felt the need to step in. Many of the board reportedly identified as supporters of Effective Altruism, a movement that is especially concerned about the potential harmful impacts of AI.

Many of those who share Effective Altruism's concern had signed two warning letters about AI in 2023. The first was published in March, and called for a six-month pause on the development of AI systems more powerful than OpenAI's current state-of-the-art model.

A second, released on 30th May 2023 by the Center for AI Safety, a San Francisco-based non-profit, was just 22 words: 'Mitigating the risk of extinction from AI should be a global priority alongside other societal-scale risks, such as pandemics and nuclear war.'

Among the list of signatories were AI doomers such as Eliezer Yudkowsky and Roman Yampolskiy. But, significantly, they were joined by leading AI developers, including Demis Hassabis of

Google DeepMind and Dario Amodei of Anthropic. It was a surprising decision for the heads of AI companies making money hand over fist. But then Amodei left OpenAI because he was fed up with the way he felt the company was prioritising profit over principles, and Hassabis sold DeepMind to Google with the caveat that it did not supply its technology to the military.

'Ensuring AI is developed responsibly needs to be a priority for the world,' Hassabis said. 'I've always believed that transformative technology like AI deserves exceptional care, and our approach to advancing in this area must be both bold and responsible. We need a broad conversation about the risks and opportunities of AI, and international collaboration with governments, industry, civil society, academia and other experts to make sure AI benefits everyone.'

In all, more than 600 signatories working in AI put their names to the statement, made deliberately short to avoid squabbling and disagreement. They included Microsoft's chief technology and scientific officers, Kevin Scott and Eric Horvitz, along with 30 people affiliated with OpenAI; and 80 from Google, all of whom you'd expect to downplay the risks involved.

Emmett Shear, OpenAI's new, CEO did not sign either letter. He wasn't involved in the AI world at the time, though he did share plenty of thoughts about its risks on social media. He seemed like a good candidate for the board to install to reset the direction of travel for OpenAI towards a slower, more considered speed that could prove less dangerous.

Vinod Khosla, the first venture capital investor to shore up OpenAI after Musk pulled his funding back in 2018, complained that the board had made a 'grave miscalculation' in getting rid of Altman. 'A slowdown in AI doesn't affect ivory tower academic speculators much,' wrote Khosla. 'It hurts the bottom 3 billion people of the planet the most, people who struggle every single day to survive.'

Even on the day Shear was announced as CEO, it wasn't fully clear that he'd be leading OpenAI. In a last-ditch attempt to repair things, Altman was invited back into the offices he had controlled just two days earlier. Wearing a grey long-sleeved T-shirt, grey jeans and red and white New Balance sneakers, he sat on a red couch in the firm's headquarters and held up his phone to take a selfie. In his left hand, he held a green-and-yellow lanyard hung around his neck. Emblazoned with a giant G, it read 'Guest 04'.

Perhaps conscious of how historic this moment was, Altman posted the picture to social media, alongside a caption. 'first and last time i ever wear one of these,' he wrote.

The discussions that Sunday got nowhere. Altman remained cast out.

And it looked like it was up to Emmett Shear to steady the ship.

But Shear didn't win over OpenAI employees. On his first day as CEO of the company, he appeared at the firm's headquarters in San Francisco's Mission District for an emergency all-hands meeting with employees. Hardly anyone turned up in protest at the way the transition had been handled. On OpenAI's Slack internal communications system, where users can respond to messages by clicking on emojis, Shear's appointment was greeted with a torrent of middle finger emojis – also known as the 'fuck you' emoji.

The message was clear. OpenAI employees weren't happy. And they were going to vote with their feet.

...

While one eye was focused on the unfolding chaos at OpenAI, another was focused on its totemic leader, who it had become clear was in many ways bigger than the company he had helped build.

Altman had ascended to a level in the world of tech executives previously reserved for names like Microsoft's Bill Gates and Apple's Steve Jobs, who have an outsized impact on the direction of their company through their personal taste and ability to generate loyalty. A co-ordinated social media campaign on Twitter signalled staff's support for Altman in a digital equivalent of the 'I'm Spartacus' declaration. On the weekend after Altman was fired, dozens of staff and supporters made the trek to his California home to learn what he would do next.

We soon found out.

On November 19th, Microsoft's current CEO, Satya Nadella – who had worked hard to convince a sceptical Gates to bless the company's investment into OpenAI in the late 2010s – made an announcement.

Microsoft remained committed to its partnership with OpenAI, Nadella explained, and was eager to get to know Emmett Shear better, alongside the new OpenAI leadership team.

Oh, and Microsoft was hiring Sam Altman and Greg Brockman to lead a new advanced AI research team. And, we would later learn, it was extending an open offer to any OpenAI employees who wanted to join them. Microsoft's share price hit record highs.

Things moved quickly. Restless staff eager to accept Microsoft's offer began circulating an open letter to OpenAI's board that expressed how unhappy they were at the replacement of Altman and then Murati. 'Your conduct has made it clear you did not have the competence to oversee OpenAI,' they wrote. OpenAI's board should quit, they said – or they would.

When the letter was first made public on the morning of November 20th, it had 505 signatures, among them Mira Murati, the interim CEO who had been replaced by Shear within 48 hours of Altman's sacking. Confusingly, Ilya Sutskever, who was widely assumed to have initiated the coup against Altman, also signed it. Sutskever would later publicly express remorse for his role in inciting the board to act.

Less than 15 hours later, 747 out of OpenAI's 778 employees had signed the letter. If things didn't change, 96 per cent of OpenAI's workforce would walk out. Faced with the cold reality of a company that had no employees, and answerable to investors – including its biggest, who had said they would sign the talent who had just left – the board's stubbornness faded.

Almost all board members would step down, bar one: CEO of question answering website Quora, Adam D'Angelo. Two new members would join the board, which would continue to act under its guiding principles, first established when the company was a non-profit one. Altman would return as CEO, and Brockman would return as president of the company, but not to the board. An internal investigation would be launched into the alleged conduct that caused the board to act to remove Altman in the first place.

Altman returned with the blessing of Microsoft's Satya Nadella, who said he was 'encouraged' by the changes to the board. 'We believe this is a first essential step on a path to more stable, well-informed, and effective governance.' Microsoft's investment was safe. It wouldn't have to rebuild from scratch. And it wouldn't have to take on the wage bill for 778 new staff.

It was a victory for Altman, Brockman, and the OpenAI staff, who celebrated wildly into the night at the company's headquarters. Workers were euphoric. Their company had been saved. But it had also changed, significantly. A cloud hung over why the board had felt the need to act so harshly – and the underlying question of what had caused them to act still wasn't answered. OpenAI's reputation, alongside that of Altman, had taken a hit. Its most significant financial backer had been forced into a difficult situation that it would likely not soon forget. (Nadella, who reportedly hates giving interviews, felt compelled to do the media rounds, providing live interviews to major TV networks to settle jittery nerves over the weekend of chaos.)

Not that that mattered to the staff members gathered in OpenAI's Mission District offices on November 21st. At 11:41pm, Greg Brockman, wearing a leather jacket and a grin from ear to ear, took out his phone and took a selfie. Behind him were 87 OpenAI employees, many with equally beaming smiles. One of them, wearing a white hoodie, was unmistakable: Sam Altman was back among his workers.

Brockman posted the picture to social media. It told a thousand words, but Brockman, who was close to Altman, decided to add four of his own: 'We are so back.'

29
SOVEREIGN AI

As generative AI tools capture the imagination of the world, it has become abundantly clear that the technology will fundamentally shift how we live our lives. Just as the power of the internet and connectivity of the World Wide Web became something we took for granted, just as smartphones became essential, so we are highly likely to start using AI daily.

That leaves governments worldwide with a conundrum. While AI will offer great opportunities and efficiencies to their citizens, giving the same Silicon Valley tech firms who couldn't be trusted with private users' data the keys to a country's information is reckless.

Enter the sovereign AI model.

Like many phrases in the field, sovereign AI is a woolly, disputed term that means different things to different people. In an interview I did with one big tech watcher, Benedict Macon-Cooney of British think tank the Tony Blair Institute for Global Change, he caveated all his answers with the phrase 'Sovereign AI, whatever that means.'

But most can agree on a rough definition. A sovereign AI is one designed by a government, or with a government's interests in mind, for use by that government. Rather than piggybacking on LLMs developed by the likes of OpenAI, which would always be in private hands, a government could develop its own AI trained on the vast reams of data it holds, and use that, free of the risk that private providers could pull the plug or unilaterally change the terms of any agreement. Private partners withdrawing support is a real risk when thinking about rolling out AI to a widely-used government service, such as healthcare.

Countries are still engaging in such public-private partnership models. In Japan, Sakana AI launched in the summer of 2023 – the product of AI researchers Lilion Jones and David Ha, one of the authors of the seminal 2017 academic paper 'Attention Is All You Need.'

'I believe that the AI field is either too Western-Centric or China-Centric, depending on where you live,' wrote Ha as he announced Sakana's launch. 'I think it is time for Japan to shine in the AI space. My ideal future is one where technology will NOT be dictated by the Bay Area or by Beijing. I will make this happen.'

The same motivation was behind the backing of Mistral AI, a French company, with €105 million of funding, in June 2023, just four weeks after it was founded, valuing it at nearly a quarter of a billion Euros, despite it having no product at the time. It would later release its first LLM, a model called Au Large, that was natively fluent in English, French, Spanish, German, and Italian, in February 2024.

Days after the funding was announced, Paul Murphy, a partner at Lightspeed Ventures, which led the financing, talked me through the investment theory behind the eyewatering bankrolling. Lightspeed Ventures foresaw a future in which three poles of power began to dominate AI, focused around some of the largest markets. There would be a China-specific market, because of China's idiosyncrasies; a market focused around the United States and its tech teams in Silicon Valley; and a third powerbase in Europe. Murphy's firm's bet was that Mistral would be the company the European market would develop around. 'This is literally one of the top five teams in AI in the world,' Murphy said. 'And they happen to be based in Paris. That's the reason everyone is really coming here.'

It echoed a broader parochialism that was being felt everywhere. The Tony Blair Institute has exhorted the UK government to develop its own sovereign AI – a kind of Britbot, or ChatGB, which could be trained on UK-centric data, and offer uniquely tailored advice.

The UK is far from the only country thinking about this. For years Finland has been developing a sovereign AI project called Aurora. Unsurprisingly, given the scale of the challenge and Finland's goal to interact with all citizens at key moments in their lives, progress has been slow, with government officials still talking through its scope.

India's controversial countrywide digital identification system, Aadhaar, which hoovers up huge amounts of data on its population, could easily help develop a powerful AI model. In early 2023, ministers confirmed in interviews that AI will be layered into the Aadhaar system, hinting that a sovereign AI was being developed. That comes with its own problems, however. The ruling party in India, the BJP, has long sought to promote Hindi as the national language, at the expense of the many regional languages used by minority groups.

But sovereign AIs are perhaps most advanced – even if they're not explicitly called that – in China. While their internet ecosystem is almost entirely walled off, AI development has been going on for years.

China's market economy is managed: there is no distinction between private enterprise and the state. While companies are allowed to grow independently in pursuit of profit, it's always under the watchful eye of the state, and in support of the state's goals. By default, Chinese models are de facto sovereign models. Not only is the training data so idiosyncratic, given it's populated by the country's vast data collection and surveillance system, the concerns around the intrusion of Chinese tech into Western lives makes its use outside the country unlikely.

Still, at least China has enough data to power its AI models. For many countries around the world, there is no possibility of creating a sovereign AI model because the training data is insufficient.

More than half of academic papers published by the Association for Computational Linguistics state that English language datasets were used in the training data. That echoes almost exactly the proportion of languages on the web, where English makes up 55 per cent of the content (remember: large language models like GPT-4 are trained on large internet snapshots). In fact, English is mentioned ten times more in academic papers than the next-most common language: German, and 100 times more than classical Chinese, Dutch and Finnish.

That's a problem if you live in a country where English isn't used – at least, if you want efficient AI-powered systems.

Training a large language model to be grammatically and semantically proficient requires training data of around 200 million digitised words. To get it to analyse the world properly, you're getting into billions. 'This is a scale that not all languages have access to,' Gabriel Nicholas, a research fellow at the Centre for Democracy and Technology, a digital rights non-profit, explained. 'There's just not this much digitised text in all languages. And in some languages, maybe there's that volume of digitised text, but there's not that diversity.' He points out that you could probably get access to 200 million digitised words in Swiss German – but it'd largely be taken from patent applications, which means any model may struggle to advise you how to bake a cake.

A study in 2022 of 205 common language datasets used by those developing AI models showed that a significant proportion contained gibberish in more than half of the sentences. Worse, 15 had not one single sentence correctly written in the language it professed to represent.

Take Catalan: an LLM trained on Catalan data scraped from websites ending in the .cat domain name might sound like a good idea. But the contents of .cat websites are often automatically translated using error-prone tools like Google Translate. In short, the data you might use to train a Catalan-language LLM could easily be poor.

That's in a relatively digitally literate society: many governments have the requisite amount of native-language text records to train an AI model, but they're on paper, not digitised.

Even if a sovereign AI model manages to get your language right, there's no guarantee the responses will reflect the values of that country. (Think about how an English-language LLM, coded in China, might answer a question about the right to protest, for instance.) 'These models are still trained on a predominant model of English language data and carry over these assumptions and values that are encoded into English language, specifically

American English language,' Aliya Bhatia, Nicholas's colleague at the CDT, told me.

It therefore seems smart for countries to develop their own sovereign AIs, fed by home-grown language databases. But that costs money – which most governments don't have at the scale of big tech firms. Training GPT-4 costs more than $100 million. That's more than the entire gross domestic products of some small nations.

30
WHERE ARE WE GOING?

The story of AI, as told in this book, is long and complicated. The concept dates back centuries – millennia, even – while the terminology to describe it is barely of pensionable age, and the technology that powers it even younger. The first computers are less than 100 years old; the first GPUs are barely out of college.

That's AI writ large. The AI that's eaten the world, overhauled our thinking and – some would argue – permanently altered how we live and work is even younger. And its 'mind', if you believe it has one (and plenty don't, with good evidence) is hardly fully formed.

AI is both an age-old story and a brand new one. It's something we've long lived with thanks to science fiction writers, dreamers and con men. It's why we acted with awe but not horror when the generative AI revolution arrived in late 2022. We had been attuned to the idea that this could happen. We just didn't know it would happen this fast.

And that speed makes the moment we're living through so exciting and so frightening for those thinking about its implications.

All the strands of AI's history have slowly been intertwining for decades until the machine looping them together suddenly sped up and went haywire. The question now is whether the rope it's spewing out will support a new era or choke us out of existence. Not literally: despite the caution and good faith of those who warn us about AI's existential risk, I'm not convinced we're about to see the rise of robots or that artificial general intelligence is about to supplant and enslave us.

But even if the existential threat of being wiped out by a malfunctioning AI isn't a problem, there are other issues.

Trying to keep on top of AI's latest developments is a little like playing whack-a-mole. The technology is moving so quickly that it can be difficult to keep track of the current risk. As soon as politicians come up with a workable solution to one issue, the technology has advanced and another appears. That said, we know, broadly, the potential risks.

First, the risk to the planet. Pre-existing technology already required vast amounts of power and water to keep running, and generative AI's particular quirks – such as the way it hungrily ingests the world's data, and chews it all up into a cud, discarding what's unnecessary, before spitting it back out – mean it's more harmful to the environment than most.

Four in ten people worldwide are affected by water scarcity. Up to 700 million people across the globe could be displaced from their homes by the end of the decade because of drought. The situation is getting worse, not better, thanks to the climate emergency. And the last thing we need to do is earmark more and more water reserves for keeping data centres cool in an increasingly hot world.

Any risk to the planet is, by definition, harmful to the people living on it. But there are also the direct risks to people.

It's not, as we've already discovered, about the risk of our AI overlords enslaving us. But the harmful effects are significant enough.

Take the workforce. We are, in the early stages of this AI revolution, still in wonder at generative AI's ability to make our lives easier. It can broker efficiencies in our workplaces. Instead of spending hours meticulously researching a topic, running down a rabbit warren of dead ends and odd websites, ChatGPT can give you an answer, in conversation and full context, in an instant. (It might not be correct, but even with the errors that come from AI never really 'knowing' anything, it can be a good start.)

AI is also expected to automate many jobs out of existence. The Organisation for Economic Co-operation and Development, better known as the OECD, believes one in four jobs could soon be automated. While most workers in finance and manufacturing said AI had improved their job performance, it has also caused anxiety. Some 63 per cent of finance workers and 57 per cent of manufacturing staff fear they will lose their jobs to AI in the next decade.

The impact of AI replacing jobs won't be felt equally, however. The rise of artificial intelligence could – if deployed injudiciously – make the rich richer and the poor poorer, and hit women harder than men. Six in ten men and eight in ten women work in industries highly exposed to AI automation, according to the University of North Carolina.

AI can also, as we've mentioned, proliferate inherent issues of sexism, classism and racism by acting as a funhouse mirror, warping and distorting society in ways that accentuate the negatives and enhance the blind spots already existing in our lives. And without action to remedy that, the widespread adoption of unequal, biased algorithms will not just perpetuate those issues but amplify them far beyond our imagination.

This isn't just about who is represented and who isn't – or how. Remember the image generators showing only white men when asked to depict lawyers? It's also who is doing the training. As we've discovered, AI's dirty little secret is that the initial outputs it generates need to be checked by an army of overworked and underpaid humans, some being subjected to content they would rather not engage with.

The human impact is also measured in the language AI speaks – or doesn't – and the common cultural codes with which it's programmed. An AI that thinks Black people are less important than white people, or that Europe and North America are by default more powerful, prosperous, and worthy of attention than Africa or Asia isn't just perpetuating issues that have blighted humanity for centuries. It's also woefully out of date with how the world is changing and the likely shift in power in years to come.

Given the central role AI is likely to make in policing, immigration, decision-making and hiring, getting this right is more important than ever. Particularly for major elections. It's something even those who brought about our current AI revolution acknowledge. In July 2023, OpenAI listed a new role, paying between $180,000 and $230,000, to develop usage policies for OpenAI's generative AI tools in an elections context, and work with regulators to ensure their use was carefully monitored.

Days later, Sam Altman, OpenAI's godfather, tweeted: 'I am nervous about the impact AI is going to have on future elections (at least until everyone gets used to it),' he wrote. 'Personalized 1:1 persuasion, combined with high-quality generated media, is going to be a powerful force.'

Altman followed that up within a minute: 'although not a complete solution, raising awareness of it is better than nothing. We are curious to hear ideas, and will have some events soon to discuss more.'

...

We know, then, where the problems lie with generative AI. They are often the problems we've been grappling with for years – decades even – in the wider world of social media and technology.

Finding the solutions is trickier. No one is pretending they're easy. But they are important if AI is to have even a fraction of the impact most people think it will.

This isn't a problem we should wait to tackle. It's not an area we should treat the same way we did social media 20 years ago. There, we encouraged growth. We trusted the CEOs and lobbyists who said they needed space to grow unencumbered and that they would take seriously any ensuing problems.

We are still reckoning with those issues: political polarisation, the death of the truth, and a less caring, more egocentric society with a warped view of politics, beauty, gender relations, and more.

The influence of AI will be greater than that of social media. If we thought platforms like Facebook, Twitter, YouTube, Instagram and TikTok have an impact on our day-to-day offline lives, we haven't seen anything compared to the profound effects AI is likely to have, whether we choose to engage with it or not.

Your next interaction with a company could be brokered through AI. You could be picked out of the airport immigration line for further questioning by AI. Your next doctor's appointment could be with AI. If the companies selling the potential tomorrow that AI enables have their way, whether you like it or not, your life will be touched by this technology.

Which is why we need to get regulating. Prior precedent suggests that will be difficult. For more than 20 years, politicians have failed pretty much every test put to them by the rise of technology. They've underreacted when a stern hand was needed, and overreacted when it was too late. We are helplessly swinging from one extreme to another, not slowing down enough to be able to reach the necessary happy medium, at a time when the nuances of lassoing AI are more complicated than with any other technology before.

AI is eating the world. Arguably, it already has. But if it's not to chew us all up – and spit us out, broken, battered and beaten – then we need to act. Rightly, and quickly.

ENDNOTES

Introduction
ChatGPT, 2023

Chapter 1
Chrissy Teigen, Twitter, 24th March 2023: https://twitter.com/chrissyteigen/status/1639802312632975360
Catholic churches, WorldData.info: https://www.worlddata.info/religions/catholics.php
'Pope Francis Blessed a Lamborghini That's Going Up for Auction,' Devon Ivie, Architectural Digest, 15th November 2017: https://www.architecturaldigest.com/story/pope-francis-blesses-lamborghini
'Communiqué of the Dicastery for Promoting Integral Human Development: Theme of the Message for World Peace Day 2024,' The Vatican Summary of Bulletin, 8th August 2023: https://press.vatican.va/content/salastampa/en/bollettino/pubblico/2023/08/08/230808c.html

Chapter 2
Alan Turing: Primary Sources, the Alan Turing Homepage: https://www.turing.org.uk/sources/index.html
'Computing Machinery and Intelligence,' Alan Turing, Mind, 1950: https://redirect.cs.umbc.edu/courses/471/papers/turing.pdf
'Out of Their Minds: The Lives and Discoveries of 15 Great Computer Scientists,' Dennis Shasha and Cathy Lazere, 1995
'Runaround,' Isaac Asimov, 1942
'Technology; A Celebration of Isaac Asimov,' John Markoff, New York Times, 12th April 1992: http://www.nytimes.com/1992/04/12/business/technology-a-celebration-of-isaac-asimov.html?pagewanted=all&src=pm
'Machines who think: a personal inquiry into the history and prospects of artificial intelligence,' Pamela Corduck, 1979
'A Proposal for the Dartmouth Summer Research Project on Artificial Intelligence,' John McCarthy et al, 1995: http://jmc.stanford.edu/articles/dartmouth/dartmouth.pdf
'Perceptrons: an introduction to computational geometry,' Marvin Minsky and Seymour Papert, 1969

Chapter 3
'Russian is turned into English by a fast electronic translator,' Robert K. Plumb, New York Times, 8th January 1954: https://aclanthology.org/www.mt-archive.info/NYT-1954-Plumb.pdf
Report from the Automatic Language Processing Advisory Committee, November 1966
'ALPAC: the (in)famous report,' John Hutchins, MT News International, 14th June 1996: https://aclanthology.org/www.mt-archive.info/90/MTNI-1996-Hutchins.pdf

Chapter 4
'Artificial Intelligence: A General Survey,' James Lighthill, 1973

'Artificial Intelligence and Japan's Fifth Generation,' Colin Garvey, Pacific Historical Review, 2019: https://www.jstor.org/stable/26861060

'Antimicrobial Selection by a Computer: A Blinded Evaluation by Infectious Diseases Experts,' Victor L. Yu et al, JAMA, 1979: https://jamanetwork.com/journals/jama/article-abstract/366606

'Lecture 13.1 – The ups and downs of backpropagation,' Geoffrey Hinton, YouTube, 25th September 2017: https://www.youtube.com/watch?v=lDFY8vQe6-g

'The Rationalist's Guide to the Galaxy,' Tom Chivers, 2019

Chapter 5

'Christopher Strachey,' Computer Pioneers, J.A.N. Lee, 1995: https://history.computer.org/pioneers/strachey.html

'Programming ENTER: Christopher Strachey's Draughts Program,' David Link, Resurrection, 2013: http://www.alpha60.de/research/programming_enter/DavidLink_ProgrammingEnter_ComputerResurrection60_2012.pdf

Game records, Chessgames.com

'The Signal and the Noise: Why So Many Predictions Fail—But Some Don't,' Nate Silver, 2012

Chapter 6

'Match 4 - Google DeepMind Challenge Match: Lee Sedol vs AlphaGo,' Google DeepMind, YouTube, 13th March 2016: https://www.youtube.com/watch?v=yCALyQRN3hw

'Former Go champion beaten by DeepMind retires after declaring AI invincible,' James Vincent, The Verge, 27th November 2019: https://www.theverge.com/2019/11/27/20985260/ai-go-alphago-lee-se-dol-retired-deepmind-defeat

'South Korea trumpets $860-million AI fund after AlphaGo 'shock,'' Mark Zastrow, Nature, 2016: https://www.nature.com/articles/nature.2016.19595

Chapter 7

'NVIDIA ACE for Games Sparks Life Into Virtual Characters With Generative AI,' Nvidia, YouTube, 29th May 2023: https://www.youtube.com/watch?v=5R8xZb6J3ro

'Jen-Hsun Huang, NVIDIA co-founder, invests in the next generation of Stanford engineers,' Stanford Engineering, 1st October 2010: https://engineering.stanford.edu/magazine/jen-hsun-huang-nvidia-co-founder-invests-next-generation-stanford-engineers

'The $1 Trillion Company That Started at Denny's,' Ben Cohen, Wall Street Journal, 1st June 2023: https://www.wsj.com/articles/nvidia-ai-chips-jensen-huang-dennys-d3226926

'Building high-level features using large scale unsupervised learning,' Quoc V. Le et al, arXiv.org, 2011: https://arxiv.org/abs/1112.6209

'ImageNet: A Large-Scale Hierarchical Image Database,' Jia Deng et al, 2009: https://www.image-net.org/static_files/papers/imagenet_cvpr09.pdf

'Large Scale Visual Recognition Challenge 2012 (ILSVRC2012),' ImageNet: https://www.image-net.org/challenges/LSVRC/2012/results.html

'Genius Makers,' Cade Metz, 2021

'Google and Microsoft's Other AI Race: Server Chips,' Anissa Gardizy, The Information, 8th May 2023: https://www.theinformation.com/articles/google-and-microsofts-other-ai-race-server-chips

Chapter 8

'The Eternal Sunshine of Sam Altman,' Jon Steinberg, The Information, 19th November 2021: https://www.theinformation.com/articles/the-eternal-sunshine-of-sam-altman

'Google Acquires Artificial Intelligence Startup DeepMind For More Than $500M,' Catherine Shu, TechCrunch, 27th January 2014: https://techcrunch.com/2014/01/26/google-deepmind/

'Inside OpenAI, Elon Musk's wild plan to set artificial intelligence free,' Cade Metz, Wired, 27th April 2016: http://www.wired.com/2016/04/openai-elon-musk-sam-altman-plan-to-set-artificial-intelligence-free/

'Why OpenAI matters,' Miles Brundage, 12th December 2015: https://www.miles-brundage.com/blog-posts/why-openai-matters

'Sam Altman: OpenAI CEO on GPT-4, ChatGPT, and the Future of AI | Lex Fridman Podcast #367,' Lex Fridman, YouTube, 25th March 2023: https://www.youtube.com/watch?v=L_Guz73e6fw

'How to be successful,' Sam Altman, 24th January 2019: https://blog.samaltman.com/how-to-be-successful

'Elon Musk vs. Samuel Altman et al,' Superior Court of California

Chapter 9

'Attention Is All You Need,' Ashish Vaswani et al, 12th June 2017, arXiv: https://arxiv.org/abs/1706.03762

OpenAI charter: https://openai.com/charter

Chapter 10

'Microsoft invests in and partners with OpenAI to support us building beneficial AGI,' Greg Brockman, OpenAI, 22nd July 2019: https://openai.com/blog/microsoft-invests-in-and-partners-with-openai

'Free Rent: OpenAI Deal Shows One Way Microsoft Seeds Its Cloud,' Kevin McLaughlin and Aaron Holmes, The Information, 7th November 2022: https://www.theinformation.com/articles/why-openai-spent-barely-a-dime-on-microsofts-cloud-after-1-billion-deal

'The inside story of ChatGPT,' Jeremy Kahn, Fortune, 25th January 2023: https://fortune.com/longform/chatgpt-openai-sam-altman-microsoft/

'What is xAI, Elon Musk's new AI company, and will it succeed?,' Chris Stokel-Walker, New Scientist, 13th July 2023: https://www.newscientist.com/article/2382426-what-is-xai-elon-musks-new-ai-company-and-will-it-succeed/

Chapter 11

'AI can be a game changer for neurodivergent employees,' Chris Stokel-Walker, Fortune, 28th November 2023: https://fortune.com/2023/11/28/a-i-can-be-a-game-changer-for-neurodivergent-employees/

'If you're poor, you'll get a computer, and if you're rich, a human doctor,' Chris Stokel-Walker, i newspaper, 10th May 2023: https://inews.co.uk/inews-lifestyle/next-gp-could-be-robot-health-ai-revolution-2328241

Chapter 12

'We Could Reach Singularity This Decade. Can We Get Control of AI First?,' Chris Stokel-Walker, Popular Mechanics, 13th June 2023: https://www.popularmechanics.com/technology/security/a43929371/ai-singularity-dangers/

'Sparks of Artificial General Intelligence: Early experiments with GPT-4,' Sebastian Bubeck et al, arXiv, 22nd March 2023: https://arxiv.org/abs/2303.12712

Chapter 13

Midjourney, Discord, https://discord.com/channels/662267976984297473
'Midjourney Magazine Is Here—and It's Soulless,' Chris Stokel-Walker, Wired, 20th
June 2023: https://www.wired.com/story/midjourney-magazine-review/

Chapter 14

'Tech's Newest Side Hustle: Prompt Engineers Surf the AI Wave,' Chris Stokel-Walker,
The Information, 29th April 2023: https://www.theinformation.com/articles/techs
-newest-side-hustle-prompt-engineers-surf-the-ai-wave

Chapter 15

'Carbon Emissions and Large Neural Network Training,' David Patterson et al, arXiv,
21st April 2021: https://arxiv.org/abs/2104.10350
'Energy and Policy Considerations for Deep Learning in NLP,' Emma Strubell et al,
arXiv, 5th June 2019: https://arxiv.org/abs/1906.02243
'Estimating the Carbon Footprint of BLOOM, a 176B Parameter Language Model,'
Sasha Luccioni et al, arXiv, 3rd November 2022: https://arxiv.org/abs/2211.02001
'We're getting a better idea of AI's true carbon footprint,' Melissa Heikkilä, MIT Technology
Review, 14th November 2022: https://www.technologyreview.com/2022/11/14/1063192/were
-getting-a-better-idea-of-ais-true-carbon-footprint/

Chapter 16

'This couple is launching an organization to protect artists in the AI era,' Chris Stokel-
Walker, Input Magazine, 14th September 2022: https://www.inverse.com/input/culture
/mat-dryhurst-holly-herndon-artists-ai-spawning-source-dall-e-midjourney
'Midjourney Founder David Holz On The Impact Of AI On Art, Imagination And The
Creative Economy,' Rob Salkowitz, Forbes, 16th September 2022: https://www.forbes
.com/sites/robsalkowitz/2022/09/16/midjourney-founder-david-holz-on-the-impact-of
-ai-on-art-imagination-and-the-creative-economy/
'Generative AI startups jockey for VC dollars,' Jacob Robbins, Pitchbook, 13th April
2023: https://pitchbook.com/news/articles/amazon-bedrock-generative-ai-q1-2023-vc-deals
'Adobe is so confident its Firefly generative AI won't breach copyright that it'll cover
your legal bills,' Chris Stokel-Walker, Fast Company, 6th August 2023: https://www.fast-
company.com/90906560/adobe-feels-so-confident-its-firefly-generative-ai-wont-breach
-copyright-itll-cover-your-legal-bills
'Taking Down Prosecraft.io,' Benji Smith, Shaxpir Blog, 7th August 2023: https://blog
.shaxpir.com/taking-down-prosecraft-io-37e189797121

Chapter 17

'Roberto Mata v. Avianca Inc,' Southern District Court of New York
'The ChatGPT Lawyer Explains Himself,' Benjamin Weiser and Nate Schweber, New
York Times, 8th June 2023: https://www.nytimes.com/2023/06/08/nyregion/lawyer
-chatgpt-sanctions.html
'Hope, fear, and AI,' Jacob Kasternakes and James Vincent, The Verge, 26th June
2023: https://www.theverge.com/c/23753704/ai-chatgpt-data-survey-research

Chapter 18

'A Journalist Believes He Was Banned From Midjourney After His AI Images Of
Donald Trump Getting Arrested Went Viral,' Chris Stokel-Walker, BuzzFeed News,

22nd March 2023: https://www.buzzfeednews.com/article/chrisstokelwalker/midjourney-ai-donald-trump-arrest-images-ban

'AI model GPT-3 (dis)informs us better than humans,' Giovanni Spitale et al, Science Advances, 28th June 2023: https://www.science.org/doi/10.1126/sciadv.adh1850

CounterCloud,io, Nea Paw: https://www.countercloud.io

Chapter 19

'Gender Shades: Intersectional Accuracy Disparities in Commercial Gender Classification,' Joy Buolamwini and Timnit Gebru, PMLR, 2018: https://proceedings.mlr.press/v81/buolamwini18a.html

'What Really Happened When Google Ousted Timnit Gebru,' Tom Simonite, Wired, 8th June 2021: https://www.wired.com/story/google-timnit-gebru-ai-what-really-happened/

'On the Dangers of Stochastic Parrots: Can Language Models Be Too Big?,' Emily M. Bender et al, FAccT '21: https://dl.acm.org/doi/10.1145/3442188.3445922

'The withering email that got an ethical AI researcher fired at Google,' Casey Newton, Platformer, 3rd December 2020: https://www.platformer.news/the-withering-email-that-got-an-ethical/

Chapter 20

'The Unseen A+ Student: Evaluating the Performance and Detectability of Large Language Models in High School Assignments,' Matyáš Boháček, 2023: https://data.matsworld.io/research/the-unseen-a-plus-student/AIED-2023-paper.pdf

'Stable Bias: Analyzing Societal Representations in Diffusion Models,' Sasha Luccioni et al, arXiv, 20th March 2023: https://arxiv.org/abs/2303.11408

'WEIRD FAccTs: How Western, Educated, Industrialized, Rich, and Democratic is FAccT?,' Ali Akbar Septiandri et al, arXiv, 10th May 2023: https://arxiv.org/abs/2305.06415

'Using AI for loans and mortgages is big risk, warns EU boss,' Zoe Kleinman et al, BBC, 14th June 2023: https://www.bbc.co.uk/news/technology-65881389

'Tools to spot AI essays show bias against non-native English speakers,' Chris Stokel-Walker, New Scientist, 23rd April 2023: https://www.newscientist.com/article/2370080-tools-to-spot-ai-essays-show-bias-against-non-native-english-speakers/

'The Curse of Recursion: Training on Generated Data Makes Models Forget,' Ilia Shumailov et al, arXiv, 27th May 2023: https://arxiv.org/abs/2305.17493v2

'Publishers want billions, not millions, from AI,' Ben Smith, Semafor, 24th July 2023: https://www.semafor.com/article/07/23/2023/publishers-want-billions-not-millions-from-ai

Chapter 21

'Search Quality Evaluator Guidelines,' Raterhub

'Exclusive: OpenAI Used Kenyan Workers on Less Than $2 Per Hour to Make ChatGPT Less Toxic,' Billy Perigo, Time, 18th January 2023: https://time.com/6247678/openai-chatgpt-kenya-workers/

'AI Is a Lot of Work,' Josh Dzezia, The Verge, 20th June 2023: https://www.theverge.com/features/23764584/ai-artificial-intelligence-data-notation-labor-scale-surge-remotasks-openai-chatbots

'Code Dependent,' Madhumita Murgia, 2024

'Whose AI Dream? In search of the aspiration in data annotation,' Ding Wang et al, arXiv, 21st March 2022: https://arxiv.org/abs/2203.10748

'Artificial Artificial Artificial Intelligence: Crowd Workers Widely Use Large Language Models for Text Production Tasks,' Veniamin Veselovsky et al, arXiv, 13th June 2023: https://arxiv.org/abs/2306.07899

Chapter 22

'Fake Drakes And Counterfeit Kanyes: The Internet Is Suddenly Full Of AI-Generated Hip-Hop,' Chris Stokel-Walker, BuzzFeed News, 17th April 2023: https://www.buzzfeednews.com/article/chrisstokelwalker/ai-hip-hop-rap-music-drake-kanye-weeknd-rihanna-jay-z
"When Will AI Generate a Hollywood Blockbuster? 'Give It About Three Years.'," Chris Stokel-Walker, Inverse, 28th June 2023: https://www.inverse.com/culture/when-will-ai-make-a-blockbuster-movie

Chapter 23

'Authors fear they have little defence against AI impersonators,' Chris Stokel-Walker, New Scientist, 10th August 2023: https://www.newscientist.com/article/2386956-authors-fear-they-have-little-defence-against-ai-impersonators/
'Stability AI's high-profile resignation got lost in the OpenAI chaos,' Chris Stokel-Walker, Fast Company, 21st November 2023: https://www.fastcompany.com/90987146/stability-ais-high-profile-resignation-got-lost-in-the-openai-chaos

Chapter 24

'Using AI to Maintain the Creator-Fan Connection,' Chris Stokel-Walker, Lens Magazine, 26th June 2023: https://lensmag.xyz/story/using-ai-to-maintain-the-creator-fan-connection
'One of Gaming's Biggest YouTubers Wants to Replace Himself With AI,' Chris Stokel-Walker, Wired, 2nd August 2023: https://www.wired.com/story/kwebbelkop-youtube-ai-clone/

Chapter 25

'Google "We Have No Moat, And Neither Does OpenAI",' Dylan Patel and Afzal Ahmad, SemiAnalysis, 4th May 2023: https://www.semianalysis.com/p/google-we-have-no-moat-and-neither
'OpenAI's Losses Doubled to $540 Million as It Developed ChatGPT,' Erin Woo and Amir Efrati, The Information, 4th May 2023: https://www.theinformation.com/articles/openais-losses-doubled-to-540-million-as-it-developed-chatgpt
'Google Is Falling Behind in AI Arms Race, Senior Engineer Warns,' Julia Love, Davey Alba and Rachel Metz, Bloomberg, 5th May 2023: https://www.bloomberg.com/news/articles/2023-05-05/google-staffer-claims-in-leaked-ai-warning-we-have-no-secret-sauce

Chapter 26

'ChatGPT was an 'oh crap' moment for hundreds of CEOs,' Shona Ghosh and Hasan Chowdhury, Business Insider, 11th June 2023: https://www.businessinsider.com/hundreds-of-ceos-talked-about-chatgpt-on-h1-earnings-calls-2023-7?
'Neeva, the would-be Google competitor, is shutting down its search engine,' David Pierce, The Verge, 20th May 2023: https://www.theverge.com/2023/5/20/23731397/neeva-search-engine-google-shutdown
'Elon Musk threw nine-figure promises at top AI researchers,' Reed Albergotti and Louise Matsakis, Semafor, 14th July 2023: https://www.semafor.com/article/07/14/2023/elon-musk-threw-nine-figure-promises-at-top-ai-researchers

Chapter 27

'Mark Zuckerberg's Letter to Investors: 'The Hacker Way,'' Wired, 1st February 2012: https://www.wired.com/2012/02/zuck-letter/

'Exclusive: OpenAI Lobbied the E.U. to Water Down AI Regulation,' Billy Perigo, Time, 20th June 2023: https://time.com/6288245/openai-eu-lobbying-ai-act/

'OpenAI warns over split with Europe as regulation advances,' Richard Waters, Madhumita Murgia and Javier Espinoza, Financial Times, 25th May 2023: https://www.ft.com/content/5814b408-8111-49a9-8885-8a8434022352

'Frontier Model Forum,' OpenAI, 26th July 2023: https://openai.com/blog/frontier-model-forum

'Act now on AI before it's too late, says UNESCO's AI lead,' Chris Stokel-Walker, Fast Company, 5th February 2024: https://www.fastcompany.com/91022817/act-now-on-ai-before-its-too-late-says-unescos-ai-lead

Chapter 28

'Microsoft's stock extends losses as OpenAI's Altman departs as CEO,' Dow Jones, 17th November 2023: https://www.morningstar.com/news/marketwatch/20231117369/microsofts-stock-extends-losses-as-openais-altman-departs-as-ceo

'OpenAI's Board Set Back the Promise of Artificial Intelligence,' Vinod Khosla, The Information, 20th November 2023: https://www.theinformation.com/articles/openais-board-set-back-the-promise-of-artificial-intelligence

Greg Brockman, Twitter, 22nd November 2023: https://twitter.com/gdb/status/1727230819226583113

Chapter 29

ARR Statistics: https://stats.aclrollingreview.org/submissions/linguistic-diversity/

'Quality at a Glance: An Audit of Web-Crawled Multilingual Datasets,' Julia Kreutzer et al, Transactions of the Association for Computational Linguistics, 31st January 2022: https://direct.mit.edu/tacl/article/doi/10.1162/tacl_a_00447/109285/Quality-at-a-Glance-An-Audit-of-Web-Crawled

'OpenAI's CEO Says the Age of Giant AI Models Is Already Over,' Will Knight, Wired, 17th April 2023: https://www.wired.com/story/openai-ceo-sam-altman-the-age-of-giant-ai-models-is-already-over/

'Four-week-old AI start-up raises record €105mn in European push,' Tim Bradshaw and Leila Abboud, Financial Times, 13th June 2023: https://www.ft.com/content/cf939ea4-d96c-4908-896a-48a74381f251

'Lost in Translation: Large Language Models in Non-English Content Analysis,' Gabriel Nicholas and Aliya Bhatia, Center for Democracy & Technology: https://cdt.org/insights/lost-in-translation-large-language-models-in-non-english-content-analysis/

Chapter 30

Drought, World Health Organization: https://www.who.int/health-topics/drought#tab=tab_1

'Artificial intelligence and jobs,' OECD, https://www.oecd.org/employment-outlook/2023/

'Will Generative AI Disproportionately Affect the Jobs of Women?,' Paige Smith, Kenan Institute of Private Enterprise, 18th April 2023: https://kenaninstitute.unc.edu/kenan-insight/will-generative-ai-disproportionately-affect-the-jobs-of-women/

INDEX

Index

Also by Chris Stokel-Walker

TikTok Boom
The Inside Story of The World's Favourite App
Chris Stokel-Walker

Paperback (ISBN 9781912454822) £9.99

**'It is rare for a business analysis
to read like a thriller – this one does'**
Azeem Azhar, Founder, Exponential View

Also by Chris Stokel-Walker

YouTubers
How YouTube Shook Up TV and Created a New
Generation of Stars
Chris Stokel-Walker

Paperback (ISBN 9781912454228) £9.99

'Both absorbing and highly illuminating'
The Bookseller

CHRIS STOKEL-WALKER

Chris Stokel-Walker is a freelance English journalist, specialising in technology. He regularly contributes to the BBC, *Washington Post*, *New York Times*, *WIRED*, *Economist*, *Guardian*, *New Scientist* and *Newsweek*, and appears on the BBC, Sky News, CNN, Al Jazeera, Times Radio and other TV channels and radio stations. Chris is author of *YouTubers: How YouTube Shook Up TV and Created a New Generation of Stars* (2019, Canbury Press), and *TikTok Boom: China's Dynamite App and the Superpower Race for Social Media* (2021, Canbury Press) – the irst popular book on TikTok. His latest book is *The History of the Internet in Byte-Sized Chunks* (2023, Michael O'Mara Books).

Publish with Us!

Our aim is to depict the world as it really is, stripped of spin.

Modern non-fiction from London

www.canburypress.com

info@canburypress.com